COMMITTEE FOR ECONOMIC DEVELOPMENT
RESEARCH STUDY

# NATIONAL SECURITY AND
# INDIVIDUAL FREEDOM

# COMMITTEE FOR ECONOMIC DEVELOPMENT

## RESEARCH STUDIES

PRODUCTION, JOBS AND TAXES — *Harold M. Groves*

POSTWAR TAXATION AND ECONOMIC PROGRESS — *Harold M. Groves*

AGRICULTURE IN AN UNSTABLE ECONOMY — *Theodore W. Schultz*

INTERNATIONAL TRADE AND DOMESTIC EMPLOYMENT — *Calvin B. Hoover*

CONTROLLING WORLD TRADE — *Edward S. Mason*

SMALL BUSINESS: ITS PLACE AND PROBLEMS — *A. D. H. Kaplan*

MONETARY MANAGEMENT — *E. A. Goldenweiser*

NATIONAL SECURITY AND INDIVIDUAL FREEDOM — *Harold D. Lasswell*

*Studies That Dealt with the Transition Period from War to Peace*

THE LIQUIDATION OF WAR PRODUCTION — *A. D. H. Kaplan*

DEMOBILIZATION OF WARTIME ECONOMIC CONTROLS — *John Maurice Clark*

PROVIDING FOR UNEMPLOYED WORKERS IN THE TRANSITION — *Richard A. Lester*

FINANCING BUSINESS DURING THE TRANSITION — *Charles C. Abbott*

JOBS AND MARKETS — *CED Research Staff*

## SUPPLEMENTARY RESEARCH PAPERS

WORLD POLITICS FACES ECONOMICS — *Harold D. Lasswell*

THE ECONOMICS OF A FREE SOCIETY * — *William Benton*

PERSONNEL PROBLEMS OF THE POSTWAR TRANSITION PERIOD * — *Charles A. Myers*

*\* Published by CED*

COMMITTEE FOR ECONOMIC DEVELOPMENT
RESEARCH STUDY

# National Security and Individual Freedom

BY

## HAROLD D. LASSWELL

*Professor of Law*
*Yale University*

FIRST EDITION

McGRAW–HILL BOOK COMPANY, INC.

NEW YORK    TORONTO    LONDON    1950

NATIONAL SECURITY AND INDIVIDUAL FREEDOM

# FOREWORD

THE RESEARCH PROGRAM initiated in 1942, during World War II, by the Committee for Economic Development has as its focus a study of the chief economic factors affecting the maintenance of high stable production and employment. It is revealing of the tumult in the postwar world that this report on *National Security and Individual Freedom* has a place in such a research program. It is apparent, however, that the economic strength of our country is vital to our national security; and freedom of the individual as well as a free economy have been, and are, pillars of our economic strength.

This report examines the problems that confront us in seeking national security without forfeit of the basic values and principles of American life.

Other studies in the CED research program already issued and those under way are described in a note on pages 239 to 247.

HOWARD B. MYERS
*Research Director*

# PREFACE

I N PREFACES it is customary to acknowledge the assistance received from various sources and to conclude by absolving everyone save the author from culpability for the final result. Both operations are more than perfunctory in the present instance. Generous aid has come from many quarters. Since very controversial issues of policy are involved, the responsibility of the author for the outcome is correspondingly increased.

Among those who have been or are members of the staff of CED I am especially aware of the encouragement and help coming from Theodore O. Yntema, Howard B. Myers, Gardiner C. Means, Herbert Stein, Robert F. Lenhart, and Sylvia Stone. The discussions of the CED committee, under the chairmanship of Fred Lazarus, Jr., which issued a policy statement on the subject, were richly informative and suggestive. The members of this committee were Messrs. William Benton, James F. Brownlee, S. Sloan Colt, Gardner Cowles, John M. Hancock, Robert Heller, Philip D. Reed, Beardsley Ruml, Sidney J. Weinberg, W. Walter Williams, and Dr. Sarah G. Blanding. The ground was cleared by a preliminary group initiated by Beardsley Ruml, which included Messrs. Hiland G. Batcheller, Herbert Emmerich, William Tudor Gardiner, Harry Scherman, and Joseph E. McLean. In the preparation of Chapter VI, dealing with the courts, I have relied heavily upon Adam Yarmolinsky, of the New York Bar. I have benefited, though perhaps not sufficiently, from many criticisms, notably by Professor Myres S. McDougal and Ralph Brown, Yale Law School; Professor James L. McCamy, Chairman, Department of Political Science, University of Wisconsin; Professor Joseph E. McLean, Political Scientist, Princeton University;

## Preface

Joseph M. Goldsen, RAND Corporation, Santa Monica, California; Philip L. Graham, *The Washington Post*; Professor David F. Cavers, Harvard Law School; Don K. Price, Public Administration Clearing House; and various members of the armed services.

HAROLD D. LASSWELL

NEW HAVEN, CONNECTICUT
*June,* 1950

# CONTENTS

FOREWORD . . . . . . . . . . . . . . . . . . . . . . . vii

PREFACE . . . . . . . . . . . . . . . . . . . . . . . ix

I. THE CONTINUING CRISIS OF NATIONAL DEFENSE . 1

The Continuing Crisis . . . . . . . . . . . . . . 2
International Anarchy . . . . . . . . . . . . . . 2
The Bipolar Structure of World Politics . . . . . . . . 3
America Is No Longer at the Periphery . . . . . . . . 3
The Reduced Value of Distance as Defense . . . . . . . 6
The Willingness to Play with Fire . . . . . . . . . . 7
Despotisms Exist and Can Act Quickly . . . . . . . . 9
Despotisms Are Aggressive . . . . . . . . . . . . 10
Energetic Despotisms Are Most Aggressive . . . . . . . 10
The Appeal of Communism beyond Russia . . . . . . . 11
The Relative Failure of Russian Propaganda . . . . . . 14
The Communist Appeal in the United States . . . . . . 17
U. S. Assets in the War of Ideas . . . . . . . . . . 19
The Ideological Vulnerability of Soviet Russia . . . . . . 20
The World Revolution of Our Time . . . . . . . . . 22

II. THE THREAT INHERENT IN THE GARRISON-POLICE
STATE . . . . . . . . . . . . . . . . . . . . 23

The Uneasy Coalition . . . . . . . . . . . . . . 24
The Atomic Weapon . . . . . . . . . . . . . . . 25
Pressure for Defense Expenditures . . . . . . . . . . 26
Expansion of Government . . . . . . . . . . . . . 27
Centralization of Government . . . . . . . . . . . 29
Withholding of Information . . . . . . . . . . . . 30
Atmosphere of Suspicion . . . . . . . . . . . . . 31
Press and Public Opinion Decline . . . . . . . . . . 33
Weakening of Political Parties . . . . . . . . . . . 36
Decline of the Congress . . . . . . . . . . . . . 38
Decline of Most Civilian Executives . . . . . . . . . 41
Decline of the Courts . . . . . . . . . . . . . . 45
Changes in Group Influence . . . . . . . . . . . . 46

# Contents

III. THE MEANING OF NATIONAL SECURITY POLICY . . 50

A Comprehensive Program of National Defense Does Not Rely
  Solely on Armament . . . . . . . . . . . . . . . 52
The Best Balance of All Instruments of Foreign Policy . . . 53
Security and the Impact Inside America of the Measures
  Adopted for the Primary Purposes of Foreign Policy . . . 53
Security and the Impact at Home and Abroad of Policies
  Primarily Aimed at Internal Conditions . . . . . . . 55
Security Calls for a Comprehensive and Balanced Reviewing
  Procedure . . . . . . . . . . . . . . . . . . 56
Four Principles of National Policy . . . . . . . . . . 57
  Civilian Supremacy . . . . . . . . . . . . . . . 58
  Freedom of Information . . . . . . . . . . . . . 63
  Civil Liberties . . . . . . . . . . . . . . . . 65
  A Free Economy . . . . . . . . . . . . . . . . 68

IV. ACTION BY THE PRESIDENT AND THE EXECUTIVE . 76

Planning and Reviewing Are Essential . . . . . . . . 81
The Potentialities of the National Security Council . . . . 82
Why Not the Cabinet? . . . . . . . . . . . . . . 84
How About the Vice-Presidency? . . . . . . . . . . 86
Keep Political Policing to a Minimum . . . . . . . . 87
Special Measures against Unnecessary Secrecy . . . . . . 90
The Place of Propaganda and Information . . . . . . . 93
What Are Information and Propaganda? . . . . . . . 94
Addressing Foreign and Home Audiences . . . . . . . 94
Minimum Interference with the Free Economy . . . . . 96
Effective Civilian Authority in the Department of Defense . 98
In-Service Training: A National Policy College . . . . . 100
Annual Reports by the President on Security and Freedom . 101

V. WHAT THE CONGRESS CAN DO . . . . . . . . 103

The Congress Lacks the Over-all View of Security . . . . 105
National Security Committees Are Needed . . . . . . . 106
Genuine and Spurious Bipartisanship . . . . . . . . 108
Trends toward Party Responsibility . . . . . . . . . 110
Can Ideas Divide Parties? . . . . . . . . . . . . 111
Shall It Be Cabinet Government? . . . . . . . . . . 113
Congress Can Represent the Nation . . . . . . . . . 115
A Revised Conception of Responsibility . . . . . . . . 119
The Disclosure of Lobbying and Propaganda . . . . . . 121
Checking Up on Results . . . . . . . . . . . . . 124

# Contents

Congress Can Use Civilian Panels . . . . . . . . . . 126
Congress Can Inform the Public More Fully . . . . . . 126
Fair Play at Committee Hearings . . . . . . . . . . 129
New Agencies of Congressional-Executive Action . . . . . 129

VI. WHAT THE COURTS CAN DO . . . . . . . . . . 133

The War Power . . . . . . . . . . . . . . . . . 136
Due Process Restrictions . . . . . . . . . . . . . 137
The Judicial Function of the Executive: . . . . . . . 143
Military Law . . . . . . . . . . . . . . . . . 143
Military Government . . . . . . . . . . . . . 144
Martial Law . . . . . . . . . . . . . . . . . 147

VII. WHAT THE PUBLIC CAN DO . . . . . . . . . . . 154

1. The Responsibility of the Free Press . . . . . . . 157
2. Committees on National Security and Individual Freedom 158
3. Community Councils on Human Rights . . . . . . . 161
4. Observe National Security and Freedom Days . . . . . 161
5. The Full Use of Modern Media . . . . . . . . . . 162
6. Fostering Unofficial Sources of Information and Interpretation . . . . . . . . . . . . . . . . . . . 170
Holding Public Officials Accountable . . . . . . . . 178
Preventing Hysteria . . . . . . . . . . . . . . . 180
Preventing Complacency . . . . . . . . . . . . . 182
Individual Responsibility . . . . . . . . . . . . . 184

APPENDIX A . . . . . . . . . . . . . . . . . . . . 189

APPENDIX B . . . . . . . . . . . . . . . . . . . . 195

NOTES . . . . . . . . . . . . . . . . . . . . . . 201

A NOTE ON THE COMMITTEE FOR ECONOMIC DEVELOPMENT AND ITS
RESEARCH PROGRAM . . . . . . . . . . . . . . . . 235

RESEARCH AND POLICY COMMITTEE . . . . . . . . . . . 251

RESEARCH ADVISORY BOARD . . . . . . . . . . . . . . 253

INDEX . . . . . . . . . . . . . . . . . . . . . . 255

# I. THE CONTINUING CRISIS OF NATIONAL DEFENSE

THE CENTRAL PROBLEM with which this book deals is how to maintain a proper balance between national security and individual freedom in a continuing crisis of national defense.

The aim is more restricted, therefore, than considering how to bring the crisis to an end. The task is the more modest and less gratifying one of thinking how to endure the crisis with the least loss of fundamental freedoms. The immediate problem is not unrelated to the ending of the crisis itself, however, since the capacity and will of the whole people to cope with the eventuality of war is affected by our success in keeping the freedoms worth fighting to protect. It is also true that daily concern for all that touches the dignity of man will keep alive our determination to fan every spark of reasonable hope for a practicable means of escape by peaceable agreement from the suicidal situation in which mankind lives today.

The nature of the problem precludes the possibility of definitive treatment, since quick change and instant improvision are the distinctive characteristics of crisis and of crisis statesmanship. The positive suggestions offered are bound to be partial and somewhat inconclusive, subject to rapid obsolescence by the quick march of affairs. It is less important, perhaps, that a brief book about our problem arrive at definitive recommendations than that it does something to focus attention upon the issues at stake, and helps to create a climate of opinion in which the talents of scholars and statesmen are challenged to cope with immediate emergencies with an eye upon enduring goals and principles.

## National Security and Individual Freedom

The factors which contribute to the continuing crisis are here looked into first, and some of the formidable dangers ahead are assessed. The basic values and principles of American policy are reviewed, and consideration given some of the alternatives of action open to the President, the Congress, the courts, and the public.

### THE CONTINUING CRISIS

There is no longer any doubt that we are in a world crisis of insecurity that may last for a generation. We are in the midst of an armament race for the command of weapons of unprecedented destructive strength. The continuing crisis of national defense is reflected in peacetime conscription and in unprecedented peacetime appropriations for the armed forces. Between World War I and World War II the armed services expended each year on the average less than one per cent of our national product (about one billion dollars). After a sharp decline immediately after World War II, our appropriations rose again, and show every prospect of remaining at a high level. The sense of crisis is communicated by the leaders of opinion in this country, and throughout the world, whether the forum is the United Nations, a national government, or a private gathering.

### INTERNATIONAL ANARCHY

Many factors account for the crisis. Not the least important is the universal realization that existing international institutions are too feeble for the government of mankind. The United Nations is not powerful enough to spread confidence in public order. The Security Council is handcuffed by the voting arrangements and the lack of effective power. The existence of the veto testifies to the unwillingness of governments and peoples to trust one another when the United Nations was organized. We are warned by the continuation of the veto that national defense must be strong enough to protect America in the event that the new institutions of international action are brought to a full stop in the midst of crisis.

## THE BIPOLAR STRUCTURE OF WORLD POLITICS

A dominating feature of the present crisis is the bipolar structure of world politics. Policies in every sphere of human activity are affected to an increasing extent by calculations of the relative strength of America and Russia. In many circles it is already true that

. . . A good crop in Western Germany is chiefly evaluated, not in economic or humanitarian terms, but according to its effect upon Soviet-American power. The question whether Italy is to receive economic assistance is entangled with estimates of how the economic recuperation of the Italian peoples will affect the spread of communism. Whether Koreans or Chinese are to have medical aid becomes subordinated to the Russo-American balance of power in Asia. Every expansion of population, every decline in the death rate, every upswing in production, every drop or rise in the standard of living, every amelioration in the respect position of the colored peoples, every advance in scientific knowledge, every radio broadcast, every movement of students or traders or tourists or displaced persons across frontier lines, every addition to transportation facilities (by air, sea, or land), every movement of raw materials, foodstuffs, semi-processed products, machine tools or consumer goods: In a word every social change is promptly weighed in the scale pans of power and responded to accordingly. [1] *

## AMERICA IS NO LONGER AT THE PERIPHERY

The defense position of America is profoundly affected by recent developments. We are no longer at the periphery of the principal conflicts of world politics. Up to the present, our country has been protected by the rivalries and antagonisms pre-

* All footnotes and references are assembled by chapter in the section labeled Notes at the back of the book.

vailing among the major European powers. A crucial factor in the Revolutionary War was the support obtained from France, the Continental rival of England. Having lost the Seven Years' War, the French monarchy began to plot revenge immediately after the peace of 1763. The French government saw what seemed an excellent opportunity to weaken England by giving secret support to the Colonies against the mother country. In April, 1776, the foreign minister of Louis XVI, Vergennes, read a memorandum to the King and Council which outlined the advantages of aiding the American Colonies:

First, it will diminish the power of England and proportionately raise that of France. Second, it will cause irreparable loss to English trade, while it will considerably extend ours. Third, it presents to us as very probable the recovery of a part of the possessions which the English have taken from us in America, such as the fisheries of Newfoundland and of the Gulf of St. Lawrence, Isle Royale, etc. We do not speak of Canada.[2]

On May 2, 1776, secret assistance was decreed to the Colonies in the form of munitions from the royal arsenals. An equal amount was furnished by another enemy of England, Charles III of Spain. (All this occurred before the Declaration of Independence.) All told, France subsidized the Colonies to the extent of $1,996,500 and extended loans of $6,352,500. Spain gave $397,230 in subsidies, and $248,098 in loans.[3] In addition, Dutch loans reached America at first by way of France, and later directly. A French expeditionary force arrived on this side of the water in 1780, and as is well remembered, the combination of French armies and fleets with the forces of General Washington culminated in Yorktown.

Besides giving direct aid to the Colonies, the European rivals of England prevented the mother country from assembling armed forces in sufficient strength to suppress the American rebellion. Spain declared war on England in 1779, and England was soon embroiled with the Netherlands. The armed neutrality included Denmark-Norway, Russia, Prussia, Portugal, Hapsburg Dominions, and the Holy Roman Empire.

Forty years later we were able to improve our defense position in relation to Europe when the American Colonies of Spain revolted, and we took advantage of the balance of power to prevent united action on the part of Europe to reconquer the Colonies. This time we threw our weight on the side of the English against the French, Spanish, and Russians. Canning, British foreign minister, turned to our ambassador in London for a joint declaration. Although we gave no joint statement, we presently issued the independent declaration of policy known to history as the Monroe Doctrine (December 2, 1823). One immediate occasion of Monroe's message was alarm at the expansion of a Russian-American company along the Pacific Coast.[4]

We were able to benefit also from the European balance of power during one of our gravest internal crises. The Civil War was an obvious opportunity for outside powers to step in for the purpose of dividing the United States permanently, and of reestablishing European control in Central and South America. But the relations of England, France, Austria, and Russia were such that prompt, united action was not taken.[5]

Situated as we were on the periphery of the European arena, it was possible to keep out of, and to be relatively unaffected by, several struggles which came to a head during the nineteenth century. We stood apart from the Crimean War, the Franco-Prussian War, and the many clashes that arose when Europe began the partition of Africa.

Gradually we were drawn into colonial commitments of our own. As a result of our intervention against Spain in Cuba, we took over the Philippines, which brought our territory close to Asia, and particularly to Japan and China. However, these developments still left us somewhat to one side of the European balance of power. Hence, for two and one-half years we were able to stay out of World War I while the British-French-Russian coalition fought the Germans and Austro-Hungarians. In World War II we kept out of a full shooting war for about the same length of time.

Today we are no longer at the periphery of power. On the contrary, we are one of the giant poles around which all power alignments are made. The major European states are eclipsed to a degree that constrains them to lean toward us or to succumb to the Soviet Union. In a century and a half we have been transformed from a tiny peripheral element in the power process into a middle power, a major power, a superpower, and finally a giant power in a bipolarizing world. We are no longer protected by the possibility of playing one European coalition against another and stalling for time in the event of a major outbreak.[6]

### THE REDUCED VALUE OF DISTANCE AS DEFENSE

The present crisis of defense is intensified by the degree to which recent developments have reduced the value of distance. In World War I the airplane was of some limited use for reconnaissance purposes. Only thirty years later, great bombing fleets were major instruments of war. In World War I the submarine was rather closely tied to bases and compelled to surface frequently. By the end of World War II the problem was solved of cutting the submarine loose from bases for long periods of time; and the snorkel made it possible to remain under water. In World War I a German gun dropped a few shells on Paris from a distance of about seventy miles. By the closing months of World War II, V-2 rockets were raining death on London at a distance of two hundred and twenty miles. The most drastic development of all, obviously, was the atomic weapon, whereby one B-29 superfortress with one bomb could do as much damage in one raid as 270 B-29's each carrying ten tons of conventional bombs.[7]

Since the war America and Russia have been engaged in a race for the improvement and discovery of weapons. It is now common for aircraft to exceed the speed of sound (a development long believed by many reputable scientists to be impossible). Research on guided missiles is one of the most active areas of technical progress. We hear of the possibility of pilotless planes loaded with atomic and hydrogen explosives, and of rockets with devastating and toxic warheads. An alternative to the manufacture of A-bombs is the use of the same raw material for the purpose of preparing small pellets of destructive radiation. Hostile submarines, planes, or missiles (or saboteurs) are possible carriers of radioactive material, not exclusively to render ports unusable, but to contaminate water supplies. When medical services are reduced from bombing or radiation attack, bacteriological warfare can spread epidemics among survivors. Chemical weapons of many types are known to be in existence (some kill, others cripple permanently, some discommode temporarily). Taken together, these developments are reducing not only the importance of distance as an element in defense but the usefulness of natural barriers like water, icecaps, mountains, and deserts.[8]

### THE WILLINGNESS TO PLAY WITH FIRE

A serious factor contributing to the tension of our time is the willingness of many influential leaders to take a chance that the destructiveness of another general war is currently exaggerated. It might be supposed that the frightful potentialities of modern weapons would impel all responsible leaders to do everything to prevent war. We know from history, however, that fear of technology has not brought peace. When Benjamin Franklin witnessed the first ascent of Dr. Charles's hydrogen-filled balloon, he thought it might "convince sovereigns of the folly of wars . . .

since it will be impracticable for the most potent of them to guard their own dominions." [9] But the hardheaded Franklin was wrong. Since 1783 we have lived through miracles of invention and unexampled orgies of destructive warfare.[10]

What prevents the fear of destruction from preventing war? For one thing, annihilation has never been guaranteed. Even today no scientist can promise that the setting off of large numbers of A-bombs or H-bombs by one side will automatically generate a chain reaction which will result in the extermination not only of the enemy but of the aggressor.[11] The scientist can testify that some finite number of superbombs exploded in a short period of time by known methods will generate "atomic dust clouds" which may circle round and round the globe killing persons anywhere on the face of the earth by radiation. But this still gives an "out": after all, so many bombs may not be released; the clouds may not get close to the surface; and if the clouds get close, they will annihilate people in a limited area.

Since annihilation cannot (as yet) be guaranteed when any known weapon is resorted to, a margin is left for political manipulation. The human factor, not the gadget, remains decisive. Thanks to the human factor, planners on one side can hope to surprise and outwit the other. Owing to the human element, agents may be slipped into vital spots in the enemy's defense. Agents may be recruited by persuasion (or other means) from the enemy population. In a word, enough doubt exists to keep alive in some minds the willingness to play with fire rather than to make the apparent sacrifices of power involved in organizing an effective world government. Further, some leaders are in honest doubt about the desirability of the kind of world government that can be obtained under present conditions.

## The Continuing Crisis of National Defense

### DESPOTISMS EXIST AND CAN ACT QUICKLY

The world crisis is sustained by the existence of despotism, especially in Russia. It is apparent to all that despotisms are at an advantage in planning secretly and striking without warning. We saw despotism in action at Pearl Harbor. We now know that the idea had long germinated in the mind of an imaginative naval officer and that final preparations were begun in January, 1941. The plan was approved by the Supreme War Council on September 6, 1941.[12] We also saw despotism at work in Nazi Germany. When Hitler determined to act against the Soviet Union, plans were begun several months in advance. As early as December 18, 1940, nine copies of a secret directive were issued to the chiefs of the German services.[13]

That the top leadership of democratic countries is at a disadvantage in the game of secrecy and surprise assault is well known to Americans from our own history. Consider the case of President Roosevelt before Pearl Harbor. There is every reason to believe that the President was convinced from an early date of the importance of stopping Hitler, and that he wanted the United States to join the anti-Nazi coalition. Dependent as he was in a democracy upon public support, Roosevelt could not shut off debate or declare war at will. The President used his position to give indirect aid to our future allies and to block our future enemies. He was determined to defer our full participation in a shooting war until the country was substantially united. The contrast with Hitler is obvious and enormous. And this conclusion holds, whatever criticisms may be made of President Roosevelt, either because he went too fast or too slowly, or because of his tactics.[14] The contrast with Lenin or Stalin and associates is equally striking. Without preparing the Russian people or taking them into consultation, Stalin was able to make the surprise Pact with Hitler in 1939 and to inaugurate a "tough" policy against America and England in 1945. (It need scarcely be said that all news reaching the Russian people through Russian media of communication is heavily censored and that public objection to the official line is not permitted.)

Perhaps we should point out for our own reassurance that the advantage of despotism in matters of secrecy and surprise does not imply that democracies are ineffective in holding secrets essential to their defense. Before the war England developed radar as a means of detecting planes, and this paid off handsomely in the Battle of Britain when the radar-aided R.A.F. was able to stave off the Luftwaffe. Some secret advance planning was done with the United States (especially with the Navy), but this, too, was of a strictly limited and defensive character. One effect of the bipolar structure of world politics is to clarify the policy alternatives open in world affairs and to enable public as well as expert opinion to become crystallized in advance of a possible "hot war" in support of large-scale measures of national preparedness.

## DESPOTISMS ARE AGGRESSIVE

Despotisms are well known to be aggressive. The affinity of despotic regimes for aggressive action comes from the internal stresses generated by arbitrary power. In absolute governments the head men of the state are conspicuous targets for the hostilities that accumulate against the established order. In democratic systems, on the other hand, the level of hostility can be kept comparatively low by debates and elections. Despotisms tend to protect themselves by turning mass grievances against outside targets. This is the technique of the war scare (and of actual war).[15]

## ENERGETIC DESPOTISMS ARE
## MOST AGGRESSIVE

An energetic despotism is more disturbing to the peace than a sluggish one, and there is no denying the enormous pressure which the rulers of Russia impose upon their own people. The Soviet elite makes use of every means at its disposal to speed up the pace of Russian production and industrialization. After the Revolution the communist leaders undertook the total transformation of Russian society. The new industrialization is indicated by the rapid growth of cities and towns. Soviet agriculture changed from independent proprietorship to socialized forms of production.[16] The human cost of this reconstruction is feebly reflected in such figures as the peasants who were allowed to starve as a disciplinary measure or the many millions in the forced labor camps.

All this was accomplished with the aid of the war-scare technique, which was promptly resumed after the defeat of Germany and Japan, and which has been of decisive importance in maintaining the mood of perpetual crisis.[17]

## THE APPEAL OF COMMUNISM BEYOND RUSSIA

International tension has been heightened by the appeal of communist ideology to individuals and groups beyond the borders of the Soviet Union. The defensive potential of the United States is unquestionably weakened by whatever support is given to communism by Americans and by the peoples occupying an intermediate position between the Soviet Union and the United States.

As a political weapon in the hands of the Russian leadership, communist doctrine still contains an element of surprise in relation to America. Americans have been accustomed to think of themselves as the most progressive nation in the world, materially, morally, and politically. It is with some sense of shock and incredulity that we hear ourselves denounced as the spearhead of all that is old, rotten, and corrupt. We do not recognize ourselves as the "putrifying corpse" of capitalism, soon to be interred among the has-beens of history. If the communists are to be believed, we have made an astonishing descent from the proud days of self-confident "manifest destiny" to the graveside of "inevitable" extinction.

Since our security is affected by the appeal of communism, however weak or strong, it is important to appraise in a spirit of candor the points which give plausibility to the doctrines propagated by the communists.

Communism derives plausibility from some theses of Marx, which have been of political importance for a century. The longevity of Marxism suggests that there must be elements which gain apparent corroboration from the experience of men and women living under modern industrial conditions.

One such thesis is that there is a tendency toward monopoly in capitalistic countries. The plausibility of this cannot be denied. In the United States the danger of monopoly has been a standard complaint in political platforms and public statements for decades.[18]

Another thesis is that the capitalistic system generates periodic crises of mass unemployment. Here again the doctrine is plausible in the light of the well-known history of "panics," "crises," and "depressions." [19]

A third doctrine is that movements of protest arise among the nonowners in capitalistic societies. This is also plausible in view of the support gained by the socialist, labor, and other parties in many countries.[20]

It is further asserted that in parliamentary countries when the owning groups feel themselves to be seriously threatened by movements of protest, they abandon the ways of democracy and support dictatorships. Some plausibility is given to this by the aid received from big industrialists and landlords in the formative stages of Mussolini's Fascism, Hitler's Nazism, and Franco's Falangism.[21]

Another thesis is that imperialism is a result of capitalistic rivalries for the control of markets and raw materials. This gains plausibility from the scramble for colonies which enlarged the empires of England, France, Germany, and Belgium, and which put the United States in the Philippines.[22]

A further thesis is that imperialistic rivalries generate wars among the imperial powers. This, too, is not without plausibility in view of the clash between England and Germany before 1914 and the German demand for "living space" in more recent times.[23]

It is not surprising that a body of doctrine which contains so many plausible theses is a powerful instrument of politics. Yet the doctrines that have just been cited are far from accounting for the degree of success which Russian propaganda has had since the 1917 Revolution. Generally speaking, the response to the Soviet message is greatest where the knowledge of modern industrialism is least. We have not seen the greatest communist triumphs in the cities and towns of industrial Europe or America. Rather, the impact is at its height among the nonindustrial peoples of Europe and Asia.

The crux of the matter is that the Russians have been able to exploit many of the hostilities and fears which were fostered by the domination of Europe over several generations of "colonial" peoples. The United States inherits the resentment against the "white man" nourished by succeeding waves of expansion by the Portuguese, Spanish, Dutch, French, British, Belgian, German, and Italian empires. The fact that American imperial expansion beyond the North American continent was recent and relatively slight does not count for much. For we are the power that props up what is left of the empires of Europe in Asia, Africa, and the islands. No one doubts what would happen to the Dutch, French, or British in their remaining toeholds on the continent of Asia and the adjacent islands if we were to provide no further support.

Another major factor accounts for our vulnerability to propaganda assault by the Russians among the nonindustrialized peoples. Not only is the overwhelming portion of most of the population colonial. It is colored. All the humiliations, fancied or real, experienced at the hands of the "white imperialist" by the colored Asiatic, of whatever class or caste, are turned against the "final citadel of white imperialism," the U.S.A. Every lynched Negro, every public declaration of "white supremacy," every clash over alleged acts of discrimination in jobs or votes or education provides material which is eagerly disseminated by the propaganda machine of communism to the colored millions of mankind.

### THE RELATIVE FAILURE OF RUSSIAN PROPAGANDA

Despite the plausibility of many points of Marxist doctrine and the festering antagonism of colonial and colored peoples against "white imperialism," it cannot be successfully maintained that Russian propaganda since the Revolution has been a series of impressive victories. On the contrary, the history of world revolutionary propaganda is a story of successive disillusionments.

The Russian leaders of world communism who organized the Third International in 1919 were hopeful of winning the support of revolutionists throughout the world. And for a brief period in 1919 and 1920 the postwar chaos appeared to provide a fertile soil. With the exception of a transient dictatorship in Hungary and a local seizure of power in Bavaria, no sizeable positive gains were scored beyond the borders of Russia, and these were soon erased. The leaders of communism became so pessimistic about the chances of revolution elsewhere that they reacted with too little too late when Germany went through the inflationary crisis of 1923. Hoping to score in China, the Third International was used to cooperate with the Kuomintang party in the drive in 1927 from Canton to take over power in central and northern China. With victory in sight the armies of Chiang Kai-shek turned on the communists, beginning the long civil war which during the first few years drove the communists into the north-west.

Turning away from collaboration, the communists adopted a separatist line that threw such weight as they could muster against the social democrats and liberals anywhere in the world. Not until the sensational seizure of power by Hitler in Germany did it dawn on the leadership that they were splitting the strength of the left and middle forces for the benefit of fascism. The favorable response to communist propaganda during the early months of the Great Depression obscured from the high command of the Communist International the seriousness of the German situation.

After the damage was done in Germany, the communists changed tactics and entered a period of "united front" action against "fascism" in all countries. Since, however, the slogans of unity were exploited by communist factions to seize control of cooperating organizations, internecine struggles continued among the labor and liberal elements of most countries. The communists did receive some favorable recognition throughout the left and center groups of the world when they led vigorous fights against Franco in Spain. Unfavorable opinion crystallized in 1939 with the signature of the Pact between Russia and Nazi Germany. Disillusionment reached a climax when Russia attacked "little Finland." By this time it was relatively clear that the façade of world revolutionary socialism was worn by the Russians as an adjunct of the power politics of the new state.

Hitler's attack on Russia and the stubborn defense which culminated at Stalingrad initiated a change of feeling in the West. But positive sentiment was not directed toward communism as a product exportable from Russia. The liquidation of the Comintern in 1943 was widely held to symbolize an admission that Soviet communism was a Russian form of national socialism and that the fifth-column tactic of world revolution was being abandoned.

In certain countries Communist parties gained stature as a result of daring and intrepid leadership of resistance movements. In the concentration camps of German Europe and in the active resistance movement of France, for example, the communists won power based on respect for heroism. Communist tactics in northern China which were directed against the Japanese invader were generally admired and imitated by movements of resistance and liberation in Europe. After the liberation of France, the Communist party was a powerful factor for national discipline, since strikes were at first opposed.

The Russians were not successful in winning over the people in the countries which they occupied. In Rumania, Poland, Hungary, Austria, and other central and southern European nations the standard of living was higher than in Russia, and the conduct of the Russians was generally judged to be "naïve" or "barbarous," testifying to the low standards of Soviet Russia. In Czechoslovakia, where the Russians evacuated quickly, they received the greatest popular support.

All during the war close observers of the Soviet Union were aware that the world revolutionary aspects of Russian ideology, though subdued, were not eliminated. The special press intended for the use of party leaders and members continued to repeat traditional doctrine, even though the newspapers and the radio were de-emphasizing slogans of the kind. By late 1945 it was becoming apparent that Russia was changing the dominant tactics of the wartime coalition. Now began a train of incidents that puzzled, annoyed, and angered the groups in the West who had hoped to draw Russia into genuine cooperation after the war. Recognizing that they could not win the voluntary support of the masses in the countries adjacent to the Soviet Union, the communists began to engineer seizures of power by local stooges. At the same time, the slogans of world revolution were revived as a means of gaining access, in a psychological sense, to labor and liberal groups beyond the zone under full Soviet control. It became obvious once more to serious observers that the Soviet leaders were making use of the world revolutionary appeal as a tool of psychological warfare.

When the United States began to react against Russian pressure by using economic means to strengthen Western Europe, the tactic of the Communist parties became more transparent than ever. The French party abandoned the former policy of economic discipline and became the instigator of sabotage against recovery. Through the newly reconstituted Communist International (now called the Cominform), the communists intensified the propaganda against "capitalistic imperialism."

Only in China (and only in certain regions of China) can it be truthfully said that the communists have been successful in winning over broad layers of the population behind communist leadership. Possibly Czechoslovakia should be added, since two of every five voters in predictatorship Czechoslovakia were willing to vote a communist ballot.

Although it is true that communist propaganda has always achieved some acceptance outside the Soviet Union, these successes have been modest in the sense that mass support has seldom been attained. Enough has been done, however, to recruit potential stooges with at least some popular strength. When supplied with coercive means by the Russian leadership, such elements have been available to take over adjacent countries and to bring them unequivocally into the Soviet orbit.[24]

### THE COMMUNIST APPEAL IN THE UNITED STATES

The overthrow of the Czar was greeted in the United States with enthusiasm, but the second, or October, Revolution was widely stigmatized as the work of a German agent (Lenin had been permitted to cross Germany in the famous sealed car). When it was obvious that a social revolution was under way, sentiment divided sharply in this country, with liberal and labor elements tending to take a tolerant view of what was going on. Top industrial leaders were alarmed, and use was made of the fear of Bolshevism in the "open-shop" drive at the close of the war. The government also participated for a time in armed intervention in Siberia, principally with the object of acting as a check on Japanese expansion.[25]

The Communist party in the United States has never been significant either in the top politics of this country or of the Communist International. Members have been recruited from scattered groups in the population. First of all, many Americans of foreign birth, intensely hostile to the regimes in control of their mother countries, were overjoyed at any political movement to bring an end to the older absolutisms or feudalisms. Foreign language associations among recent immigrants were early recruiting grounds for communism. A second source was pre-1917 labor and political movements. Many radical elements were disgusted when most of the socialist and labor leaders of America became "social patriots" and supported the war. A former syndicalist (I.W.W.) leader like William Z. Foster or Bill Haywood is in this category. A third reservoir of communist support overlaps with the first and second. Workers in certain industries, whether recruited from disaffected Europeans or not, were subjected to working conditions which alienated them from the American community. An example is migratory labor in the West, a long-time stronghold of the I.W.W. A fourth source of communist strength was ethnic targets of discrimination, notably the Negro. A fifth source that should be noted is the less discernible but no less real group of persons with personalities hostile to authority. Owing to certain difficulties of personal development, they are intensely hostile to the conventions of American life. Psychiatric research has shown that such persons are often compensating against strong impulses to be submissive, the result being what at first sight is a remarkable combination. As a means of satisfying strong drives against the authority of the system into which he was born, the individual becomes a member of one of the most authoritarian political parties on record.[26]

Many of those whose conversion depended upon very intimate motivations were young people, most of whom kept their connection with communist organizations for short periods, especially at the time of the Great Depression, the seizure of power by the Nazis, and the Spanish Civil War. Among journalists, writers, teachers, and other professional people, there were many who responded to the humanitarian idealism of communist teaching, and to the systematic conceptions of Marx, Engels, and Lenin.

### U.S. ASSETS IN THE WAR OF IDEAS

The relative failure of Russian communism in the United States and elsewhere suggests that the United States has powerful assets in the war of ideas. Whatever the blemishes, America is still the "miracle" of our age. It is possible to assert categorically that for at least a century the U.S. has maintained the longest sustained rise in the standard of living in the history of mankind.[27] Thus the Marxist thesis of the inevitable and progressive impoverishment of the masses is emphatically contradicted by the facts. Millions of human beings have found a new birth of personal dignity in the freedom of this country. Any exceptions to the ideal of respect for human personality are under vehement attack among ourselves and are steadily giving ground in the face of unceasing pressure to narrow the gap between ideals and practice. America has fostered the release of the energies of man on a scale without parallel.

It is safe to say that chronic mass unemployment will no longer be tolerated in this country. No qualified observer believes that it will be morally or politically possible for the government to refrain from adopting whatever measures are necessary to restore high job levels in case a substantial recession occurs.

The powerful program of economic assistance to European and other nations is a vital demonstration of the capacity of the United States to adjust to new emergencies and to rise to the responsibilities of the leadership so unexpectedly thrust upon us. Although a victor in two world wars against aggressive powers, the United States has not engaged in imperial aggrandizement. In 1918 and in 1945 the leadership of the nation gave substantial support to the growth of international institutions.

## THE IDEOLOGICAL VULNERABILITY OF SOVIET RUSSIA

Through the years it has been slowly dawning upon the observers of Russia that the most important thing to be discovered about Soviet Russia is that it is not what it purports to be. This discovery has been made, often at great personal and social cost, by ever-enlarging circles of laymen, writers, scholars, and politicians. The spokesmen for Russia have done everything in their power over the years to induce or compel the Russian people and the rest of the world to take the Russian leadership at its own evaluation. There is ample reason to believe that this self-evaluation is false, and that in this falseness lies the ideological weakness of the Russian regime.

The official myth spread at home and abroad by the ruling class of Russia is that they, the leaders of the Soviet Union, are the infallible interpreters of Marx, and that they are installing democracy, socialism, and communism in successive stages throughout Russia and the Russia-centered world. The evidence accumulates that the regime is neither communist nor socialist nor democratic.

## The Continuing Crisis of National Defense

The noncommunist character of the present regime has already opened a running sore adjacent to the Soviet sphere of control in Europe. The revolt led by Tito in Yugoslavia is more than a routine border incident. It has profound ideological importance. Titoism is opposed to the subordination of every nation to the political convenience of the Moscow machine. Instead of permitting each nation to evolve its communist institutions in a genuine federation of communist states, the Moscow regime appears to be substituting a new form of Russian imperialism—this time speaking the language of Marx—for czarist imperialism.

It has long been denied by the liberal left of other countries that the Russian regime can properly call itself socialistic or democratic. The evolution of the perpetual dictatorship in Moscow has brilliantly confirmed the forecasts of Rosa Luxembourg and Karl Kautsky, for example, in the protests which they made against the autocratic centralization inaugurated and defended by Lenin and Trotsky. Trotsky himself fell victim at a later stage to the process which he had done so much to start.

What, then, is the true nature of the regime in Moscow? The answer is not too difficult. Soviet Russia is a garrison-police state, in which the political police are exercising a dominant role. It has been characterized as an oriental despotism [28] in modern clothes, speaking a language borrowed from European political philosophy and applying the gadgets of Western science and industry to the problem of power. The Kremlin is the headquarters of a vast system of forced labor camps; and it is only some exaggeration to say that the whole Soviet area is a concentration camp operated by the Political Bureau of the Communist Party at the head of a huge bureaucratic apparatus.

Already the moral foundations of the Russian regime are cracking at the seams as its falseness is discovered and exposed by free or disillusioned minds. It is the Kremlin elite that fears what can happen to its power once the masses of the Russian people can receive honest news of the outside world. It is the Kremlin clique that keeps the globe divided into two great garrisons, while it searches for weapons strong enough to give them the power of enlarging the Russian prison until it admits the world. It is the Kremlin machine that must take principal responsibility for rejecting overtures for peace through understanding and for blocking inspection as a means of weapon control.

There are many hateful and dangerous philosophies and modes of conduct in the world. But in this period of crisis, the principal enemy of national security and individual freedom is the ruling class of Soviet Russia. Kremlinism exploits the nations under Russian dominion. Kremlinism threatens the security and even the physical existence of mankind by keeping alive the global anarchy.

### THE WORLD REVOLUTION OF OUR TIME

This is not the place to discuss the larger meaning of the continuing crisis of national security in which we live. Scholars and scientists have proposed many clues to the understanding of the historical developments of our epoch. Whether we look at the panorama of civilizations described by historian Toynbee or examine the stages of culture outlined by sociologist Sorokin or consider some other major interpretation, this much stands out: Ours is an epoch of changes profound enough to be called revolutionary and of sufficient scope to cover the globe.[29] These transformations are not likely to work themselves out in a year or even a decade. Although we assume that a third world war is not inevitable, we also must assume that there is little prospect of genuine peace in the next few years.

Hence the timeliness of our search for policies by which we can reasonably hope to attain a high level of national security without at the same time making an unnecessary sacrifice of individual freedom.

## II. THE THREAT INHERENT IN THE GARRISON-POLICE STATE

THE PRESENT CRISIS of defense is likely to be with us for years. Public alarm about the danger of war will rise and fall with the headlines, but the danger will probably continue. No one needs to be told that a third world war would devastate man and his works on a scale without precedent. A more insidious menace is that even if we avoid a general war, continuing crisis may undermine and eventually destroy free institutions. This is the time to remember what James Madison wrote to Thomas Jefferson during another tense period in our history (May 13, 1798) : "Perhaps it is a universal truth that the loss of liberty at home is to be charged to provisions against danger, real or pretended, from abroad." We want to prepare against dangers which are real, not pretended, and to keep the loss of liberty at home at the lowest possible point.

If we are to take adequate measures in time to cope with the continuing crisis in which we live, we need to be fully conscious of the dangerous possibilities that lie ahead. The purpose of this chapter is to outline these possible threats. No genuine American needs to be persuaded that the loss of national independence to a totalitarian despotism would be a crushing blow to freedom of every kind. We take for granted the readiness of the American people to sacrifice for national security. The immediate point is that overzealousness in the cause of national defense weakens rather than strengthens total security.

Knowledge of past crises can be utilized to show what can happen to individual freedom in a continuing crisis of defense. Under some conditions officials and the public at large are likely to develop a "state of nerves," of crisis impatience, that can burst into full hysteria and encroach unnecessarily and perilously upon individual freedom. The inference is not that citizens ought to refuse to sacrifice individual freedom on behalf of measures proposed in the name of national security, but rather that any sacrifice should be made knowingly, with full consciousness of what is being given up, and why. It should always be necessary to make a positive case for any limitation upon individual freedom, and also for the specific method to be employed in administering the limitation. By viewing these dangerous possibilities in advance, we can reasonably hope to prevent or mitigate their occurrence. The picture projected is what might happen, not what must happen.

### THE UNEASY COALITION

During World War II the Russian leaders were haunted by the possibility that a successful conspiracy by German conservatives would kill Hitler, put an end to Nazism, and clear the way for a united German-British-American attack on the Soviet Union. At the same time our top leaders were alert to the possibility that Germany and Russia might revive the Pact of 1939 and release Germany to spring once more against the West.

Top American leaders believed that the best way to prevent a separate deal between Russia and Germany, and to lay the foundation for successful cooperation in rebuilding the postwar world, was to allay Russian suspicions by offering and giving lavish support to the Soviet war effort.[1] The Russians evidently concluded that only by keeping the greatest possible pressure on the Western Allies could the Allies be kept convinced that the Russians were still in the war, while the Russians themselves would be in a position to judge when and if the Allies were preparing to leave Russia in the lurch. Any reluctance on the part of the United States to promise or provide supplies, for instance, would be a "tip" that Britain and America were swinging toward a separate deal with German conservatives. There is reason to believe that for the reasons indicated the Russians demanded supplies even when they were not needed.

## THE ATOMIC WEAPON

The explosion of the atomic bomb dramatized to the world the scientific and technical superiority of the United States. Hardly any development could have been more terrifying to the leaders of the Soviet, who were indoctrinated with respect for the influence of material factors in history. Having reached immense technical superiority, would not the capitalist world assail Russia after disposing of Nazi Germany and Japan?

The Russians began to bend every effort to get on a basis of at least weapon parity with the United States. German laboratories were dismantled and sent to Russia, and thousands of German scientists and weapons technicians have found a home in the Soviet Union.

The years immediately after our demonstration of the atomic bomb can be called the period of "American technical supremacy" in new weapons. Then we moved into a second period in which there were ever more plausible rumors of "progress by the Russians." During the first period these rumors were dismissed as boasts intended to impress the gullible. But there was not much doubt that the Russians could achieve formidable results by concentrating manpower, facilities, and resources upon selected problems. Although the general level of Soviet industrial development remains much below that of the West, Russia's centralized system can allocate vast facilities to priority projects.

More recently we have entered the third period after the bomb, "weapon parity" in the technology of new weapons. Parity does not mean equality. Between two powers it means the capacity of each to inflict such grave damage upon the other that it exercises a very strong deterring effect against aggression. This concept of weapon parity is useful to emphasize the narrowing of the gap in "know-how." The H-bomb has not, so far as we can tell, as yet modified the relative position of the rivals in the arms race.

The knowledge that Russia possesses atomic weapons has not increased, but rather diminished, our sense of security. It will be necessary to keep Russia under perpetual surveillance in the hope of being forewarned of aggression. The girdle of radar stations will no doubt be strengthened and pushed nearer to the borders of Russia and Russian satellites. Hence the globe will become even more sharply divided into a Russia-centered and an America-centered world. We will probably extend our system of alliances beyond the countries covered by the Atlantic Pact. In order to keep potential aggressors away from our borders, we will continue to build economic, political, and social relations throughout the non-Russian world.

### PRESSURE FOR DEFENSE EXPENDITURES

The continuing crisis will doubtless strengthen pressure for defense expenditures. This is in harmony with the principle that crisis intensifies demands for defense. In addition to popular sources, we must take into account the initiative of the expert on arms. The expert on planes wants more planes. The expert on ships wants more ships. The expert on guns wants more guns. And this pressure is not in bad faith. On the contrary, it is a natural and basically healthy tendency. Any professional worth his salt has a mind full of projects and lays hands on all the facilities he can use.

Crisis strengthens the plausibility of the military way of thinking. Experts on any subject exaggerate what they know best. The expert concentrates on one set of relationships. The other dimensions of reality seem less prominent and less important. The professional strategist thinks of all the contingencies connected with the use of weapons in war. The result is to emphasize in the minds of all who are exposed to his thinking the most extreme possibilities and the importance of physical weapons.

The professionals of the Army, Navy, and Air Force may be expected to push hard and in good conscience for weapon research, development, and equipment. In our country the tradition is to starve the services between wars. With full knowledge of this history no professional suffers from pangs of conscience when he gets a favorable "break" in public sentiment.

The American people have a favorable attitude toward experts, and this tends to support the pressure for defense appropriations in crises. Nearly everybody thinks he is an expert on something, and in the area of his competence assumes that he should be deferred to. (America is famous for the new occupations which have sprung up here and which want to be accepted as "professions.") Since laymen usually think of national defense in terms of physical weapons, there is a tendency to listen to the advice of experts on armament.

Once large expenditure programs are undertaken, special interests develop. When rearmament begins, many firms accept orders reluctantly and only in response to patriotic pressure since they have gone into business to produce some peacetime product for a civilian market. As productive capacity becomes committed to defense materials, businesses gradually begin to rely on defense projects. Since defense embraces economic assistance to foreign lands, agriculture becomes no less directly interested than business in defending whatever level of exports is reached.

## EXPANSION OF GOVERNMENT

When we divert resources to large-scale arms and other defense programs, we automatically enlarge the scope of government in industry, in politics, in science and education, and in every sphere of life.

In 1948 the President's Economic Advisers warned that arms expenditures much above fourteen billion dollars would make necessary a considerable imposition of controls in order to avoid profiteering and to cope with emerging shortages of certain materials. The ceiling figure chosen by the Advisers may be incorrect, but nearly everyone will agree that at some point the volume of expenditures would set off a strong agitation for controls.

The imposing of controls would be mechanically simpler now than it was before the war, since we have the experience of the war to guide us. Moreover, the National Security Resources Board has been set up and has even experimented for a time with several thousand stand-by committees to cover the nation's industry. The impact of industry controls on agriculture can be met, since the government is supposed to sustain price parity between farm and industrial products in order to protect the buying position of the farmers. As part of the economic recovery program many of our exports are now controlled.

As business comes to depend upon defense contracts, businessmen tend in fact, though not in form, to be hired administrators of government programs. They are dependent on central decisions for allocations of machine tools, plant, credit, raw materials, specifications, and price. Government becomes the risk bearer. Profit-making opportunities within the defense program are cut down as a matter of legislative policy in the hope of forestalling criticism of the defense program by wage workers, salaried workers, professional groups, and farmers.

It is unlikely that the volume of private investment would sustain crisis programs. The private investor is intimidated by the uncertainties connected with continuing crisis, by profit limitations, and by the expansion of controls. Consequently, to correct or forestall shortages and other "unbalances," the government takes the initiative and the risk to enlarge production facilities, and in general to perform top investment and managerial functions.

The starting of new enterprises under these circumstances is handicapped by the timidity of private risk capital and by the administrative complexities that multiply as controls spread. Another handicap is the security blackout on many new inventions. Inventions always attend the billion-dollar research and development projects underwritten by the government. But difficulties arise in making new inventions known in sufficient detail to attract promoters and investors without compromising security.

As crisis continues, scientific and educational activities become more dependent upon government. The high taxes that accompany high defense expenditures have their repercussions, among other spots, on educational funds. As support diminishes from private donors, the government is asked to step in. New institutions have already come into existence in order to bring government facilities and university talent together. (The Brookhaven interuniversity laboratory, Long Island, New York, is a recent example. The National Science Foundation is a new mechanism of the same sort.)

An insidious outcome of continuing crisis is the tendency to slide into a new conception of normality that takes vastly extended controls for granted, and thinks of freedom in smaller and smaller dimensions.

## CENTRALIZATION OF GOVERNMENT

Expanded government can be expected to be more centralized government. The long-term trend of recent decades has been toward the centralization of functions in the Federal government. This is an outcome of the increasing interdependencies of modern industrial life, and is a process which is stimulated by such crises as the two world wars which have been fought in this century. In the continuing crisis of the bipolar world, state and local governments are likely to come under the fiscal and regulatory arrangements of Washington to an increasing extent. The technological conditions of modern weapon development have already made it necessary to put great tracts of land under the direct control of Federal authorities. The Atomic Energy Commission and the armed services have taken over the land in many localities and assumed direct responsibility for administration. This is a precursor of further crisis adjustments.

## WITHHOLDING OF INFORMATION

The continuing crisis gradually imposes a dim-out on the sources and channels of public information. This is a result of the steady pressure of "security consciousness" in spite of the general admission that the public must have facts if it is to reach rational opinions on defense policy.

The principal of disclosure is recognized in the security regulations of the armed services. They lay down procedures for making information accessible to wider groups and to the public at large. "Downgrading" reduces the classification of an item from "top secret," for example, to "secret" or lower. "Declassification" removes all secrecy.

It is less the content than the administration of security regulations that endangers public information. The security officer has strong incentives to overclassify. At officers' training school, indoctrination emphasizes secrecy and not disclosure. On duty, an officer soon learns that it is safer to forestall criticism by stamping a document "secret" than by taking the risks involved in leaving off the stamp. It is not customary to reward acts of declassification; it is, however, commonplace to discipline a breach of security.

With the expansion of defense activities the government becomes a more important primary source of information, and as the armed forces grow, the military personnel has more influence on what is told the public.

### ATMOSPHERE OF SUSPICION

Connected with the cutting off of information is a thickening atmosphere of suspicion. All communists do not speak with Russian accents or have Russian parents. Communists often have permission to deny that they are members of the party. Communists conspire to create "fifth columns."

All this is confusing to the public in locating hostile elements. The citizen cannot be expected to make fine distinctions between communists who adore Stalin and those who adore Trotsky. The citizen cannot even be sure of distinguishing between socialists, liberals, and communists. The public has a general hostility against "reds," which is favorable soil for a propaganda smear by "pinning the red label" on someone.

The psychological warfare of the communists will not overlook opportunities to weaken America by widening every seam in our society. In some cases scientists and engineers can be kept away from national defense work if they are publicly and privately smeared as "reds." As it becomes more common to attack rivals as "red," cleavages in politics and business can be widened. The trade-union leader is in a particularly exposed position. When genuine communists and communist sympathizers are driven out of office at international union headquarters, they are freed of direct responsibility for union policy, and can agitate at the workbench and shop level against union leaders, whom they accuse of "selling out to the bosses." Since some rank-and-file grievances are always at hand, and can be intensified by agitation, workbench leadership is an effective ambush. If union leaders offer too many concessions, they run the risk of being attacked as "reds" or "fellow travelers." In such an atmosphere of recrimination and distrust the solidarity of labor and of the nation is impaired.

The crisis has already brought special measures into use to test the loyalty of government employees, thus giving a foretaste of what can be anticipated in a continuing and deepening crisis. It would be a new and strange experience for Americans to wonder if the office or home telephone is tapped; or whether a microphone has been installed in the room; or whether the reading of the meter yesterday was done by an agent who was actually sent to look over the books in the library; or whether the new girl at the office is a police agent; or whether an old friend is now adding to his income by writing reports about what goes on at private dinner parties; or whether one ought to cancel a subscription to a "liberal" magazine for fear a hostile neighbor will send in a denunciation; or whether one should stop writing letters to a schoolmate (who may possibly belong to a "front" organization) for fear private correspondence is being tampered with by police agents; or whether one should express no views whatever about matters of controversial public policy for fear of adding to a dossier in the police department; or whether one should caution his wife and children to avoid controversial topics so that suspicious acquaintances will not gossip about a "subversive" atmosphere in the home. In deepening crisis, life would be darkened by rumors (no doubt greatly exaggerated) of why John Jones has had his "vacation" extended or why Tom Brown was passed over for promotion or why Mary Williams can't get a government job. The initiative and outspokenness which have been the daily evidence of life in a free society would be slowly throttled. So far as government is concerned, John Lord O'Brian summed up an experienced judgment in these words:

No one familiar with the administration of a government department, however, can doubt that the mere existence of any law or order authorizing secret investigation will encourage suspicion, distrust, gossip, malevolent talebearing, character assassination and a general undermining of morale.[2]

In business organizations supplying the defense program, the discretion of management is reduced in the selection of employees at all levels, since contractors and subcontractors of the defense program are subject to loyalty checks. Labor unions, in turn, are scrutinized in connection with access to defense plants.

Existing restrictions on freedom of movement can be expected to become even more severe as the crisis continues. This applies to the granting of passports to Americans to travel abroad and to citizens of other countries to visit here. Within the country freedom of movement must be progressively curtailed as more acres are turned into proving grounds and more plants and other facilities are involved in the defense program.

Scientists, educators, and students engaged in research and development are drawn into the net of police surveillance. This comes about in connection with subcontracts to universities originating with the defense program, and the granting of scholarships and grants-in-aid.

The spread of political police activities is alien to our tradition and repugnant to our convictions, since we believe that an agency of this kind degenerates all too quickly into an organ of oppression and intimidation. Even without great abuse of authority, the simple fact of its enormously expanded role cannot fail to intensify the atmosphere of suspiciousness. The path is cleared for something comparatively new and unmistakably sinister in this country, namely, personal advancement by denunciation.

### PRESS AND PUBLIC OPINION DECLINE

In some ways the most insidious effect of continuing crisis is the undermining of the press and public opinion. The process resembles death by slow strangulation more than heart failure. Suffocation will not show its first effects in Washington or in the most influential organs of the press. The press corps in Washington prides itself upon its ability to dig out whatever it goes after. "There are no secrets in Washington" is a frequent boast. Americans are accustomed to "government by leak." It is common practice for a correspondent or a commentator to cultivate a "source" by playing down unfavorable news of the official or giving him favorable publicity. Mr. A, of one New York City paper, may find out what is going on in the Foreign Relations Committee from Senator Y. Commentator B gets a tip on what Prime Minister Churchill says in a confidential dispatch to a British officer about Greece. Correspondent C, of the competing big city paper, may get his inside story of the Air Force from a contact man in the Navy. In the thicket of agencies in Washington and in the innumerable rivalries among the subdivisions of the armed services, the press has learned to live on leaks and love it.

Security has already begun to tighten in Washington, and it is reasonable to foresee that security will be tighter as the crisis prolongs and deepens. Perhaps it will always be possible for a powerful newspaper to publish secret war plans and get off scot free. Possibly a columnist or commentator can reveal a secret paper from the files of the Department of State and bring no roof tumbling about his or his informant's ears. But evasions of security restrictions are likely to become less easy, partly because the press will usually be in active sympathy with a program of strong defense.

The drying up of information will first hit the smaller communities and the smaller units of the press. The formation of public opinion in America is a complex process. In local communities throughout America there are individuals who are turned to by their neighbors for the interpretation of the main happenings of the day. It may be a local banker. Often it is the editor of the local paper. Sometimes it is a clergyman, or the principal of the high school, or the teacher of history and civics. Many times it is a well-to-do and well-read farmer. It may be a trade-union leader. Possibly it is a leading merchant, and not infrequently it is a local lawyer or judge.

It is true that most of the members of a local community have access to the same radio broadcasts, and even to the same newspapers and periodicals, as the opinion makers. But the opinion makers are the interpreters of the content of the mass channels for their neighbors. They are deferred to by those who know them as more experienced or more judicious or better educated, or merely more successful, than others. In the daily processes of living, neighbors specialize their relations to one another, even including the interpretation of large questions of public policy.[3]

The range of the local opinion leader is not restricted to his immediate vicinity. Typically, the local leaders are among those summoned to take an active part in regional or even national conventions of country bankers, fraternal orders, the church, the high school principals' or teachers' association, the grange, or the union. At county, state, regional, and national conventions there is talk about major and general as well as local and special issues. Men and measures are judged and rejudged in the forums that spring up in the lobby, the bar, and the "smoke-filled rooms."

From studies that have been made of factories and unions, we know that the opinion-making process proceeds in much the same way as it does for the neighborhood. At nearly every workbench there is a member of the crew who is the opinion specialist. He may impress his fellow workers because he is more traveled or more acute or better read or better educated than they are. Often he is active in union affairs, whether with the faction in office or the opposition. The opinion leader has a tongue in the endless chain of formal and informal talk that Senator X is a "bum" and Y is a "hero." In somewhat more polished accents the same process of evaluation goes on at the Union League or the country club.

If public information dries up, and the level of suspiciousness goes up, the first casualty is the man of independent mind. When the caliber of the news in the media is reduced, the honest man finds the ground slipping out from under his feet. He sees that he does not have the raw material of judgment. As the fog deepens from the progressive blackout of information, it is apparent to the citizen that he is less and less qualified for effective citizenship.

When the independent citizen loses confidence that his opinion can be something more than a gripe or a hope, he may suspect that he is the target of propaganda; but he also admits that he has nothing beyond his suspicions to contribute to public opinion.

It is not necessary to assume that the State Department or the armed services will deliberately engage in fomenting war scares in order to protect their appropriations or to bolster the solidarity of the nation. Given the possible state of tension such measures are hardly necessary in any case. But we must allow for honest exaggerations, such as occurred in early 1948 when Washington was thrown into a dither by a few intelligence reports. Correspondents were summoned with great urgency and secrecy to hear the "background." Almost without exception they came away believing that they were being "had," not necessarily because the brass was trying to "put something over" for the sake of appropriations, but because of honest exaggeration. They were helpless to do much more than keep quiet, ask questions, and ride it out.

## WEAKENING OF POLITICAL PARTIES

Whatever their limitations, political parties are powerful agencies through which American opinion is organized, changed, and stabilized on great national questions. The hundreds of pressure organizations which mediate between the citizen and his government do not abolish the party system. On the contrary, the ordinary activity of a pressure group is to mobilize citizens in the hope of influencing the parties. Candidates and party campaign managers rely on one coalition of organized groups at one moment and then on another. Mitigating and giving some direction to the pressure struggle are the "grass-roots" leaders of opinion.

By weakening the "grass-roots" opinion leader, the drying up of public information undermines the vitality of the party system. The independent leader subsides into apathy, or becomes wholly dependent upon the handouts of pressure groups and government. The local editor, clergyman, teacher, lawyer, official, trade unionist, businessman, or farmer loses confidence in the validity of his criticism, not only of government policy as a whole, but of what the pressure organizations say who speak in his name. The Washington bureaucracy of the pressure group has even more freedom than usual from rank-and-file control. National policy increasingly becomes a matter of deals made between national pressure-group officials and the bureaucracy of executive departments and agencies. What the pressure organization is able to "deliver" more than ever depends upon what the officials of a centralizing government find it expedient to give.

As a result of these changes, congressmen and party managers are caught in a squeeze. With the weakening of the "grass-roots" leader, a moderating element within each pressure organization and constituency is lost. Continuing crisis leads to the withdrawal of the party from many of the gravest issues. We have seen this in the field of foreign affairs as the "bipartisan principle" has taken form. Cordell Hull and his succeeding Secretaries of State, together with many of the ablest leaders of the Senate and House, have applied the idea that "party differences stop at the water's edge." As the information curtain goes down, the temptation exists for the executive branch of the government to justify and invoke the "bipartisan principle" to close off debate.

The principle of party responsibility already rests on sandy foundations in American government. As everybody knows, the Congress and the Presidency may be held by different parties, so that in the maneuvering it is not easy for the voter to decide who is responsible for the conflicts that follow. It is perhaps less generally understood how the seniority principle operates to break up party responsibility in the Senate and the House. A President with the majority of his party behind him may find that important committee chairmanships are in the hands of party members who are out of sympathy with him. Our party system, in fact, is poorly geared to withstand the forces that would undermine it during a continuing crisis of defense.

### DECLINE OF THE CONGRESS

With the drying up of informed public opinion, the Senate and the House can be expected to decline as effective agencies for controlling the executive. As in other spheres of national life, the process would be gradual and undramatic. No patriotic member of the Congress will deny that some secrecy is essential to security. Recognizing the rapid tempo of modern science and invention, Senators and Representatives will be willing to dedicate large sums to weapon research and development. (The billions which the Congress allowed to go into atomic research "paid off.") Nobody doubts that nuclear physics is making vast strides and that constant vigilance is needed to translate basic knowledge into national armor. Bacteriological warfare, jet propulsion and guided missiles, chemical warfare: no branch can be safely left to languish. Certainly the Congress will be unwilling to bring into the open all the facts on the basis of which rational judgments could be made among weapon categories, or concerning the advantages of physical versus psychological, economic, and other weapons. Because of the risk of disclosure, there will be some reluctance to have detailed descriptions given even at closed and secret hearings.

Such feelings would inevitably intensify as congressmen begin to distrust one another more actively. They will believe it unwise to make certain kinds of information available to the Senate or the House as a whole if they suspect the loyalty or the gullibility of their colleagues. Some members have already come under the suspicion of their colleagues because they received election support from communist blocs. As the communists go underground, and the atmosphere of suspicion is intensified, the moral position of the patriotic Senator or Representative grows more difficult in relation to the executive branch. He cannot in good conscience insist upon as much disclosure as he needs if he doubts the trustworthiness of "weak links" in either chamber. ( Judgments of a sound security risk depend partly on ideology but also on self-control when and if intoxicated, for example.) Our Senators and Representatives are not officially screened to determine whether they are good security risks. That the members of Congress will allow the executive to subject them to loyalty checks is, to say the least, highly doubtful. It is necessary only to recall the commotion made by Representatives Hoffman and Busbey when they discovered that the Civil Service Commission had dossiers on them.

However great his initial reluctance, a patriotic Senator or Representative would undoubtedly find it necessary to acquiesce in further expansion of executive authority. As the danger of conflict increases, the executive may be authorized to negotiate secretly with foreign powers, acting with very general advice. The practice of enabling the exccutive to act, subject to later veto by the Congress, would probably be extended. If the gravity of the crisis reaches this stage, the "power to declare war" which under the Constitution rests with the Congress will have faded nearly to zero.

Caught in the circumstances we have been examining, the member of Congress who takes up a critical attitude toward the executive on national defense issues will find himself in a less and less tenable position. Often he cannot satisfactorily substantiate his public statements without revealing facts which he believes it contrary to the national interest to disseminate. At the same time, he cannot reasonably expect the public to believe him without evidence. No man of integrity can fail to suffer crises of conscience under such conditions. There is not much doubt, however, that the issue will be resolved more often than not by silence.

Such conditions heighten the cumulative impact of the "little pressures" on the Congress from the executive branch. It is reasonable to expect that the billions required by the armed forces, for instance, will exert many side effects, some of which bear upon the ordinary member of the Congress. It is more than that the services are heavily represented on Capitol Hill by lobbyists working for legislation. In many little ways the services can help or hurt the rank-and-file member with his constituency. Publicity and cooperation can be given to the legislator, or withheld, in connection with the opening of training schools, the dedication of memorials, and tours of inspection. Appointments for visitors can be arranged with alacrity or quietly ignored. No official is unappreciative of courtesies, such as rides on planes belonging to the armed services or a physical checkup at the Naval Hospital. There are traditional rights of appointment to Annapolis and West Point and continuing appropriations for "rivers and harbors" which "bring money into the district," and there are defense contracts and subcontracts for local business. Fortunately it is rarely a question of bribery in these matters but rather of the dulling of personal incentive to scrutinize or cut doubtful estimates. Any arm of government, indeed any institution, that has no less than fifteen billion dollars a year to spend cannot fail to exercise a species of charm that discourages tactless outspokenness in dealing with it. Unwillingness to give offense can go beyond the point of good manners and impair the public interest in the efficient use of manpower, facilities, and resources.

The Congress is always open to attack as a "gab shop" because of the very nature of the lawmaking function. All this is highlighted by the occasional filibuster, and the times when Congress is a target of attack by the chief executive as well as by disappointed pressure-group operators and party politicians. National crisis spotlights the executive or "action" arms of government and breeds impatience with "more talk." Since the withholding of information often prevents the Senator or the Representative from telling what he knows, the impression is heightened that congressmen are "talking through their hats."

## DECLINE OF MOST CIVILIAN EXECUTIVES

A continuing crisis favors the rise of the executive branch of the government at the expense of the legislature. This tendency toward centralization in times of crisis is one of the oldest and best established relationships in political science.[4] The advantages, however, are not uniformly enjoyed by all departments and agencies of the executive. With one important exception, the civilian agencies decline in effective power as the influence of the armed services rises. The exception is the political police.

At the outset, the role of the armed forces specialist is advisory and technical. When the State Department and the President were weighing our line of action toward Greece, the armed services were asked to estimate our position if a considerable amount of resistance appeared. Estimates of this kind are typical of the proper and necessary way to use the particular competence of the Army, Navy, and Air Force heads. (The National Security Council has been a channel for the evaluation of such possibilities.)

As the crisis continues, the number of strategic issues which are thought about is extended to cover all imaginable contingencies. Suppose there are further communist penetrations in southeastern Asia? How much armed force, handled in what way, would be necessary to contain the communists? Suppose that a Soviet-inspired coup occurs in northern Iran, what would be necessary to protect the oil fields of the south? Or to aid the Iranians to upset the coup? Suppose certain Turkish territories are invaded? Assume that Soviet-directed armies from Bulgaria, Rumania, and Hungary invade Jugoslavia? Such questions are representative of the contingencies that suggest themselves when the potentialities of the future are in review.

The specter of crisis shapes men's minds into the strategic mold of thought. Other features of social life are given meaning in so far as they can be translated in terms of ultimate fighting effectiveness. Owing to the continuing emergency, the armed services are able to command the talent of men of ability who would normally devote themselves to business and other peaceful pursuits. Furthermore, the vast administrative mechanism of the services provides a means of accomplishing purposes which the civilian sector of society is reluctant to contemplate. (This applies, for example, to advance preparations against surprise bomb raids.) Provided with a comparatively clear standard of judgment and schooled to doing staff work and to following instructions, the weight of the services makes itself felt in widening spheres of decision. Hence the roles which were initially advisory and technical become operational and comprehensive. The civilian heads of administration are influenced by their advisers and assistants who are in sympathy with the basic aims of the armed services to begin with and who are likely to rely upon facts and interpretations originating in the services.

If the civilian administrator is at odds with the services, he is trapped by the same considerations that stop the mouth of the conscientious member of the Congress. He does not feel free to state in public, or in some cases to the Congress, the facts that might convince most of his fellow citizens that he is right. Such an administrator is a vulnerable target for rivals who may imply or assert that he is sabotaging the national defense effort. Given the atmosphere of suspicion which prevails in a crisis, only a few men of outstanding prestige derived from years of conspicuous public service can hope to survive. The supply of such men is always short, and they are not always where they can do the most good.

In the continuing crisis the role of the investigative services is bound to grow. The function of the political police is to gather information on the basis of which determinations can be made as to whether a person serves America or a foreign power.

This vitally necessary function in any continuing crisis of national security is carried on under conditions which readily lend themselves to abuse, and which have often been described. The procedure of political police the world over has a certain similarity since the job is basically similar. Much of the work is secret. A dossier (or file) of any "suspect" is kept (and one can be made suspect by an anonymous denunciation). Into the file, besides denunciations which are volunteered, go the reports of hired investigators. There is an understandable tendency to give more rewards of pay and praise to agents who supply "derogatory" material. The agent who "clears" more suspects than his fellow agent may be viewed with some doubt. Is he, by chance, a secret agent? His position is similar to that of the manager of a department of a business who appears to hire an unusual number of "subversives." A mist of doubt begins to accumulate around his name. The same pressure is on the chief of the agencies doing police work. What if they fail to turn up dangerous characters? Does this mean they are "sluggish," "overcautious," or actually "subversive"?

In the protracted security crisis which we are here considering, the political police function can be expected to play a part of growing influence. In the past America has had little direct experience with political agencies or methods, and we have inherited the English tradition of aversion to all forms of arbitrary power, and to practices such as secret denunciation and trial which are peculiarly susceptible to abuse. Under continued crisis, a great expansion in the number of official and unofficial associations and individuals who concern themselves with the political police function can be anticipated.

Activities of this kind have been carried on in America on a comparatively modest scale, and the fact that there is a political police function has only recently been recognized by any large sector of the public. The publicity attending the imposition of "loyalty" investigations upon Federal employees brought the role of the FBI in this connection into public notice. A great many special intelligence units which conduct their own inquiries have been scattered through the government. The Immigration Service (Treasury) and the Department of State are examples. Some reserve officers in the armed forces devote themselves on a part-time and voluntary basis to political police intelligence. Federal police agencies rely upon the voluntary cooperation of state and municipal police to assist in political work. The larger cities have long had special squads devoted to such problems. The Haymarket Riot in Chicago, for instance, produced the "Industrial Squad," later known as the "Red Squad," when communists took the place of anarchists as the chief problem.

Voluntary organizations have engaged or are engaging in

espionage on their fellow citizens for the purpose of detecting political attitudes which are regarded as dangerous. For years this has been an activity of many White Russian officers and officials who have found refuge in this country. Members of groups possessing a distinct religious or cultural loyalty have often acted as informers on political opponents (even when fellow Americans were involved). Some "patriotic" and local organizations of veterans carry on similar projects.

Private intelligence services offer businessmen lists of workers and unions who are alleged to be communist. Part of their sales appeal has been that the businessman could expose strike leaders as "subversive" and win public opinion on his side in a strike. Private detective services offer themselves to business corporations to do spying on employees. One of the appeals here, as in the other case, is that dangerous persons may be exposed. (Major businesses do not believe that espionage is a sound method of industrial relations.)

Under the impact of a continuing crisis the "man with the dossier" takes an important advisory place in personnel choices at every level. Beginning as an adviser, the head of a political police agency tends to get his men accepted in operating spots, first of all in personnel departments.

### DECLINE OF THE COURTS

Under the American system we place an enormous degree of trust in courts. The first ten amendments to the Constitution provide binding written texts which give the courts a peg on which to justify their defense of private rights and civilian supremacy. How far can we depend upon the courts to withstand the pressure generated by a continuing crisis and to act as a barrier against the strangulation of free institutions?

It is important to view the court system as a whole, and not limit ourselves entirely to the words uttered by the Supreme

Court. The damage to private rights and civilian principles can be accomplished in the thousands of minor jurisdictions (Federal, state, local) into which our country is divided. Much of this damage is not brought to the notice of the highest tribunal in the land, if at all, until years have elapsed. In one of our earliest crises of national security, for example, the Alien and Sedition Acts were passed (1798). Thousands of persons were imprisoned, and the Acts were presently repealed. Their constitutionality was never passed upon by the Supreme Court. On the basis of past performance we expect the courts to provide some defense in future crises, even though the defense gradually crumbles.

### CHANGES IN GROUP INFLUENCE

This preview of the serious possibilities for the loss of freedom if the crisis continues and intensifies can be summed up in terms of changing institutions: rising defense expenditures, expansion of government, centralization of government, withholding of information, police investigation, decline of the press and public opinion, weakening of the political parties, decline of the Congress, decline of civilian administrators (except the political police), weakening of the courts. These changes imply that free institutions are crippled, not alone in the government, but in the market, in the forums of public enlightenment, and in the laboratories and libraries of science and scholarship.

Parallel with these developments and interacting with them are shifts in the relative power and influence of groups. The obvious change is the rise of official at the expense of such unofficial groups as businessmen, free trade-unions, the press, and private pressure and party groups. Within the official category the most significant shift is the rise of the soldier and the political police and the relative decline in weight of other officials. The businessman, for instance, declines as the free market disappears. Privately owned and operated enterprises would continue to be called by the name "businesses," but the reality would have turned into something else. The businessman would resemble the enterpriser in a free market only in superficial traits. He would in fact be an administrative official dependent upon the approval of the superiors who wrote the regulations under which he works, and issued the contract which he fulfills. The classical description of the businessman as a "higgler of the market" assumes that there is very considerable scope for bargaining or at least for alternative choices. With the extension of controls the choices that were once made by bargaining become administrative decisions made by pressure and negotiation. From the economic "market," production and distribution pass into the political "arena."

In view of the expectation of war, and the importance of national security as a value, the new state of affairs could be called a "garrison state." To the extent that intimidation is threatened or applied at home, we have a police state. In the garrison-police state the dominant group is constituted by the specialists on violence, since force is the distinctive skill of soldiers and police. The specialist on violence rises in power as other skill groups subside, such as the specialists on civil administration, party and pressure-group administration, and specialists on propaganda or persuasion.

This transformation would come about gradually as men abandon their former roles and take up new ones, which are thought of as temporary. The owner or active head of a business notes that he is losing able associates to the civil or military services. Sensing that his own activities are becoming more stereotyped, the executive may himself "put on a suit." A credit manager connects with the political police because of his knowledge of the network of industrial-information contacts across the nation. A trade-unionist joins up in order to spy on communists and supposed fellow travelers in the labor movement. It is on the basis of thousands of choices of this kind that the transformation in American society would take place. At any given moment

· 47 ·

the currents appear to be running as usual in all directions. Closer inspection would show drift away from the activities comparatively untouched by the crisis into operations immediately involved. The garrison-police state is both a "state of mind" and a "state of readiness." It is when the state of mind gets set that the transformation is well along.

If the crisis continues for five, ten, fifteen, or more years, the factors making for the transformation of American life will gain in depth and breadth. Nearly all choices and decisions will be made with the expectation of violence in mind. The atmosphere of threat and suspicion provides the incentive for the weak to seek protection from the stronger, which brings about an informal stratification of society. Relationships become less fluid and more fixed, as in a feudal form of social organization. Every person of influence is surrounded by dependents and retainers who fasten themselves upon him more tenaciously than under peaceful conditions. As human relations are determined to an increasing extent by the status of one's protector, the channels open to the individual merit of the "unknown" are clogged by the intense suspiciousness and place-consciousness of a hierarchy living in an insecure world. The long-run trend under these conditions is to formalize the relations of dependency-protection, and to create a social structure which is molded according to the principle of status and not upon the merit of the individual. The American dream has been the achievement of a mobile form of society, an organization of human relationships in which there is effective equality of opportunity. A social organization based upon protection-dependency tends to transmit status relations from one generation to the next, slowly evolving a true caste society, which is the very opposite of a mobile society.

Not only America, but all Western civilization, has been the scene of a vast struggle to unfetter the individual from the bonds of preceding status forms of society. Liberalism and socialism were two wings of the attack against status (caste) tendencies carried over from earlier times. The spokesmen of modern liberalism and of socialism are alike in arguing the case for the free man living in a free society. They differ about some of the social institutions capable of translating the dream of freedom into fact.

As matters stand today the continuing crisis of insecurity may bring disaster to both conceptions. For the most drastic fate that could befall mankind, aside from physical annihilation, is the turning of the clock back from the hour of freedom and the forging anew of the chains of caste in the heat of chronic crisis. This is the true measure of the peril represented by the garrison-police state, which has already emerged in the Soviet Union, and which it is the aim of sound policy to prevent in the United States and elsewhere on the globe.[5]

Plainly the national security of America demands all the sacrifices necessary to preserve American independence. This calls for the development of an American garrison to be defended against aggression. If the crisis continues for years, as seems probable, and rises to even higher levels of intensity, as seems likely, effective freedom of choice will be restricted by the necessities of defense. One urgent problem, which is the problem with which this book is particularly concerned, is how to keep these sacrifices of freedom at the lowest point consistent with national security, since an unnecessary loss of freedom is an unnecessary blow to security. Our aim is to prevent successful aggression by a totalitarian dictatorship without becoming transformed in the process into a garrison prison.

# III.  THE  MEANING  OF  NATIONAL
## SECURITY  POLICY

IF THE POLICIES of defense are to safeguard the fundamental
values of America, the requirements of national security must
be clearly related to the over-all goals of the commonwealth.
These have been expressed by the leaders of the nation on occasions that have become historic.

There have been in the past, as no doubt there will be in the
future, discrepancies between the ideal goals of the nation and the
prevailing level of practice. But there is "stress toward consistency" between the ideal and the actual which it is the task of
statesmanship to further.

In the free climate of opinion in this country everyone can tell
in his own way what he thinks are the goals of America. We may
differ in choice of words, but we have a common stock of ideas
from living the life of an American. Not many would deny that
the aim of American life is to realize the dignity and worth of the
human personality in theory and practice. We have in mind a
commonwealth of individual merit rather than inherited privilege.
We depend upon institutions which give the greatest possible lee-
way to individual choice and turn to coercion reluctantly as a last
resort. The life of man in American society, as in all human
associations, is the shaping and sharing of values by means of
institutions which he uses to utilize resources. The values are
"life, liberty and the pursuit of happiness." Or, to spell out the
values at somewhat greater length, there is well-being and
abundance, coupled with skill in the exercise of favorite talents.
There is democracy in politics and shared respect in all human
relations, by which is meant the absence of discrimination based

on religion, race, sex, family position, or any criterion other than personal worth. Enlightenment is a basic value, and rectitude, which is a sense of responsibility to the community. And there are the intimate values of love and loyalty.[1]

If we assume that the overriding goal of the American commonwealth is the dignity of man, what does national security signify? The distinctive meaning of national security is *freedom from foreign dictation*. National security policy implies a state of readiness to use force if necessary to maintain national independence.

There is also a secondary meaning. When we provide for the common defense, we hope to defend ourselves against the tragedy and horror of war by deterring a potential disturber of the peace from daring to take aggressive action. But this is not the ultimate meaning of defense. If the only object were to do away with the danger of war, the aim could be accomplished without benefit of arms. We could install a communist leadership in this country and alter American institutions according to the directives of Moscow. We would then apply for admission into the Union of Socialist Soviet Republics.

Apart from a small minority of communists, hardly anyone dreams of avoiding war by submitting to outside dictation. Peace on such terms is peace at too high a price.

The conception of national security does not mean dictating to other peoples. From the beginning of our life as a nation we have looked upon the United States as part of a world community of peoples who are both independent and interdependent. Our Constitution has no place for imperialistic arrogance in dealing with other peoples. The paragraphs that spell out the authority of the Congress authorize that body "to define and punish piracies and felonies on the high seas, and offenses against the law of nations." The mention of the law of nations provides a key to the American idea of world order. Not by conquest but by the volun-

· 51 ·

tary expansion of the institutions of world law do we propose to cooperate in perfecting a world community.

We must be strong enough to defend the United States from any invader. We must be able to prevent an aggressor from taking and holding strategic positions from which he can directly menace this country. Our arms must at all times deter potential aggressors.

In a word, a basic aim of American policy is the prevention of war by all lawful and equitable means and the winning of all unavoidable wars. To win a war is to bring an end to military resistance and to succeed in encouraging a successor regime that is likely to cooperate as a peaceful member of the world community.

Under modern scientific and technical conditions the cost of armament adequate to these tasks is a heavy burden on our national income.

## A COMPREHENSIVE PROGRAM OF NATIONAL DEFENSE DOES NOT RELY SOLELY ON ARMAMENT

National defense is more than the possession of weapons of physical destruction. A comprehensive program also uses diplomacy, information, and economic instruments of foreign policy. By the proper application of these instruments we may improve our security position by reducing the foreign menace. Perhaps we can separate an actual or potential enemy from his allies, or prevent him from bringing another ally or satellite into camp. It may be possible to weaken a hostile power by encouraging secession or revolt. By diplomacy and allied methods we can prepare and maintain "positions in readiness" across the seas, notably in the British Isles and Western Europe, and we can prevent the Soviet Union, for example, from achieving comparable positions in the Western Hemisphere near our territory.

The best result is had, of course, if we can transform a hostile into a friendly member of the world community, willing to co-operate in protecting public order and in advancing the welfare and freedom of all. This in fact is the highest test of efficiency in the foreign policy of a free people: to preserve the security of the nation while bringing about by voluntary methods a situation in which all are made more secure and free. The greatest success in the use of armament is not in destroying life and property but in deterring aggressors from imposing themselves upon others until they can be dealt with at home by the people most immediately affected.

There is truth in the celebrated maxim of Clausewitz to the effect that war is the pursuit of policy by other than peaceful means. It is no less true to affirm with another German general that "war is the bankruptcy of policy." [2]

## THE BEST BALANCE OF ALL INSTRUMENTS OF FOREIGN POLICY

The inference is that national defense calls for the best balance of all instruments of foreign policy (arms, diplomacy, economics, information). A continuing campaign for peace and security must be based upon military preparedness, an intelligent and comprehensive foreign policy, and the strengthening of our non-military defenses. This calls for an active information program at home and abroad to strengthen liberty, and for the continuation of economic aid to peoples struggling to maintain or attain democratic freedom.

## SECURITY AND THE IMPACT INSIDE AMERICA OF THE MEASURES ADOPTED FOR THE PRIMARY PURPOSES OF FOREIGN POLICY

National defense is not limited to foreign affairs. Our security is also affected by the impact inside America of the measures adopted for the primary purposes of foreign policy.

## National Security and Individual Freedom

The cost of arms and of economic, informational, and diplomatic programs in foreign countries comes out of the pockets of the American people. We must be prepared to foot the bill for independence as well as to enjoy its benefits.

The American citizen wants to be reasonably certain that he is getting the most return in security for his defense dollar. He must be convinced that our foreign policies are realistically adapted to the world in which we live and that we are not responsible for the continuing crisis. For example, when we give military, economic, and other aid to nondemocracies abroad, it must be apparent that we are concerned in good faith not alone with immediate strategic gains but with the long-range advantage of guiding development to a point where sound economic and social foundations exist for free institutions.

The American citizen wants to feel assured, too, that wasteful and duplicating expenditures are kept at the lowest possible point.

He must also be convinced that the methods chosen to put the defense program into effect bring about the least possible loss of freedom at home. If the nation is to be free, it must be secure; and if it is to be secure, the nation must be free.

Our security is affected not only by what the citizen thinks of our defense program; it is also affected by the impact of the program upon our physical resources. If we overspend in the name of national defense, we weaken American security. Instead of readying the nation to defend itself in the hour of need, defense expenditures can have the opposite effect by reducing the assets on hand for the emergency. Every man-hour, facility, and resource spent unnecessarily on armament wastes the economic strength of the nation. Excessive mobilization of assets for security purposes is in fact an immobilization of resources for all purposes, including security.*

* As Hamilton phrased it in No. XXVIII of *The Federalist,* "The extent of the military force must, at all events, be regulated by the resources of the country."

## The Meaning of National Security Policy

This principle applies with particular force to the problem of security in the kind of crisis in which we are involved today. Although all competent analysts agree that World War III might break out at any time, the weight of opinion is that the chances are against it. Rather, the present variable crisis—now a little more, now a little less, grave—is held likely to continue for years to come. If we give in to "crisis mentality," we lay ourselves open to psychological attack by a power who employs a series of hostile moves of limited scope in order to induce us to heap up equipment out of proportion to the actual threat. Such waste of resources is an internal bleeding that ends in weakness.

### SECURITY AND THE IMPACT AT HOME AND ABROAD OF POLICIES PRIMARILY AIMED AT INTERNAL CONDITIONS

It has been noted that our security is affected by the foreign and domestic impact of policies undertaken with foreign policy primarily in view. The fact that policies primarily aimed at internal conditions affect our security at home and abroad needs equal recognition. Two of the chief points of attack against the United States in foreign countries, for instance, are the alleged inherent instability of our economic system and the prevalence of discrimination against colored peoples. Whatever measures are taken at home to maintain high levels of productive employment and to reduce discrimination also strengthen our position abroad. Security policies are thus being made whenever any decision influences the stability of our economic life or the degree to which opportunity is made to depend upon individual merit.

*The conclusion is that American security measures should be the outcome of a comprehensive process of balancing the costs and benefits of all policies in the foreign and domestic fields.*[3]

The determination of how strong America needs to be in physical weapons (or in any other respect) is properly a policy judgment rather than an expert opinion. There are no experts on national security. There are only experts on aspects of the problem. Judgments of security are balance sheets of our present and prospective position as a nation under all thinkable conditions and policies.

There are bound to be risks in connection with security. Any idea that there can be absolute security through defense preparations is a delusion, since in our kind of world, dominated by the expectation of violence, there is always risk of war. The only way to be sure exactly when a war will break out is to start one. But this sort of aggressive planning is only for a despotism or dictatorship. Even a despotism fully preoccupied with war cannot be sure of its calculations. A recent example: Nazi Germany was not prepared for the kind of war that the last war proved to be.

## SECURITY CALLS FOR A COMPREHENSIVE AND BALANCED REVIEWING PROCEDURE

Since all security policies entail risk, the public interest calls for the calculation of risk by a *procedure* that balances each policy against every policy and arrives at a judgment to which many minds have contributed. Only by developing proper procedures can public confidence be gained or vindicated in the long-run wisdom of the outcome. At any given moment well-informed persons may disagree as to whether defense expenditures are too high or too low, or whether the over-all defense program is in balance or seriously unbalanced. The public must estimate the bias and competence of rival leaders. The public interest can be protected by the use of a procedure that takes conflicting views into account and subjects them to the discipline of debate and exposure to available knowledge.

The initial responsibility for the review and balancing of security policies is with the executive branch of the government. But the responsibility of the Congress for reviewing the initiatives taken by the executive is heavy. The courts are involved in guarding our traditional system from overzealous encroachment in the name of security. Ultimate responsibility for the review and balancing of policy lies, however, with public opinion.

## FOUR PRINCIPLES OF NATIONAL POLICY

At all levels of review of measures proposed in the name of security, special attention needs to be paid to the relation of the program to four traditional principles of national policy. These principles are more specific applications of the fundamental values of America. They merit emphasis because they are peculiarly likely to be violated during a prolonged period of crisis, when the domain proper to freedom may be unnecessarily curtailed without sufficient notice being taken of basic issues. Every program put forward on behalf of national security needs scrutiny in terms of four questions:

1. Is there a threat to the principle of civilian supremacy in our system of government?
2. Does the policy involve a threat to freedom of information?
3. Is there danger to the civil liberties of the individual?
4. Does the policy violate the principle of a free as against a controlled economy?

If the answer to any question is in the affirmative, the problem is to determine whether the potential loss of freedom can be avoided or reduced without endangering national security beyond the margin of reasonable risk.

Strictly speaking, all measures proposed in the name of security are capable of being examined according to the impact which they are likely to have on all the goal values and institutions of America. The principle of civilian supremacy is a characteristic

of democratic government, and has obvious and immediate rele-
vance to the defense crisis. Freedom of information is an essential
feature of that public enlightenment which is valued in its own
right, and is also an essential means to sound public opinion. The
civil liberties of the individual are means of safeguarding the
equality of respect which is a basic value in a free society. The
preference for a free as against a controlled economy rises from
the respect for individual choice which is a fundamental value.
The preference also rests upon the ground that when the economy
is free, it is most productive, and contributes most to the standard
of living.

### CIVILIAN SUPREMACY

Let us consider at somewhat greater length the traditional
principle of civilian supremacy.

From the early days of our life as a people we have been aware
of the problem of subordinating military to civilian authority and
control. Prominent among the grievances stated in the Declaration of Independence, from Jefferson's first draft to the appearance of the document in its final form, was that "He [the King]
has kept among us in time of peace standing armies without the
consent of our Legislatures," and that "He has affected to render
the Military independent of and superior to the Civil power."

Foreign prophets of doom believed that the American experiment in free government would end with a Caesar in the saddle.
At the very beginning, however, a model of correct military-
civilian relations was set by General Washington, who patiently
endured the vexation of control by an inexperienced Congress
representing a poorly united country. As he wrote in 1777:

I confess, I have felt myself greatly embarrassed with respect to a
vigorous exercise of Military power. An ill placed humanity perhaps
and a reluctance to give distress may have restrained me too far. But
these were not all. I have been aware of the prevalent jealousy of

military power, and that this has been considered as an evil much to be apprehended even by the best and most sensible among us. Under this Idea, I have been cautious and wished to avoid as much as possible any Act that might improve it. On [acts] of Military power, whether immediate or derived originally from another Source, they [the people] have ever looked with a jealous and suspicious Eye.

Fear of military rule was expressed in opposition to a standing army in peacetime. The Virginia Declaration of Rights (June 12, 1776), for example, had proclaimed,

. . . that standing armies, in time of peace, should be avoided, as dangerous to liberty; and that in all cases the military should be under strict subordination to, and governed by, the civil power.

It is not always remembered that John Adams and other founders of the Republic thought of the system of checks and balances as an alternative to the dangers of army rule. In "A Defense of the Constitutions of Government of the United States of America," Adams wrote, in the conclusion to Volume 1:

All nations, under all governments, must have parties; the great secret is how to control them. There are but two ways, either by a monarchy and standing army, or by a balance in the constitution. Where the people have a voice, and there is no balance, there will be everlasting fluctuations, revolutions, and horrors, until a standing army, with a general at its head, commands the peace, or the necessity of an equilibrium is made appear to all, and is adopted by all.

In the debates of the Constitutional Convention, the issue loomed large. The power to raise armies, in Article 1, Section 8, was discussed at some length, and proposals to limit the peacetime size of the army to a specific figure were defeated only when it was pointed out that revenue appropriations were limited to a two-year period. It was even suggested by one delegate that the militia clause include the words, "that the liberties may be better secured against the danger of standing armies in time of peace," but the motion to that effect was defeated as "setting a dishonorable mark of distinction on the military class of citizens," in the words of Gouverneur Morris.

*The Federalist* deals, in several numbers, with the issues connected with defense. Hamilton, in Number 41, found it necessary to answer the objection that appropriations were made for two years rather than one. In Number 8 he argued that the army authorized in the proposed Constitution would be no danger to freedom because of its smallness and the prevailing attitudes of the people:

> The smallness of the army renders the natural strength of the community an over-match for it; and the citizens, not habituated to look up to the military power for protection, or to submit to its oppressions, neither love nor fear the soldiery; they view them with a spirit of jealous acquiescence in a necessary evil, and stand ready to resist a power which they suppose may be exerted to the prejudice of their rights. The army under such circumstances may usefully aid the magistrate to suppress a small faction, or an occasional mob, or insurrection; but it will be unable to enforce encroachments against the united efforts of the great body of the people.

In Number 41, Hamilton states the dangers and expediencies of a military establishment with great clarity:

> Not the less true is it, that the liberties of Rome proved the final victim to her military triumphs; and that the liberties of Europe, as far as they ever existed, have, with few exceptions, been the price of her military establishments. A standing force, therefore, is dangerous, at the same time that it may be a necessary, provision. On the smallest scale it has its inconveniences. On an extensive scale its consequences may be fatal. On any scale it is an object of laudable circumspection and precaution. A wise nation will combine all these considerations; and, whilst it does not rashly preclude itself from any resource which may become essential to its safety, will exert all its prudence in diminishing both the necessity and the danger of resorting to one which may be inauspicious to its liberties.

## The Meaning of National Security Policy

The best safeguards are "the effectual establishment of the Union" and "a limitation of the term for which revenue may be appropriated to their support."

When Washington was president, he grasped more than one opportunity to underline the proper subordination of the armed forces to civilian control. He wrote to Governor Henry Lee at the time of the Whisky Rebellion:

> There is but one point on which I think it proper to add a special recommendation. It is this, that every officer and soldier will constantly bear in mind that he comes to support the laws and that it would be peculiarly unbecoming in him to be in any way the infractor of them; that the essential principles of a free government confine the provinces of the Military to these two objects: 1st: to combat and subdue all who may be found in arms in opposition to the National will and authority; 2dly: to aid and support the civil Magistrate in bringing offenders to justice. The dispensation of this justice belongs to the civil Magistrate and let it ever be our pride and our glory to leave the sacred deposit there unviolated. . . .[4]

In many succeeding situations our chief executives have found it important to reaffirm the basic principle of civilian supremacy. General Andrew Jackson reassured the country in his first inaugural address (March 4, 1829):

> Considering standing armies as dangerous to free governments in time of peace, I shall not seek to enlarge our present establishment, nor disregard that salutary lesson of political experience which teaches that the military should be held subordinate to the civilian power.

Thoroughly entrenched during the first generations of national history, the principle was not seriously challenged even during the Civil War and Reconstruction period, and certainly not in subsequent years.

Civilian concern with defense policies is in no way the same as a desire to hamstring the military. Civilians must be concerned with the scope and the direction of defense policies ($a$) if our traditional civilian supremacy principle is to be maintained, ($b$) if our capacity to produce is to be as great as possible, ($c$) if our defense program is to be adjusted to our capacity to produce, and ($d$) if the timing of our program is to be adapted to the situation prevailing at home and abroad. The unprecedented nature of our present defense situation is such that it is more urgent than ever that our government be responsive to the will of the people and that the principle of civilian supremacy be maintained throughout our government. The civilian principle is, of course, closely related to an informed judgment on our capacity to produce. Economic and productivity considerations, as well as military, are the basis of a sound defense program. Another important element in the retention of civilian supremacy is assurance of a proper interchange of information among appropriate agencies of government to the end that scientific and technical developments will not be retarded; there should also be a proper flow of information to a greater end that the public will better understand the nature of our defense problems and hence will fully support the basic essentials of our defense program. There is also the crucial question of *when* as well as *what* needs to be done.

Few civilians believe themselves to be in a position to pass on the technical merits of one weapon versus another. But the conspicuous failure of the services to agree on basic technical questions has reminded us that the bias of the expert needs to be resolved by resort to the judgment of nonspecialists who are put in possession of the often conflicting testimony of experts. There is need to give greater support to the President, the Secretary of Defense, and the Congress in their capacities as representatives of a civilian point of view. Military leaders should advise and indeed advocate certain programs, but the final decision must be a civilian decision, and the final appraisal of the decision should also be civilian in character. As matters stand today there is need of change in the executive branch of the government, especially to bring practice into harmony with the principle. In the words of the Hoover Commission: "The lack of central authority in the direction of the national military establishment, the rigid statutory structure established under the act, and divided responsibility have resulted in a failure to assert clear civilian control over the armed forces."

## FREEDOM OF INFORMATION

In reviewing security policies another basic question is: Does the policy involve a threat to freedom of information?

The makers of the American commonwealth were in no doubt about the necessity of an informed public opinion. James Madison gave classical statement to the point in these words:

Knowledge will forever govern ignorance: And a people who mean to be their own Governors, must arm themselves with the power which knowledge gives.

A popular government without popular information or the means of acquiring it is but a prologue to a farce or a tragedy, or, perhaps both.

Nor were the statesmen of the formative years under any illusion about the corrupting tendency of unchecked power. Power, said Hamilton, is of an "encroaching" nature, and it encroaches on the sources of informed criticism of authority. Jefferson put the whole matter this way:

The basis of our governments being the opinion of the people, the very first object should be to keep that right.

The way to prevent [errors of] the people, is to give them full information of their affairs through the channel of the public papers, and to contrive that those papers should penetrate the whole mass of the people.

Among [European governments], under the pretense of governing, they have divided their nations into two classes, wolves and sheep. Cherish . . . the spirit of our people, and keep alive their attention.

Do not be too severe upon their errors, but reclaim them by enlightening them. If once they become inattentive to public affairs, you and I, and Congress and Assemblies, Judges and Governors, shall all become wolves. It seems to be the law of our general nature, in spite of individual exceptions.

Having many memories in common of official interference with the flow of news and comment, the Bill of Rights, which was early added to the Constitution, contained several restrictions against Federal authority over communications. Congress was forbidden by the First Amendment (1791) to abridge "the freedom of speech, or of the press; or the right of the people peaceably to assemble, and to petition the government for a redress of grievances."

The First Amendment, however, applied to the Federal government, and for over a hundred and thirty years state governments and local officials could interfere with freedom of communication without subjecting their acts to review by the United States Supreme Court as violative of the Federal Constitution. Of course, free speech provisions exist in all state constitutions, but it was not until 1925 that the Fourteenth Amendment of the Federal Constitution was applied to state interference with freedom of speech. In the Gitlow case decided in that year the Supreme Court held that the "liberty" protected from arbitrary interference by the states by the "due process" clause of the Fourteenth Amendment includes liberty of speech. In 1931 and 1936 liberty of the press was added.

For many decades, with the growth of modern technology and the concentration of economic control, that it is a private monopoly has been the major complaint against the press, on the score that it blinds the eyes of the public. The indictment has run: Big technology, Big investment, Big advertisers *equal* Big Business Bias. A standing grievance among workers is that "the press as a whole is hostile to them, will not tell their story fairly, gives disproportionate space and emphasis to the employer's side in every dispute." [5] Raymond Clapper once put the matter in terms of economic and social class influences: "What I most deplore about the press, and it is the only matter which to me seems of any real moment, is that publishers and editors live too much in the world of the country club instead of the world of the people." [6]

The current crisis of insecurity revives the possibility that government will be the principal threat to public information. The government cannot proceed against a press which is protected by the First Amendment, but the government can impose severe restraints upon government personnel and others in order to prevent information of benefit to the enemy from reaching him. All this is undertaken with the utmost reluctance by American leaders who are sensitive to democratic values. As the first head of the Atomic Energy Commission said, "Democracy and secrecy are incompatible." In no problem is it more obvious that the requirements of security curtail freedom and that the task is to keep the loss at the lowest practicable level.

## CIVIL LIBERTIES

National security involves individual freedom appraised in terms of all the civil liberties. At every level of review of defense policies, therefore, a third basic question is: Is there danger to the civil liberties of the individual?

The concern of the Founding Fathers for the protection of the individual against arbitrary official action is fully reflected in the Bill of Rights. Those who argued against incorporating these safeguards in the original Constitution declared that they were entirely in favor of the principles and procedures at stake. Their argument was that the rights of the individual were so firmly embedded in the law that further provisions were not necessary, and might indeed narrow the scope of freedom by specific enumerations. The Bill of Rights amendments were, however, added to the Constitution at an early date and spelled out many of the barriers which English and American experience had learned to interpose between the private individual and official power.

We shall not attempt a technical review of the specific practices which, taken together, constitute the civil liberties so essential to the practical expression of the valuation we put upon respect for the individual. It is, however, essential to keep in mind some procedural details as a reminder of what is at stake.

We take it for granted that no one is to be punished unless his conduct is contrary to a law in force at the time his acts are committed. In short, no *ex post facto* laws are compatible with civil liberty.

We forbid officials to hold anyone in custody unless authorized by a court of law. The writ of *habeas corpus* is the technical means by which the individual brings his plight to the notice of a court.

We protect the privacy of the individual from intrusion on the part of investigators unless specific authority has been granted by a court. The purpose is to defend the home and workplace from arbitrary search and seizure of records and other objects.

Public officials are to refrain from using coercion to force confessions from individuals whom they suspect of crime. They are not to subject individuals to harassment, such as chronic interference without proper cause.

Public officials are also forbidden from inducing anyone to commit an offense. This rule is the result of the experience that crime may be increased by the zeal of police agents to entrap victims.

If an individual is charged with crime or arrested, he is to have notice that his admissions may be used against him. Experience shows that innocent persons make self-accusing statements for such reasons as the desire to shield a beloved person or as the result of blackmail. Hence we put the burden of finding proof upon the official.

The accused is entitled to receive the aid of a qualified adviser in preparing his defense.

It is of basic importance that the accused be informed not only of the nature of the charge made against him but of the identity of the accuser. It is possible to prepare a proper defense only when one knows who is alleging what.

We permit the accused to confront his accuser in open court and to examine the accuser, witnesses, and materials used against him.

Further, the authority of the court is used if necessary, at the request of the defense, to bring in reluctant witnesses.

We are also accustomed to take for granted the presumption of innocence until proof of guilt is established by an authoritative process.

We also believe that what is called a court should be constituted in a regular manner and safeguarded from biases that operate nonrationally to the disadvantage of the individual. For example, we expect judges to disqualify themselves if they have a personal grudge against the defendant. We expect jurors to have an open mind. We expect the rules of evidence to be applied to exclude irrelevant and merely derogatory references to the accused.

When serious deprivations are possible, we believe in providing means of access to a high court of appeal. We expect such a tribunal to be free of most of the local and personal factors which may affect the administration of justice at a lower level.

We insist that whatever punishments are inflicted shall apply as far as possible to the criminal and not to other persons. Hence no disqualifications for office apply to the children of a convicted person.

We are opposed to cruel and unusual punishment as an unjustifiable infringement upon human dignity. Hence the restrictions on forced labor, chastisement, mutilation, and similar practices.

We recognize that special care must be taken to see that individuals who have not attained full maturity, or who suffer from some disability which prevents maturity, shall not be discriminated against. This applies to the young or the mentally deficient and diseased.

We also recognize that some questions are matters of conscience over which men of good will can profoundly disagree. Respect for the individual implies that under such circumstances the dissenter from majority views shall be exempted from the full weight of the deprivations which would otherwise be inflicted upon him by the community. This is part of the justification for treating "political crime" with leniency.

It need scarcely be said that this inventory affords the sharpest conceivable contrast with the perspectives that prevail among the rulers of a garrison-police state. The overwhelming predominance of power as the prime value of such a state means that respect for the individual is nonexistent. The political expediency of the ruling class is the only standard applied by the top elite of a totalitarian regime.

Our regard for civil liberties is perhaps the clearest daily reminder of the difference between a free society and a state of slavery. Hence the necessity of proceeding with the utmost caution in allowing public officials to encroach upon this domain.[7]

## A FREE ECONOMY

National security affects freedom in another way. At all levels of review and balancing of security policies a fourth basic question is: Does the program involve a threat to the traditional principle of a free as against a controlled economy?

The Constitution was launched to serve the needs of a society in which private control of property in the means of production was assumed to be the norm. The makers of the Constitution were men of property, for the most part, and they were candid about the political problem that confronted them at Philadelphia. They were afraid that the owning and managing few would be swept overboard by the multitude. James Madison wrote in *The Federalist* (Number 10) :

> But the most common and durable source of factions has been the various and unequal distribution of property. Those who hold and those who are without property have ever formed distinct interests in society. Those who are creditors, and those who are debtors, fall under a like discrimination. A landed interest, a manufacturing interest, a mercantile interest, a moneyed interest, with many lesser interests, grow up of necessity in civilized nations, and divide them into different classes actuated by different sentiments and views.

Continuing :

> If a faction consists of less than a majority, relief is supplied by the republican principle, which enables the majority to defeat its sinister views by regular vote. It may clog the administration, it may convulse the society; but it will be unable to execute and mask its violence under the forms of the Constitution. When a majority is included in a faction, the form of popular government, on the other hand, enables it to sacrifice to its ruling passion or interest both the public good and the rights of other citizens. To secure the public good and private rights against the danger of such a faction, and at the same time to preserve the spirit and the form of popular government, is then the great object to which our inquiries are directed.

This is tantamount to saying that Madison wanted to set up a form of government which would not only protect the many from the few but would perpetually protect the few from the many. The makers of the Constitution sought to balance the many and the few by setting up what they called a "republic" in preference to a "democracy."

It should be understood that the term "democracy" was used in a much more restricted sense than is common in our time. Madison meant "a society consisting of a small number of citizens, who assemble and administer the government in person." A "republic" is what we now speak of as a "representative democracy." (Madison: "A republic, by which I mean a government in which the scheme of representation takes place.")

The initial slant of national policy in favor of a private as distinct from a controlled economy has continued to the present day. In part the preference for a free economy is intimately bound up with the basic valuation of respect for individual choice. We are in favor of the widest practicable scope for the choice of investment by the capitalist, the choice of business by the enterpriser, the choice of job by the worker, and the choice of product by the consumer. The principle of exalting volition over coercion implies that when factual conditions put coercive influence in the hands of a few, it is the responsibility of the commonwealth to remove these conditions if possible, and failing this, to regulate or administer the coercive activities by democratic procedures.

In a word, the valuation which American policy puts upon respect for individual judgment implies that the institutions which make a reality of this value may differ greatly in the relative balance maintained between governmental and private action. We are against government action unless this is the means by which the largest sphere of effective choice is to be maintained in the nation under prevailing circumstances. We know, for example, that official action is essential in the case of private monopolies and restrictive agreements.

The principle of preference for a free economy springs directly from the overriding goal of human dignity. When the market is genuinely free, a widespread diffusion of property occurs, regardless of the attitude of the political authorities. The possessors of property are therefore in a position to criticize public officials with minimum fear of devastating retaliation. Under these conditions the forms of democracy can be kept alive by dispersal rather than concentration of effective power.

The presumption in favor of the free market and free private competitive enterprise has been challenged in many parts of the American community. However, the challenge does not imply the rejection of democracy and respect. On the contrary, the attacks made against private capitalism allege that the institution no longer can be made to contribute to fundamental values under modern factual conditions. It is contended that many factors, including the vastly increased capitalization required by modern industry, have so greatly heightened the tendencies toward the concentration of control that government must step in to prevent private monopoly, and must thereupon retain control in order to ensure the benefits of large industrial production.

It has long been recognized by scholars that free private enterprise is a system of economic organization which is peculiarly vulnerable to the social setting in which it operates. It is, for instance, dependent upon government, and hence upon active public support. For example, the unaided free economy cannot assure the stability of over-all prices. Unless the monetary and fiscal policies which receive the sanction of public support maintain stable prices, great inflationary or deflationary movements can occur. Further, the unaided private economy cannot assure the stability of general economic activity. Here, too, proper government action is called for.

The dynamic nature of the free economy tends to put certain handicaps in the path of the government policies which are essential to it. Crises of unemployment, for instance, are scarcely conducive to the formation of rational public opinion. When millions are unemployed, the individual has no sense of personal responsibility for his predicament. When hundreds of thousands are going bankrupt, the individual bankrupt does not typically hold himself to blame. When farm prices tumble, the individual farmer does not accept responsibility. Throughout our society it is the economic "system," not the person, who is made the scapegoat. Collective action is taken in the emergency. But the emergency measures may contribute to structural transformations that imperil the ultimate viability of the economy as a free system.

Developments in the private enterprise economy which are generally held to be abuses have already been commented on. Perhaps the most conspicuous case is monopoly. The agitations necessary to initiate and to sustain public action against monopoly can go beyond the requirements of the problem, and can strengthen policies that damage as well as protect the freedom of the market. And monopoly is an example of a much larger class of abuses, which include restrictive practices of every kind.

The industrial expansion fostered by private enterprise has had some paradoxical consequences for the system of private enterprise. With the growth of vast corporations, the ratio of employees to managers and owners has increased. The fact of being an employee modifies the perspectives of the individual by making him relatively indifferent to whether his manager is hired by the government or by a private owner.

A recent report by Richard Centers states that a considerable degree of class consciousness is now present among Americans, and that opinions favorable to the free economy are, to an important extent, distributed along class lines. Centers says that over half of a national cross section of male Americans think that they are members of the "working class" (51 per cent). Two-fifths call themselves "middle class" (43 per cent). Three per cent said they were "upper class," and 1 per cent said they were "lower class." Another 1 per cent was undecided. One per cent replied to the questions about what class they belonged to by saying, "Don't believe in classes." The support of the traditional system was stronger among upper- and middle-class members than among the majority, the "working class." [8] And for the future it may be noted that the working class will doubtless increase in relation to other elements in American life.

Thus far, the preference for a free rather than a controlled economy has been considered in terms of traditional and current opinion and in reference to other than economic values. A weakening of confidence in the capacity of the institutions of a free economy to serve democratic values has been noted. For economic values, if the framework of government action is what it needs to be, the free economy is the most flexible instrument yet developed for obtaining the greatest production at lowest cost and for providing rising standards of living. What could be done by a relatively free economy was demonstrated at the end of the war. As controls relaxed, our economy shifted with remarkable speed from military to civilian production. Millions of returning veterans were absorbed, and millions of wartime workers were retained with little unemployment. Our economy overcame shortages in many areas by expanding production. It encouraged and sustained a high rate of private investment and high and widely shared standards of living. New inventions were adapted to the technique of production and to the convenience of the consuming public.

In the security crisis it is politically tempting to resort to controls in the hope of correcting a visible evil, such as glaring shortages of some materials. The crucial problem is to win significant political (public) support for a policy of patience in most of these cases. In the overwhelming majority of instances it is likely that the self-correcting mechanisms of the market will work themselves out more quickly and introduce fewer new complications than if administrative action is taken.

If the principle of freedom is to win out over control, the leaders and hence the members of the American public must grasp the basic principles of the economy. The American people are not "too dumb" to understand how the free economy operates. The American people are no strangers to the mechanism by which past shortages of many popular or necessary products have been removed. What is essential is that leaders of opinion shall vigorously remind the public of the concrete realities of everyday experience and let the people judge. All of us have seen the price system go into action when supplies are short. With rising prices the opportunity for profitable production brings new producers into the market and leads to more production by established producers. As the supply increases, prices drop and exceptional profits dwindle. Most Americans can recognize that quick resort to controls will often produce an immediate gain to some consumers and some producers at the expense of many losses to potential consumers and perhaps to potential producers and workers. Lacking objective standards of judgment, controllers look into the past and pick a period which they label "normal." Price changes which are out of line with this past period are often disapproved, even when such changes would correct current shortages or oversupplies. In this way a "freeze" is imposed on the economic system. The official schedule of allocations tends to "share the freeze," and this makes it difficult for a new business to get started or for an efficient business to expand. Private investment dries up because the investor sees that he must add to the ordinary risks of the market the risk of guessing what a number of official agencies are going to think and do. All this lays the foundation for more controls on the plea that enough private investments are not being made.

In this chapter consideration of the fundamental objectives of the American commonwealth has been turned to as a guide to the task of providing for the national security without giving up any more individual freedom than necessary. The central value of the American commonwealth is the dignity of man, and this includes the conduct of affairs in this country free of external dictation. We have national security when we are in a favorable position to protect our independence.

All measures which are proposed in the name of national security do not necessarily contribute to the avowed end. In particular, caution is needed against conceiving of national security policy in terms of foreign divorced from domestic policy; and so far as foreign policy is concerned, against confounding defense policy with armament. Our greatest security lies in the best balance of all instruments of foreign policy, and hence in the coordinated handling of arms, diplomacy, information, and economics; and in the proper correlation of all measures of foreign and domestic policy.

Security calls for procedures for arriving at comprehensive and well-balanced programs of action. The primary responsibility for making a comprehensive review of security questions lies with the executive arm of the government. But we must rely upon the Congress, the courts, and the public to take ultimate responsibility.

Whatever the procedure, the guiding aims and principles are vitally important for success. In a continuing crisis of national defense the freedoms which are most vulnerable require special vigilance on the part of everyone engaged in the review of security policies. Hence the application of four principles deserves extra care: the principle of civilian supremacy; freedom of information; civil liberty; a free rather than a controlled economy.

# IV. ACTION BY THE PRESIDENT AND THE EXECUTIVE

A MORE DETAILED consideration of the ways and means by which national security measures can be effectively integrated with the basic goals and principles of the American commonwealth will now be undertaken. In the chapters to follow, numerous recommendations will be made about routines of government. This preoccupation with procedure may push into the background the fact that fundamental questions of policy are not to be solved by "mechanics" alone.

It is not my purpose to draw the blueprint for a perpetual-motion machine capable of receiving an input of good intentions at one end and delivering an output of appropriate legislative statutes, executive regulations, court opinions, and popular votes at the other. In the rough-and-tumble of politics, all intentions are not good, and even the saints fall out among themselves over different assumptions, demands, and loyalties. The differences may be related to party alignments or to the distinctive outlook of the South, New England, the Far West, or some other region. Often the differences can be traced to the fact that a disproportionate share of the individual's experience has been in one area —agriculture, industry, labor, or the professions. Dividing lines may follow religious or ethnic groups. Besides differences which can be accounted for in terms of group affiliation and experience, personality factors count. The constituency developed by every leading figure is in some ways unique, and the traits of every leader are somewhat distinctive.

Group and personality factors, therefore, are of considerable importance for politics. But it would be a mistake to underestimate the extent to which these factors can be modified by an established procedure. A procedure constitutes an established practice when a definite set of expectations prevails as to "who does what, when, and how." A practice is not yet established when the Congress passes a statute authorizing the creation of a new agency. It is necessary to wait and see how the authorizing language is interpreted in terms of personnel, facilities, planning, and operating arrangements. A new pattern is established when the members of an agency have acquired a rather stable picture of what it is like, and expectations have crystallized at the Bureau of the Budget, the Civil Service Commission, and other parts of the vast structure of formal and informal government.

Once an activity is a "going concern," it becomes a factor of some weight, however light, in the decision-making process. Purely personal factors are sometimes of decisive importance in determining whether the organization has the ear of the President or the support of influential members of Congress and strong pressure elements in the public at large. A close and respected friend of the Chief Executive may transform a rather modest legal mandate into an effective engine of power. On the other hand, purely personal factors may have relatively little to do with the impact of an agency on politics. The elements seeking to influence policy by supporting a given branch of the executive arm of government may be so important that the President overlooks uncongenial personal considerations in order to stay on smooth working relations with the agency.

An established practice affects an organization in two fundamental ways: by recruiting personnel with somewhat distinctive predispositions, by modifying what is brought to the focus of attention of the personnel. The mode of recruitment, for example, may predispose an agency to approach national security problems with a strongly civilian or a military point of view; it may even mean that specific elements in the civilian population or the armed services will be overrepresented in relation to the nation at large or to the armed forces as a whole. Established ways of administering an agency can exert a decisive influence on what gets to the attention of decision makers. If the organization has no staff of its own, but depends upon borrowing staff members whose destiny therefore remains with another agency, the facts and interpretations that reach the policy level will, in all probability, differ from what they would be if the agency had its own staff. Or, to take another example: If the affairs of the organization head up in a group of part-time officials, each one saddled with a vast administrative machine of his own, the attention given to the work of the organization is almost certain to differ from what it would be were the agency in the hands of full-time officials.

The emphasis given here to the "mechanics" of government, therefore, arises from the importance of proper procedures in translating goal values and principles into the everyday stream of decision.

As Chief Executive and as Commander-in-Chief, the constitutional responsibility of the President for the security of the nation is clearly defined. In the discharge of his obligations the President has at his disposal a battery of facilities, the permanent agencies being supplemented from time to time by agencies to fill temporary needs. The Department of Defense is specialized to the military aspects of security. The Department of State is responsible for developing our foreign policy and for the diplomatic and propaganda instruments by which it is executed. The Economic Cooperation Administration has one of the heaviest burdens of responsibility for the economic instruments of security. Many other agencies play important roles, including the Atomic Energy Commission, the Treasury, the Department of Agriculture, and various other departments and agencies devoted to economic matters. The activities of all of these agencies must be integrated if security and freedom are to be achieved.

To assist in the task of integrating the executive branch of our government, the President relies upon an immediate circle of advisers (notably the Cabinet members) and upon staff agencies, especially the Bureau of the Budget, the Council of Economic Advisers, the National Security Council, and the National Security Resources Board.

The last two agencies, though not well known to the public, are potentially two of the most powerful and valuable agencies assisting the President on security matters. They were established as recently as 1947. The National Security Act of 1947, as amended in 1949, set up an executive department of the government, the Defense Department under a Secretary of Defense. The Secretary is designated as the principal assistant to the President in all matters relating to the Department of Defense. The Joint Chiefs of Staff are named as the principal military advisers to the President, the Secretary of Defense, and the National Security Council; the Armed Forces Policy Council is to advise the Secretary of Defense on broad armed-forces policy matters; the Munitions Board is to deal with procurement and the military phases of industrial mobilization plans; the Research and Development Board is to deal with scientific research. And there are the three military departments of Army, Navy, and Air Force.

The complexity of this structure suggests the magnitude of the burden which under our constitutional system weighs upon the President. He needs the most effective staff organization possible to provide him with a comprehensive and balanced review of security policies and their execution. Two top-level Cabinet committees created by the Unification Act were intended to perform this function, but for various reasons have not been fully effective.

The American people are in the process of adapting the instruments of government to the great new position which we occupy in world affairs. The sharp changes recently brought about in the executive branch are evidence of the severity of the need as well as the adjustive capacity of the nation. Modifications to meet new problems are a never-ending necessity, but the present need for rapid adjustment is particularly apparent. Changes that can yield important results for security and freedom are possible in these directions:

1. Develop the National Security Council as the principal executive agency on which the President relies for formulating and reviewing comprehensive and balanced security policies. Add to the Council three full-time civilian members without other governmental responsibilities.

2. Keep political police functions relating to government employees and to others at the indispensable minimum. Make one full-time civilian member of the National Security Council responsible for reviewing the effect of security measures on individual liberties and advising the President thereon.

3. Make one of the full-time civilian members of the National Security Council responsible for a more effective flow to the public of information related to national security. Let the President recognize more fully his own responsibility for informing and persuading foreign and domestic audiences on basic policies.

4. Clarify and develop the functions of the National Security Resources Board with special reference to assessing the impact of security measures upon the free economy.

5. Establish within the Department of Defense a strong civilian staff independent of control by military services to aid in developing and evaluating security policy.

6. Eliminate extraneous functions from the control of the armed forces.

7. Develop a program of advanced training within the government under civilian auspices to provide a comprehensive grasp of

security policies within the framework of our objectives as a nation.

8. The President should devote a part of his annual message to the Congress and the public on the State of the Union to a discussion of the problems involved in the national security program in relation to civilian supremacy, freedom of information, civil liberty, and a free economy.

### PLANNING AND REVIEWING ARE ESSENTIAL

The Hoover Commission performed a great national service by pointing out in a constructive spirit a number of defects in the organization of the executive arm of the government. The President, according to the Commission, lacked the staff organization necessary to provide him with a comprehensive and balanced review of security policies, of the state of their execution, and of consequences for both security and freedom. The general principle was put in the following words:

The wise exercise of authority is impossible without the aids which staff institutions can provide to assemble facts and recommendations upon which judgment may be made and to supervise and report upon the execution of decisions. The President and the heads of departments lack the tools to frame programs and policies and to supervise their execution.

Further:

The executive branch is not organized into a workable number of major departments and agencies which the President can effectively direct, but is cut up into a large number of agencies which divide responsibility and which are too great in number for effective direction from the top. The line of command and supervision from the President down through his department heads to every employee, and the line of responsibility from each employee of the executive branch up to the President, has been weakened, or actually broken, in many places and in many ways.

The limitations of the executive branch as a whole were said to be especially conspicuous in the organizations which deal directly with national security. It was generally agreed that the Unification Act of 1947 was a big step in the right direction. But the Commission summed up its judgment in these terms:

> The Commission . . . has had the benefit of an investigation into the National Security Organization by a distinguished committee. The committee found continued disharmony and lack of unified planning. Extravagance in military budgets and waste in military expenditures show a serious lack of understanding of the effect of military costs and spending upon the total economy. True national security depends more upon economic stability and political strength than upon military power. Interservice rivalries indicate a lack of understanding of the fact that military security depends upon co-operation and balance among the Army, Navy and Air Force, and upon the creation of a genuinely unified military arm.

The verdict of the Commission found general agreement, and many alterations already made can be traced directly to the recommendations put forward or to proposals advanced in the resulting debate.

### THE POTENTIALITIES OF THE NATIONAL SECURITY COUNCIL

This much seems clear: The most convenient instrument to provide the President with the planning and reviewing assistance which he so sorely needs is the National Security Council. The Council is already a force in the government. It possesses a comprehensive grant of authority by statute. A suggestion has been made for a new civilian Commission on Security Policy and Freedom to be set up as a means of strengthening civilian control. It is doubtful that this step is needed at the present time. Rather than experiment with an entirely new setup, the Council can be adapted to the job. It is, I think, generally agreed, however, that if the Council is to live up to the comprehensive role which it can perform for the President, the agency must possess a broader basis of recruitment.*

If the President, in accord with the Hoover recommendations, receives from the Congress authority to reorganize the presidential office, what changes will transform the Council into a more effective body?

Consider the opportunity and the obligation confronting the Council (in cooperation with the National Security Resources Board, the Council of Economic Advisers, and other appropriate agencies). It needs to take a long and broad view of all of the commitments of this country in relation to our human and material resources, the rapidly shifting technology brought about by modern scientific knowledge, and the goal values of the American commonwealth. Our security program needs continuous evaluation in terms of such basic and diverse questions as the integration of foreign aid and our military program; the impact of specific military programs upon our natural resources and civilian standards of living; new approaches to the stockpiling of critical materials; the utilization of island bases; propaganda as a weapon in connection with and in place of physical weapons; peacetime and wartime uses of atomic energy and other scientific developments; the character of the direct controls required in war and, if any, in peace; and the relation of security to civil liberty and the degree of information essential to sustain the vitality of a free press and a free government. Such questions are representative of the questions that appear when we consider what is at stake in defending America against external aggression in a manner that leaves our democracy intact. All of these issues must be an-

---

* The Council got under way in the early days of the Greek crisis when it was important to have regular consultations between the State Department and the armed services. The four members then sitting from the services gave an overweight to the voice of the Army, Navy, and Air Force, although there is no evidence that the numerical strength was in practice decisive.

swered in building a balanced and well-rounded security program.

In improving the work of the Council, it is recommended that three new members should be full-time civilians chosen for their great experience and outstanding judgment on national questions. They should be appointed by the President with the approval of the Senate, and serve at the will of the President. They should have the standing of Cabinet officers and attend Cabinet meetings at the discretion of the President. It is recommended that one full-time civilian member have responsibility for fostering a more effective flow to the public of information relating to national security. Another should be made responsible for reviewing the effect of security measures on individual liberties and advising the President thereon.

The present statutory members of the Council—the President, the Vice-President, the Secretaries of State and Defense, and the Chairman of the National Security Resources Board—are already overburdened with great administrative responsibilities. The three additional members, free of other operational responsibilities, would be available for continuous top-level work on security problems. The device of the "minister without portfolio" is frequently used in government and represents no innovation. In American experience, the Vice-President, when he sits with the Cabinet, can contribute by commenting from a wider perspective than any department head. In the British Cabinet it has been traditional to include an unassigned member.[1]

### WHY NOT THE CABINET?

A stranger to the American plan of government might ask why the Cabinet is not the appropriate agency to aid the President in drawing the threads of planning and execution into a coherent whole.

The traditions of the Cabinet are in many ways opposed to the function of planning and review.[2] The Cabinet is a committee of operating heads of great administrative establishments. Each officer is the focal point of pressures originating inside and outside the department for which he is responsible. Operating duties alone are a heavy drain on time and energy. Although the Presidents have differed in the use they have made of the Cabinet, there has been no tendency toward top-level planning and review of national policy as a whole. Each officer is deterred from going "outside" the scope of his administrative duties by the reflection that in return his own bailiwick may be invaded.

During the century and a half under the Constitution, the traditions of the Cabinet have been such that members have not been named with the idea that they would take a major part in over-all planning. A Cabinet is a composite in which many interests and calculations are represented. One prime consideration is party service, whether measured in terms of money given or raised or in terms of other support. (Support may take the form of public or organizational assistance during campaigns or of withdrawal of dangerous opposition in the interest of party harmony at the convention or later.) It is part of the tradition that territorial factors count, since regions are resentful if they are unable to claim a native son in the Cabinet. Some of the major functional groups comprising the American nation have a recognized, though tacit, claim to membership. If Commerce goes to business, Labor to organized labor, Agriculture to a farmer, Treasury to a banker, there are other affiliations to be "balanced" (religious, fraternal, cultural, veteran).

The size of the Cabinet has steadily increased from an original five to the present ten (including ECA), until the body is growing beyond convenient and efficient limits for intimate discussion. It is impracticable to limit the "regular" Cabinet, since each department is sustained by rather definite "constituencies," and new groups are always pressing for the prestige and power of a seat. (Education and health, for example, are almost "in.")

Under the American system of government the principle of collective responsibility does not apply to the Cabinet. The individual Cabinet member may get into trouble with the public and Congress without bringing about the resignation of the entire group. The head of each of our great departments of government learns to work with his own sustaining blocs of pressure— territorial and functional—partly in order to safeguard his appropriations on the Hill.

Since the Cabinet operates as a loose committee of busy administrators who are individually responsible to the President, we must look elsewhere for the proper agency to carry out the double task of planning and review.

## HOW ABOUT THE VICE-PRESIDENCY?

The inquisitive stranger who looks over the chart of American government might ask whether the Vice-Presidency is not the ideal spot to locate the planning function for the executive branch as a whole. In modern times the Vice-President belongs to the President's party. Why not bring him into the Cabinet and make him chairman of the general security planning commission?

The Vice-Presidency does possess one particular asset for such an assignment. That is a public following. The Vice-President speaks as the leader of significant elements in the national community. He therefore carries the weight and acquires the outlook of a top policy integrator rather than the reputation of a specialized administrator or group leader. In these respects a Vice-President is more like the President than the typical member of the Cabinet. If we look into the past career of Cabinet appointees, we find that such men have not typically run for high elective office.[3] The President does not surround himself with recent governors of states or (as a rule) with recent Senators.

When we look at the facts about the previous career of the Vice-Presidents, we see that they are from the same hard school of top politics which usually produces the President.

There is, however, a fatal disqualification which makes the Vice-President unsuitable as chief planner and reviewer. Membership in the same party is no guarantee that the Vice-President will have the confidence of the President. In the interest of party harmony it is usual for the Vice-President to represent a different trend in the party than the man who heads the ticket. The number two man is often a sop to the defeated faction, whose function is to further party harmony in the electoral campaign by healing wounds inflicted during the preconvention and convention struggle for the nomination. If the President is to have full confidence in the planner-reviewer, he must have the authority to choose his man. The National Security Council is a convenient agency for full presidential control, and for the combining of departmental voices with full-time consideration of the total needs of the nation. (As a member of the Council the Vice-President, of course, already has certain responsibilities for liaison with the Congress growing out of his constitutional role as presiding officer of the Senate.)

## KEEP POLITICAL POLICING TO A MINIMUM

Because of the crucial importance of keeping the political police function at a minimum, it is proposed that one full-time civilian member added to the National Security Council be made responsible for advising the President on the state of individual liberties in the nation, as affected by measures applied and proposed for national security.

Political policing includes the surveillance of individuals to gather facts on the basis of which a rational judgment can be made of the political attitudes of an individual, the effective control of a politically significant organization, or the performance of a politically relevant overt act. That in these years of peril there is a necessary place for political policing is beyond reasonable dispute. We must continue our foreign espionage as a means of keeping tab on the secret designs and the capabilities of possible enemies. Even after allowance has been made for the double-dealing so common among intelligence agents, it must be conceded that competent espionage is a tranquilizing factor in the prevailing state of global anarchy. We are too strong to be immediately endangered by anything short of an unforeseen technical advance which is put into effective application before we have had time to evolve countermeasures. Espionage can provide a substratum of realistic knowledge about the power position and power potentials of the nations of the world.[4]

It is in connection with counterespionage activity that the greatest danger to freedom arises. The purpose of counterespionage is to detect enemy agents. It is reasonable to look for such agents among those who are in sympathy with the ideas of foreign governments or who have some sort of dependence upon a foreign government. Fortunately our experience in fighting two wars with Germany gives us solid ground for reassurance about the unity of America, despite the diverse origins of the people. When we take into account the millions of immigrants from Germany, and the continual contact with German business, science, and culture, it is obvious that American ties were far more intimate with Germany in 1914 and in 1939 or 1941 than they are or have been with Russia. This country succeeded in assimilating the Germans to a degree that reduced the problem of effective counterespionage to a minimum in both wars. Genuine Americans did most of the work of policing their fellow ethnics, and bringing the dangerous ones to the notice of the proper authorities.

Experience appears to support the conclusion that the security of a nation depends to a very small degree upon police measures designed to keep knowledge away from the enemy. Modern business has learned to depend less on the protection of patent and copyright privileges than upon keeping a few jumps ahead of competition by excelling on the laboratory front.[5]

The President needs the assistance of the Security Council member referred to in keeping the secrecy rules revised and in estimating the proper boundary of essential restriction. In the light of continuous inquiry into these matters, government and private jobs can be classified according to "sensitivity." The highest skill then needs to be applied to the task of protecting those sensitive spots at the lowest cost in terms of dollars, freedom, and other values.

In general, it is agreed that proper censorship and police measures are needed to protect the following:

Technical details of new weapons

Technology by which new weapons are manufactured

Identity of the resources, facilities, and manpower going into new weapons, and amounts involved

Information that specific surprise weapons are being worked on

Specific plans of armed defense

Precise news of the progress of treaty and agreement negotiations (when the parties so desire)

Identity of secret friends abroad

Identity of our counteragents

Information concerning allies of the categories that we protect in our own case

We have not had much experience in administering or controlling a political police function. The nation as a whole has a healthy abhorrence for whatever smells of the police state. But one penalty of inexperience is panic when circumstances indicate that the level of insecurity has suddenly risen. The United States has recently engaged in measures out of key with the basic traditions of the nation. The holding of wholesale loyalty investigations is an example. There is no need to terrorize the population by mass surveillance.[6] The requirements of competent policing could be met by the procedure mentioned above, namely, the determining of "sensitive" agencies.

Political policing is so subject to abuse that it needs to be entrusted to personnel of the highest character and skill. Napoleon was not alone in learning that "the police invents more than it discovers."[7] Since advanced knowledge is essential to intelligent political policing, a special burden rests upon the selection and in-service training program to provide proper orientation.[8]

At present the administrative procedures by which human rights are affected are too often confused and contradictory.[9] Under these circumstances, police informers are given an effective power that endangers the values for which we stand. A foreigner who obtains a visa from the Department of State may nevertheless be denied entry by the Immigration and Naturalization Service of the Department of Justice. The impact of this sort of thing on our standing abroad is obviously dangerous to our security.

From the President needs to come the moral leadership essential to prevent hysterical interferences with the processes of freedom. With the assistance of an enlarged National Security Council, he could arrive at a more considered judgment than is today possible on questions of political policing. Certainly the objective is to keep this sort of coercion at the essential minimum.[10]

## SPECIAL MEASURES AGAINST UNNECESSARY SECRECY

The President is the official with the greatest opportunity to safeguard public opinion against a thickening fog of secrecy. It is not to be forgotten that he is the Commander in Chief of the armed forces and, subject to the acts of Congress, has legal and moral responsibility for seeing that essential secrecy is preserved.

But it is also his responsibility to see that an effective flow of information to the public is maintained on the basis of which rational judgments can be formed on over-all security policies.

Up to the present, no provision has been made for continuous government-wide planning and review in this basic area of national policy. If the National Security Council is modified to include the three civilian appointees mentioned above, one full-time member should be made responsible for maintaining the most effective possible flow of security information to the public. In this way the President can receive the assistance which he needs in fulfilling his obligations. Making such a specific assignment will in itself give proper emphasis to the importance of the policy of open information.

The duties of the civilian member of the Council charged with expediting the flow of security information are not the same as those of a press officer at the White House. The job of the press officer is to take care of the daily flow of news. The Council member is a planner and reviewer. He provides a definite focus of responsibility for the consideration of all procedures relating to the disclosure or withholding of information.

The responsible official should study all security regulations, military and civilian, and recommend to the President changes designed to provide all possible access to information without sacrifice of essential secrecy.

The Council member will need to look beyond the letter of security regulations to the spirit in which the rules are administered, with a view to creating an atmosphere favorable to legitimate disclosure to the public. And he should constantly press for the release of information since the informing of the people is so essential to security. At present in the indoctrination of officers there is one-sided emphasis upon the importance of secrecy. An officer is rarely commended for disclosure. He may, however, be reprimanded or otherwise disciplined for underclassification or for failure to classify material. Accumulations of overclassified material can be found in many offices. Among the informal administrative practices to which attention needs to be paid is the slack custom in some quarters of leaving classification in the hands of subordinates, especially clerks or secretaries. By increasing the emphasis put upon the national interest in striking the proper balance between secrecy and disclosure, the administration of security can be improved throughout the government.

There are many knotty questions connected with the limits of essential secrecy which deserve continuous study and experiment. The Atomic Energy Commission, for example, has been struggling with security problems which are in some respects similar to those that have come up elsewhere in our government, and in free governments abroad. Every scrap of experience about how security restrictions have worked in practice needs to be brought together and scrutinized by the Security Council member who works in this field.

Consider the highly controversial question of whether past releases of scientific information have damaged security by making knowledge available to an enemy, or aided security by providing a means of accelerating our tempo of scientific and technical advance. No topic is so esoteric that evidence cannot be gathered and sifted by experienced and able people (the release of the Smyth Report on atomic energy is an instance to be inquired into).

Whoever takes the job here recommended needs to look upon himself as peculiarly expendable in the public interest. In all probability he will gradually lose the confidence of the press and other influential elements in the public, since by the nature of his task he is "caught in the middle" between the demand to tell all and the necessity to keep something back. An additional factor is that he will obsolesce in his job by losing touch with what the lay public knows and wants to find out. The Security Council member who is supposed to draw the line between night and day may vanish somewhere in the twilight.[11]

### THE PLACE OF PROPAGANDA AND INFORMATION

The Security Councilman who expedites the release of information should be under strict instructions to leave propaganda to others.

Let us be candid about the problem of propaganda in a free government. The President has an opportunity and an obligation in this connection, which is to play a positive part in spreading information and propaganda at home and abroad. The machinery is already in existence in the Department of State, the Defense Department, and, above all, in the White House itself. Propaganda as a tool affecting national security requires the study and advice of the National Security Council. But the Council member charged with breaking the log jams that block the disclosure of information should not have propaganda responsibility.

Propaganda is a ticklish subject in any democracy, and especially in our country, where the influence exercised by the executive upon the channels of public intelligence is viewed with deep suspicion. In a despotism the problem does not exist. Is it good for the despotism? Let the information pass. Is it bad for the despotism? Kill it. In a free commonwealth public officials are responsible to the people, and morally bound to circulate material on the basis of which even adverse judgments can be made on their official acts. Since all men are human, including democratic officeholders, and it is human in our civilization to hang onto power and resent criticism, there is a tendency on the part of officials to narrow the stream of information available to the public. This is counteracted by the disposition of politicians out of office to keep the channel open, and the contents as unfavorable as possible to current officeholders.

It is generally understood that you control men's deeds if you control their minds, and on great public issues this is largely a matter of what is available at the focus of attention.

Democracy's fear of concentrated power over the press in the hands of the executive branch of government is justified. But democracy's security calls for an affirmative policy in the field of communication; and this can be accomplished without an invasion of the free press. Programs of information and propaganda are essential at home and abroad.

### WHAT ARE INFORMATION AND PROPAGANDA?

In any discussion of this topic it is essential to begin by laying the verbal cards on the table and showing how words are used. If the Atomic Energy Commission prints a pamphlet on the use of radioactive tracers in connection with cancer, the primary aim of the publication is to spread technical skill. On the other hand, if the Atomic Energy Commission were to put out a pamphlet in praise of itself, including no adverse comment (or scarcely any), the obvious aim of the publication would be something other than the spread of "know-how." It would be intended to influence preferences on controversial matters of public policy. Let us speak of information as the communication of know-how or of unchallenged factual ("fact-form") statements. Propaganda is mass communication designed to influence attitudes on controversial matters of policy. In applying these words to any concrete situation, it must be clear which public we have in mind. Statements are often information from the point of view of American audiences, but are propaganda in the eyes of the world audience.

### ADDRESSING FOREIGN AND HOME AUDIENCES

It is the President who has the most direct access to domestic and foreign audiences. As the leading voice of the mightiest nation on earth, his pronouncements on many questions instantly reach the top leaders of other nations. Even if these leaders distort what they allow to reach the local public, they try to receive from their intelligence sources a faithful account of what the President said. With the Voice of America at his disposal, the President has a means of penetrating the shrouds of secrecy thrown up by apprehensive dictatorships.

It is essential that the President and other members of the executive branch take an even more active hand in communicating to foreign audiences than in the past. False and distorted pictures of the United States are circulated not alone by Russia and Russian agents throughout the world. There are other interests in opposition to this country, or engaged in negotiations whose outcome will in their judgment be more favorable if the United States is criticized.[12]

Even in relation to the home audience there is a legitimate place for propaganda. The positive propaganda task of the President is historically well established, no matter how much reluctance there may be to apply this term to the championing by the Chief Executive of a controversial viewpoint. Indeed, from the earliest days government officials have always explained and defended their work on many unofficial occasions.[13] They have given press interviews or inspired press news and editorial comment. However, it is a rather recent development to use specialized personnel to inform and persuade. It was the request of the Department of Agriculture to hire a publicity man that startled Congress into enacting a law prohibiting the use of public money for such a purpose unless expressly authorized by statute.[14] The Department of Agriculture developed a system of public contact over the years which has had great influence upon the skill level of American farmers and upon their conceptions of national policy. The Department acquired vast experience in walking the tight rope between the dissemination of information, the encouragement of free discussion, and the persuasive outlining of the case for its own policies. The crucial point with reference to democracy's freedoms is whether conflicting viewpoints are allowed full expression. In the name of free and vigorous discussion, the Department has insisted upon describing all the major alternatives concerning agriculture which are before the people. The fact of survival indicates that the tight rope can be walked successfully.

In recent years the Department of State has "gone to the people" with conferences and materials intended to serve the double purpose of information and propaganda. The armed services have engaged in extensive activities along this line for a long time. Today it can be said that the taking of communication initiative is an established function of government.[15]

## MINIMUM INTERFERENCE WITH THE FREE ECONOMY

It is to the Presidency that we must turn for leadership in another area of vast importance for security and freedom. With the assistance of the Security Council the President can make a balanced, over-all review of the security program to establish the minimum expenditure on the security program that is consistent with our basic objectives. In addition, the Security Council, with the assistance of all the appropriate agencies, particularly the National Security Resources Board,* should consider the revisions of the tax structure which can reduce the harmful impact upon economic incentives of the necessary taxes resulting from the security program. Further, it is important to inquire into the

---

* The NSRB came into being on the basis of the act of 1947 and, despite early difficulties, some of which involved personalities, has an important part to play.[16] The Board's assignment is to evolve and evaluate industrial mobilization plans, to formulate stockpile policy, to relate the demands of our security policies to national capacities and resources, and in general to survey the impact of security programs upon the economy in times of peace and war.

means by which administrative interferences with the free market structure can be kept at the minimum level.

As has been noted, there is no such thing as perfect security. Nor is it possible to have a modern security program without some threat to the free economy. Obviously, a balance must be struck between the risks to security and the risks to the free economy. We are concerned with the structure of the economy, not only for the sake of economic progress and production, but in relation to the free society as a whole. By maintaining effective freedom in the economy, we reduce the role of coercion in American life. Hence the importance of the National Security Resources Board in advising the President on the impact of proposed security expenditures upon economic institutions.

In the last analysis, the decision as to the wisdom of any given volume or direction of expenditure must be made through the chain of civilian supremacy. It is essential to bring all the expertness and judgment available to bear upon the problems involved. A first step is an adequate review by a civilian agency which gives appropriate weight to the increased threat to the free economy of larger expenditure for security as well as the greater security that is sought.

Whatever the total expenditures on security may have to be, the harmful effects of the tax burden can be reduced by improvement of the tax structure. Incentives to effort and investment are weakened, not only by the total load of the present tax system, but also by the particular ways in which the total load is distributed. Thoughtful studies of the aspects of our present tax system that affect the efficiency and growth of our economy most adversely have been made, and should be given consideration.*

* See, for example, *Taxes and the Budget* (1947) and *Tax and Expenditure Policy for 1950* (1950), issued by the Research and Policy Committee of the Committee for Economic Development.

Keeping direct controls at a minimum in carrying out the peacetime security program is a further requirement of a democratic society. Hence the National Security Resources Board should look into the procedures by which necessary economic results are sought with a view to keeping administrative authority and routine at a minimum. The general point has been put in these words in a Committee for Economic Development policy statement.*

One of the main tests of the need for controls should be the responsiveness of supply to an increase of price. We believe that furnishing a strong incentive to an increase in supply by bidding up the market price of a commodity is preferable to satisfying the Government's requirements out of the more limited supplies that would be available if there were no price increase.

The behavior of the market may also have a sobering influence on the Government's demands. In many cases, particularly stockpiling, security requirements are not so rigid that they cannot be deferred or revised where it is found that to meet them would mean sharp price increases.

In a period of large defense procurement, however, the Government's bargaining position would be weak. If it were known that the Government must have certain supplies and voluntary allocations could not be made, suppliers might make speculative profits at its expense. If supply situations became tight in the future, it might become desirable for the Government to have power to issue set-aside orders to satisfy defense needs.

### EFFECTIVE CIVILIAN AUTHORITY IN THE DEPARTMENT OF DEFENSE

The Secretary of the Department of Defense is the official whose pivotal importance for the national defense is obvious to all. The President and the colleagues on the National Security

* *The Uses and Dangers of Direct Controls in Peacetime,* Research and Policy Committee of the Committee for Economic Development, New York, July, 1949.

Council must rely heavily upon his reports and judgment. The Secretary is, of course, civilian, but he cannot be effective unless his plans and operations are sifted through a civilian staff of top competence. The civilian staff is needed at every level at which policy is formulated. The staff should be related to the Secretary of Defense by a purely civilian chain of command. This civilian staff might have advisory functions only, and be part of the budgeting or planning branch of the Defense Department.[17]

In the interest of concentrating all available energies of the Defense Department on its distinctive functions, it is important to free the armed forces from extraneous civilian functions, and to prevent activities of this kind from being pushed upon them by civilian authorities unwilling to shoulder heavy responsibilities. There is also a question of principle involved, the principle of civilian supremacy. The planning agency of the Department of Defense, the Bureau of the Budget, and ultimately the President are involved in protecting the efficiency of the armed services and the integrity of the basic structure of American government.

During noncrisis periods relatively small violations of principle grow up without doing any immediate damage to the commonwealth. The Army engineers, for instance, have been active for years in constructing dams built by the government. This goes back before the Department of the Interior decided that its major function is resource development. Today the Interior Department has a competent engineering corps and can take over the job of constructing dams. Another example concerns the Navy which for years has administered outlying areas, some of which are more suitable for civilian government. (The executive branch has already approved the transfer of the two functions just referred to from the armed forces. Congressional approval is necessary.)

The danger is that such deviations from sound practice in

quiet times will impede the services in dealing with their prime responsibilities, and also accustom the nation to rely upon the armed forces to extricate the country from predicaments. It should be noted that the taking over of civilian functions is often a result of the reluctance of civilian agencies to deal with unpopular problems, such as vigorous programs of civilian defense or the administration of occupied enemy territory.

The proper partition of responsibility for military procurement and for scientific research and weapon development raises questions of principle and expediency. The negotiation and awarding of contracts is a major point of contact between governmental and private corporations and individuals, and has obvious and important implications for the structure of the economy as a whole. To say that sound principle requires the armed forces to specify their needs and to leave everything connected with the meeting of these needs in the hands of civilian authorities does not thereby abolish the operating problems that arise in a world where specifications are themselves somewhat flexible and are modifiable by knowledge of the sort that becomes known in the process of negotiation (and renegotiation).[18] In the same way there are refractory operating questions that remain if we apply the same principle to weapons, saying that the province of the armed forces is to describe the purposes to be served, and to test and administer the weapons developed by civilian scientists and engineers on the basis of these prescriptions.[19]

## IN-SERVICE TRAINING: A NATIONAL POLICY COLLEGE

The President and the National Security Council need to give careful consideration to the task of bringing our methods of policy thinking to the level of the vast tasks that confront the nation in harmonizing security and freedom. The present crisis can be shortened if we prepare to cope with it skillfully. Part of our essential preparation is clarity about the goals and capabilities of America in the modern world.

Our top policy talent needs the benefit of a comprehensive view of the interdependence of all factors affecting security. The interplay of military, diplomatic, economic, and propaganda factors cannot be understood without patient sifting of experience. The job needs to be done under civilian auspices in accord with the basic principles of the American tradition. In recent times the National War College has shown commendable initiative in providing a course of study to which officials from all parts of the government can be admitted. This is an important development, but it does not take the place of a civilian-operated institution for in-service training engaged in clarifying the goal values of this country and assessing our major lines of policy advance.

Properly conducted, such an institution could draw upon the best analytical skill of the nation, and bring it together with active experience. It has been repeatedly shown that the interplay of scholar, scientist, administrator, manager, and officer is fruitful on all sides.

### ANNUAL REPORTS BY THE PRESIDENT ON SECURITY AND FREEDOM

Since it seems probable that the security-freedom problem will be a paramount issue for many years, it would be desirable that the President report annually as part of the message on the State of the Union to the Congress and the public on the status of our security policies and their relation to freedom. This annual message could be based upon reports from the National Security Council and should be a comprehensive review of our security position and policies.

By taking the whole commonwealth into his confidence in these annual reports, the President can communicate to every citizen a sense of participation in a vast enterprise where the stakes, though formidable, depend upon the energy, character, intelligence, and training of even the humblest person. In the interdependencies of modern life it is impossible to forecast in advance who will be thrown into what decisive spot in the defense of the nation. We cannot tell upon whose alertness and competence will depend the ultimate possibility of averting Pearl Harbors in future years.

# V. WHAT THE CONGRESS CAN DO

THE GREAT expansion of government in recent times has put an unprecedented burden upon the Congress as a partner of the executive and the courts in our constitutional system. The continuing crisis of national defense superimposes another set of responsibilities upon the hard-driven legislative branch. The security crisis brings problems to the fore which have already given much concern to both houses of Congress. The challenge of big technology, big government, and chronic crisis affects the Congress in two ways:

First, as society and government grow more complicated, it becomes progressively more difficult for the legislative branch of government to achieve an over-all view of what needs to be done.

Second, as new institutions act as "intermediaries" between the people and the executive branch of government, the Congress finds it more troublesome to work out a political program that unifies the interests of the nation as a whole (and which the public recognizes as accomplishing this end). The new institutions alongside the Congress include the great network of pressure (policy) groups, the media of modern mass communication, and the polling agencies.

Both Houses have experimented with new methods of doing business in order to cope with new conditions. Staff assistants have been provided on a larger scale than before for the committees, and the Legislative Reference Service of the Library of Congress has been enlarged. In the hope of fostering party unity, policy committees have been organized. Inquiries have been made into lobbying and propaganda, and regulations laid down in order to give the public more information about the informal, as well as the formal, process of legislation.

Further changes are needed in connection with the problems of national security and individual freedom. Among the recommendations which are discussed in the present chapter are:

1. As a means of obtaining an over-all view of the security problem, and of aiding in the formation of a truly national program, the Senate and the House should establish comprehensive national security committees, representing all committees with any jurisdiction in the field.

2. In order to improve the basic technical information at the disposal of Congress, a system of auxiliary civilian panels ought to be developed as supplements to the work of committee staffs and the Legislative Reference Service of the Library of Congress.

3. The members of Congress should provide their constituents with more comprehensive and comprehensible information about the security position and problems of the nation.

4. Congress can safeguard individual freedom by providing a model of fair play in the hearings which are conducted by the several committees of the Senate and the House.

5. As a means of providing the public with full knowledge of the effective as well as the formal process of legislation, all lobbying and propaganda activities concerning national security should be matters of public record.

6. If the measures here recommended do not bring about the desired results, a more daring change ought to be seriously considered. A national civilian Commission on National Security and Individual Freedom could be set up jointly by the President and the Congress.

The chapter also evaluates recommendations for the increasing of party responsibility for the purpose of integrating national policies which touch on security. The most sweeping and conventional recommendation of this kind is that we remake the

American frame of government on the model of the cabinet system as practiced in England. I shall dissent from this view, suggesting that the nature of responsibility has been so transformed by modern industrial society that the channel of party responsibility is no longer adequate to contain the pressures involved. It is useless to try to rely upon a single instrument to give clarity and constancy to national policy in the security field. Rather, the feasible course is to tackle the problem of sustaining a dynamic consensus. Under modern conditions of mass communication and highly organized promotional activity, it is more than ever true that the price of liberty is vigilance and energy. The first step, so far as the legislative branch is concerned, is an over-all view.

## THE CONGRESS LACKS THE OVER-ALL VIEW OF SECURITY

At present, security policies and expenditures are reviewed in piecemeal fashion by several committees in Congress. This reviewing process exposes and irons out certain inconsistencies, eliminates some superfluous items, and assures a degree of economy and efficiency in the execution of the various parts of the program. Yet there is no regular procedure by which the security problem is considered as a whole.

Many of the topics which come within the field of national defense are parceled among the existing committees of the Senate and House. For lack of comprehensive review, contradictions, conflicts, and omissions in the numerous items often go unnoticed, unless the executive branch calls attention to them. At least two-thirds of the fifteen standing committees of the Senate regularly touch upon some aspect of the security problem. The fact is self-evident so far as the Foreign Relations, Armed Services, Foreign and Interstate Commerce, and Appropriations committees are concerned. More careful examination shows that the Committee on Agriculture has jurisdiction over the office concerned with international agricultural relations. The Finance Committee deals with reciprocal trade agreements as well as customs duties. Judiciary includes immigration and naturalization in addition to the control of monopoly. Labor and Public Welfare has contract labor questions referred to it, and Banking and Currency has jurisdiction over international monetary arrangements. The same sort of analysis applies to the committees of the House. Strictly speaking, it is no one's job in either House to look at all security policies in search of possible inconsistencies, duplications, and oversights, or to evaluate the impact of security upon the economy as a whole or upon the freedom of the individual.

## NATIONAL SECURITY COMMITTEES ARE NEEDED

The rational move at the present time, then, appears to be this: that the Senate and House establish committees on national security composed of members of all committees whose jurisdiction covers some fragment of the field. The Senate and House committees need to act together as fully as the constitutional differences between the two houses permit.

With the help of a competent staff, a committee on national security could keep before the eyes of its members a comprehensive and balanced picture of the security position of the country, and of the impact of security upon freedom. The proposed committees would not exist primarily for the purpose of holding hearings. Rather, they need to operate as evaluating bodies. As a means of keeping in close contact with the work of all relevant committees in both Houses, it is proposed that the security committee of each House have members who are also on standing and special committees touching upon security questions. To relieve the already overworked chairmen of the separate committees, it might be possible to utilize the services of a senior member. The member could be selected after consultation with the chairman, as was the procedure in constituting the Colmer Committee on Postwar Policy and Planning.

I am not concerned with insisting upon details of how the new committees should be set up. Many alternative arrangements are possible within the existing precedents of the two houses, such as a joint committee of the Senate and House. Actually, one of the oldest committees of the Congress is a joint one charged with supervising the Library of Congress. There is evidence of a gradual drift toward the joint-committee mechanism in order to cut down the time often consumed in duplicate hearings before separate committees. In the security field there is already the Joint Committee on Atomic Energy.

The joint committee does not usually have authority to originate legislation in its name, being limited to the making of reports. This disability is more nominal than real, however, since interested members are available to introduce legislation in harmony with the dominant view of the committee.

Up to the present, joint committees have been somewhat smaller than the average standing committee of either house. The Joint Committee on Foreign Economic Cooperation is ten. But when the subject is of special weight, the size of the joint committee expands. There are eighteen members on the Joint Committee on Atomic Energy.

Whatever difficulties are involved in two independent committees (one in each House) can be largely overcome by staff cooperation. Tasks can be parceled out according to competence, and duplication can be held down. Joint sessions can be a regular feature of committee work.

Experience shows that partisan and personal factors affect the degree of parallel action by separate committees and staffs. The joint committee has the advantage of providing a meeting ground which is particularly useful when the two Houses are under separate party control. But even this is more hypothetical than real, since it is easy to exaggerate the role of partisan factors in many security matters.

Details, then, can vary so long as the essential goal is achieved of bringing into existence on the side of Congress a mechanism which accomplishes what the National Security Council can achieve at the executive end of the avenue.

### GENUINE AND SPURIOUS BIPARTISANSHIP

Congress can create the machinery of integration without getting an integrated result. Incentives are needed to keep the mechanism in working order. Sensing the need of consistency and stability in foreign affairs, American leaders have invoked the principle of bipartisanship. Undoubtedly the security interests of the nation have been served by the loyal support given to the so-called "bipartisan" foreign policy by recent Secretaries of State and by outstanding members of the Senate and House. The aim often has been expressed in the traditional phrase about "burying party differences at the water's edge." To what extent can we rely upon bipartisanship to provide unity and discipline for the task of integrating our national security policies, while ensuring public understanding of basic premises?

It is, I suppose, necessary to begin by clearing up some misunderstandings which have arisen in connection with the principle. Before genuine two-party responsibility can exist, there must be single parties capable of behaving responsibly. Bipartisanship presupposes the existence of a party system whose units can arrive at unified decisions enforceable upon their members. No-partyship is not bipartisanship. It is absence of party government.

That the principle of party responsibility is loosely applied in American politics is a commonplace of everyday experience. The President may conflict with the leaders of his party in Congress. The practice of seniority can put key chairmanships in the custody of leaders opposed to the President. On the other hand, factions of both parties may work together on specific measures. The result is to wipe out the possibility of establishing in the minds of the voting public a clear line of separation between the parties.

There are, of course, means by which control by party leaders in Congress could be strengthened. Chairmanships might be assigned with little regard to seniority. In this way chairmen out of sympathy with the main current of party sentiment as reflected in Congress could be removed.[1]

Though contributing to the unity of parties in Congress, such an innovation would not go to the root of the problem for the government as a whole. The clash between the President and his party in Congress is not prevented by the measure referred to, and even may be made more acute. If the aim is to eliminate the possibility of such conflicts, we must look to more drastic ways of modifying our system of government.

The usual prescription is to adopt the cabinet form of government as developed in English practice.[2] The precedent of England is called upon because the prestige of cabinet government is less high in France or Italy, for example. The recommendation concerning England puts the emphasis on the principle of treating the cabinet as collectively responsible, and requiring a new election before a change of cabinet is ratified. Party leaders are thereby enabled to enforce unity by confronting the "back benchers" with the threat of going home and standing for reelection if they desert the party members in the cabinet. Where it is possible to change cabinets short of election, the cabinet system is typically associated with a continual procession of cabinet reorganizations. This is generally held to be unfortunate, partly because of the multiplicity of parties usually found under such conditions, partly because of the atmosphere of intrigue in which legislators engage in the sport of bringing down a cabinet in the hope of getting a post in the reshuffle. The consequent relative weakness of the executive can threaten national security.

When it is recalled that we adhere to the two-party system even more strictly than the British, the weakness of the principle of party responsibility in the United States is thrown into high relief. For years the House of Commons was split into four parties, the two extra being Irish and Labour. The Irish vanished with the changed status of Ireland, and the Labour party swallowed the Liberals. In this country it long has been Republican versus Democrat, and before that another pair of parties dominated the scene.

Many factors which explain the supremacy of the two-party system as the norm of British politics are at work on this side. In both countries effective executive power cannot be changed under ordinary conditions by anything short of the time, expense, and bother of a general election. Wherever general elections are involved, a premium is put upon building nationwide organizations for electioneering purposes. Since most people appear loath to "throw away" their vote on a candidate with little chance of success, the "either-or" alternatives provided by the two strongest parties are the most favored. You vote Labour or Conservative, Democrat or Republican.[3]

## TRENDS TOWARD PARTY RESPONSIBILITY

There are trends in American politics toward strengthening the rule of parties. A clear indication is the control which the President now exercises over his party. During the long tenure of Franklin D. Roosevelt the leaders of the President's party in Congress became accustomed to act as spokesmen for the President on legislative matters. As an offset to this tendency toward party consolidation under Roosevelt must be placed the tactics whereby the President frequently reached beyond the ranks of the Democratic party to appoint Republicans to office, and to build up a coalition of "liberal" elements regardless of traditional party affiliation. Roosevelt's successor felt strong enough to break with recalcitrant elements among Southern Democrats. By making an issue of Congress in the campaign of 1948, the problem of unified responsibility was given new prominence.

The rising self-confidence of the President in relation to his party and the Congress is no sudden show of ephemeral power. For decades the Presidency has been rising in influence. The favorable position of the Chief Executive is connected with the rapid expansion of the Federal government. On the whole, the American people have been in favor of positive action, and the Presidency has gravitated into the hands of the party or the faction willing to act.

A centralizing society spells centralizing government. Centralizing government means a centralizing party. However, so gradual is the evolutionary process that to this day there is no truly national political machine.[4] Nonetheless, the handwriting on the wall is clearly visible. Some city and country bosses are well aware of the trend. "The big money is in Federal stuff." From the point of view of the public, the President is the biggest figure in the party, and this improves his position both on issues and patronage.

### CAN IDEAS DIVIDE PARTIES?

A centralizing system of government and party control puts more tools for the enforcement of party responsibility at the command of the Chief Executive. Since the concentration of effective party power is but imperfectly realized at present, the question rises whether the President can force the pace by adopting new strategies. An alignment of the major parties according to principles would accomplish the purpose. Is it likely that the President as party leader will also find it expedient to resort to ideas as a means of improving party solidarity?

Fatal to the hope of aligning the parties clearly as "Right" and "Left," and achieving party responsibility in this way, is the dominant mood and direction of the American people under changing industrial conditions. There is now an effective consensus in America about where most of the people want the nation to go. And that mood and direction is not capable of being crystallized into two sharply contrasting creeds by successful major parties. "Communism" or "socialism," for example, will not go over. Nor will a "Tory" party that denounces social security, public housing, public education, price support to farmers, or labor legislation.

The balance of power in national politics has shifted toward groups which are strongly disposed to favor measures of the kind adopted by the government in recent decades. One basic fact of social structure is that the nation is becoming more urban and less rural. Most Americans are going into industry and becoming wage earners (and most factories are in towns and cities). White-collar workers, mostly on a fixed salary, are much more important than before.[5] And what do the urban middle-income groups want from the government? The question can be answered without much qualification: they hold the government responsible for preventing a drop in the standard of living. This is expressed in the social security program, which is an income maintenance device for the old or the otherwise handicapped, including the jobless. Besides social security legislation, there is strong support for the idea that the government should prevent mass interruptions of income through job loss.

These demands have come into existence as a result of the experience of Americans with modern industrialism. It has become clear that the individual acting privately cannot do much to guarantee his income (or that of his family) in the face of gigantic swells of business prosperity and depression. Also, it is clear that the government is capable of doing something positive about income maintenance. Since individuals feel less responsible for relying upon their personal efforts to maintain income, they feel few scruples in turning to their agent, the government, to act as the joint planning agency in accomplishing this result.

The demands of the urban middle-income groups are important because of their strategic political position. And they are not out of tune with the nation as a whole. Badgered by insecurities arising from the weather and other factors, the farmers now look to the government for assistance in maintaining income. Low-income groups in factories (or elsewhere) support similar demands upon the economy and the body politic.

The unification of parties along purely ideological lines, therefore, is unlikely. The main domestic controversies will be about ways and means of protecting and improving the standard of living, which are more nearly questions of relative emphasis than absolute opposition. They do not lend themselves to the formation of mass parties split according to principles.[6]

### SHALL IT BE CABINET GOVERNMENT?

It seems clear that under our system of government existing trends are not strong enough to enforce party responsibility. The current of centralization has not gone far enough to put the President in a relatively unchallengeable position at the head of his party, and the chances of achieving party discipline on the basis of principle are not great.

Is the inference that there is no hope of responsible government —that is, for clearly identified policy responsibility—unless the Congress succeeds in pressing with vigor and success toward cabinet government?

Put aside for a moment the question of immediate expediency. Let us look more closely at British experience. Contrary to much, if not indeed most, of what has been said and written, I suggest that British experience indicates that party responsibility is an inadequate means of achieving responsible government under modern industrial conditions. Britain is already groping toward other means of accomplishing this result.

Despite the nominal dependence of the cabinet upon the majority of the House of Commons, the Parliament has not proved to be an efficient instrument for supervising the executive. Under our American frame of government the many dramatic clashes between the President and Congress have been criticized for permitting the Congress to oversupervise the executive. Remember the failure of the Senate to ratify the Covenant of the League of Nations. If this was an example of too much debate and restraint on executive action, Britain provides many examples of too little debate and too little control of the executive. "A British government which makes a treaty as momentous as that of Versailles, and allows one day to the discussion, with the knowledge that either the amendment or the rejection means a dissolution, is really penalizing dissent of any kind." [7] Indeed, there is something to be said in favor of the existence of a genuine check upon executive power. This conclusion is strengthened when we remember the secret agreements entered into by the British cabinet during peacetime. In 1935, the Cabinet made the Hoare-Laval treaty which scandalized large sections of public opinion when it was inadvertently made known. The Munich agreement of 1938 was another executive arrangement.

As the weight of the executive grows in modern government, and government extends its scope, the need of efficient control of the executive is imperative. The bludgeon of party responsibility is too crude and ultimate an instrument to enable the House of Commons to adapt itself smoothly to the needs of the day. The traditional question period is now generally recognized to fall short of being an efficient means of controlling an administrative leviathan like the British government. A growing current of sentiment is in favor of organizing the House of Commons into committees modeled after the Congress. (The committees of the Senate or House are powerful instruments of legislative control, since members of the legislature with enough incentive can become expert on the work of specific bureaus, departments, and agencies.) Question time in the House of Commons does not bring the civil servant into direct contact with the legislature, since replies are given by a cabinet member or parliamentary secretary. The parliamentary speaking tube absolves the civil servant from direct contact with the legislature. The House of Commons has no mechanism comparable with Congressional committees for examining at length in the ordinary course of business representations made by private citizens and group representatives.[8]

## CONGRESS CAN REPRESENT THE NATION

Much of the demand for responsible party government in America (enforced by a cabinet system) rests upon a conception of the American Congress that caricatures the actual situation. I propose to criticize this conception and to suggest that the problem of responsible government is tied only to a limited extent to the fate of parties.

What is the chief argument for adopting cabinet government? It is that the American Congress is so organized under our system of representation that Congress is incapable of representing the nation as a whole. The analysis runs along the following lines: The President is elected by a process that makes him truly representative of the nation. The Congress is chosen in smaller constituencies where a patchwork of local interests has the upper hand. Save in times of dire national peril, the President is unable to obtain legislation corresponding to the interest of the nation as a whole, unless he relies chiefly upon his patronage power.

I am sure that no observer of the Senate or the House can deny that members of the two Houses are sensitive to what they think their constituents want. There are grotesque examples of Senators and Representatives who go "all out" for local job applicants, and use every pressure they can think of to back constituents who want more than jobs from executive agencies.

But this is not the whole picture. Let us examine the conception in detail. It assumes that members of the House and Senate act on every issue according to their calculation of how it will affect their prospects of being reelected.

It is obviously false to imagine that reelection is the ultimate ambition of every member of the two Houses. Some House members want to move into the Senate, and are sensitive to the needs and demands of wider constituencies than their own district. The presidential urge infects many able Senators; others have an eye on eventual appointment to the Federal bench, or a major Cabinet post.

The conception exaggerates the degree to which the Senator or Representative depends upon his immediate constituency, even if it is assumed that his horizon is bounded by the next election. Under modern conditions thousands of bills are introduced and voted during a session. Only a small number of measures can be regarded as crucial for the individual representative at the polls. This is not only a matter of the short memory of the public but of the limited concern in the first place for most matters.

Perhaps the gravest distortion in the picture is that all Senators and Representatives are wholly absorbed in advancing their political careers. Congressmen are also loyal Americans. A sincere claim that the security of the nation is at stake wins serious attention not only because it is good politics but because it is good for America. Congress abounds in men of conscience who are sincere in desiring to serve the common good, and who are genuinely concerned about the rights and wrongs of the questions coming before them. The Congress is hardworking (on this point, ask the physicians who tend the Senators and Representatives).

# What the Congress Can Do

There is, of course, an offset. Besides seeking security for America, or conceiving of personal success in terms of a varied pattern of power, respect, rectitude, and related values, many legislators are in pursuit of private economic advantage. This is not so much a matter of bribery as of contacts. Time on the Hill may be viewed as a steppingstone in a career devoted to the law. Or it may appear to be a step in business. And the business may be one that benefits from influence in Washington.

A major misconception in the picture of Congress to which I have been objecting is that the national interest would necessarily be betrayed by congressmen who were chiefly preoccupied with being reelected. If the picture of Congress is a caricature, the picture of the congressman's constituents is a libel. Who are these constituents who are supposed to be isolated islands of local privilege, indifferent to the fate of America? They are the products of American civilization. From early life they are entangled in the distinctive values and institutions of America. They have a common concern for national security. They are members of economic, religious, fraternal, educational, and other institutions which spread far beyond the walls of any one district. They are exposed to the same press associations, news magazines, radio newscasts, and other mass media of information that reach the nation as a whole. Religious organizations include Protestants, Catholics, and Jews who reside beyond the locality and even in foreign countries. Trade-unionists and industrialists have international affiliations. Fraternal orders usually get outside the boundaries of the continental United States. Hence every constituency is intertwined with the region, the nation, the globe. When you look into the methods of farming or manufacturing in a given constituency, you find that the technology is the same that prevails across the land. In recent years we have seen the South and West transformed so that their social structure is more nearly like that of the East and Middle West. Groups in every constituency act through parties, pressure groups, and other private channels that crisscross the nominal lines of states and Congressional districts. Even a Congress composed of reelection calculators would not typically or necessarily fail to develop national programs rather than the patchwork implied by the caricature.

The inadequacies of the conception of Congress I have been assailing go even deeper. We have been talking about conscious attitudes in the calculation of power or wealth or other goal values. What happens in Congress is also affected by unconscious traits ingrained in the lives of those who grow up in contact with American culture. The optimism of most Americans—long remarked as a national characteristic—is an influence upon policy. Optimism is expressed in the self-confident carelessness with which big expenditures and colossal projects are voted through. There is endless confidence in our capacity to improvise in any emergency. (Hence, lax planning in many fields.)

Besides the influence upon Congress of unconscious traits shared by American culture as a whole, there are class traits. It is a matter of common knowledge that children who are brought up in those poor and hopeless families where there is little interest in schooling [9] are likely to turn out differently from children from more ambitious, or from middle- or upper-income, families where schooling is taken for granted and encouraged. Special attitudes are germinated in industrial or rural environments. The urban middle classes, to which we have referred earlier, act somewhat distinctively; and we take it for granted that business executives differ from farmers. (And so on through the intricate pattern of differences in culture and class.)

Another set of unconscious patterns that influence Congress is formed in crisis or intercrisis times. People are deeply influenced by the periods of turbulence or calm through which they live.

War, depression, and boom are crises which have left their mark on tens of millions of Americans.[10]

Finally, there is the special impact of personality traits. Some men are sanguine and others are not; some are reserved where others are outgoing; some are arrogant when others are humble—and these are not without weight upon the interplay of men and measures.[11]

## A REVISED CONCEPTION OF RESPONSIBILITY

It is clear, I think, that the suggestion that Congress is unable to act for the nation as a whole is grossly exaggerated. Such an idea could live on only where old dogma obscures new facts. With a sharper look it is seen that Congress is responsive to constituents who are deeply entangled in the patterns of culture, class, crisis, and character which prevail in America. And congressmen possess consciences shaped in the same mold as their constituents. Under modern industrial conditions the processes of responsible government are enormously complex, diverse, and interconnected. It is chimerical to suppose that they can be kept within the channels of party responsibility.

And what is the meaning of responsibility? It is essential to draw a line between the formal and the effective meaning of the word. Responsibility is a relation between principal and agent (the relationship is here being considered from the point of view of general social science rather than any particular system of law). In a formal sense, the agent acts on policy knowing that he has assumed liability according to a set of authoritative rules for rewards or penalties if he fails to satisfy the principal. The principal (in the formal sense) of the Senator or the Representative is the constituency, which may endorse or reject him at the polls. In an effective sense, responsibility refers to the actual interplay of principal and agent. The actual principal is the person or group from whom indulgences and deprivations—and these must be recognized to include the rewards of esteem, prerogatives of leadership, and the like—are expected. The actual principal of the representative may be a ring of key leaders at home and in Washington upon whom he feels peculiarly dependent. If the formal accountability of the Senator or the Representative occurs at the polling booth, effective accountability is the stream of praise and blame, economic pressure, or political pressure reaching him at all times. Accountability is continuous, in no sense being limited to the outcome of periodic elections. In this industrial age of instant communication and accelerated travel, the frequency of contact between legislators and constituents has gone up manyfold.

The modern world has been evolving new modes of responsibility as the patterns of modern industrialism evolve. The nineteenth century introduced the mass franchise, mass political party, cheap and universal postal systems, and cheap daily papers—all instruments of responsibility. The twentieth century has already produced a phenomenal set of new institutional gadgets. Alongside the political party system, the pressure-group system has grown to remarkable proportions. Since Woodrow Wilson inaugurated regular press conferences at the White House, all executive and legislative branches receive similar coverage on a regular basis. The entire Washington press corps, which includes the broadcasters, has attained an eminence unthought of in 1900. Advertising, ballyhooing, and electioneering have evolved into a more formidable set of practices than ever. Today the practitioners of public relations are flanked by researchers in applied social science. Already the public opinion poll has become entrenched, and new devices of attitude reporting are coming into general use.

In the world of modern industrialism the connections between government and society have been transformed. America is far too diversified, articulate, and swift to abide the elephantine routines of party obligation. We act by consensus, a consensus shaped by a million impressions, indulgences, and deprivations. There is no letup on the unremitting pressure to which key policy makers in our mass society are continually exposed.

Within the framework of modern government, the dynamic elements of culture, class, crisis, and character smash into one another like particles battering an atomic nucleus. In a sense a special election is conducted on every one of a thousand issues reaching Congress. Any individual or organization with enough incentive can "count itself in." Mass circulation newspapers, broadcasts, and films may reach readers, listeners, and viewers by the million. Meetings by the thousand may be held throughout the land. Telegrams, letters, phone calls, delegations—all the paraphernalia of contact may be used to get the ear of Congress. All this is regular routine as the persons, factions, parties, pressure groups line up to exhaust every available pocket of motivation. Our sociopolitical process is not unlike the cloud chamber in a giant physics laboratory in which the elements and the subelements are in violent motion and brilliant clash.

And is this responsible government? Definitely yes. It may not be genteel. But it is full of opportunity for everyone in our society with push and skill to join any one of the hundreds of special elections being conducted every day under the floodlights of the "greatest show on earth," which is Washington. And there are carnival stands in every local community.

Responsibility depends in a measure upon party accountability. But it depends much more upon the daily facts of pressure and persuasion.

## THE DISCLOSURE OF LOBBYING AND PROPAGANDA

If responsible popular government under modern conditions is to pay off in terms of national security, the arena of politics must be free in fact as well as name. This calls for unhampered rivalry in persuasion. This can happen when coercion is used only for the purpose of defending the free processes of communication from coercive interference.

One condition that must be fulfilled is disclosure of source. Congress and the American public have years of experience in "considering the source" of what is said by the spokesmen of partisan, economic, sectional, religious, and other groups. For years Congress has been experimenting with measures intended to protect the Senators, Representatives, and the public from being made a fool of by statements which are anonymous or falsely attributed.[12] Rational judgments demand knowledge of "who says what." Otherwise, evidence can not be properly weighed.

To some extent it is possible to protect security and the public interest by excluding various categories of persons from Congress. The Constitution set the precedent by requiring representatives to have been for seven years a citizen of the country. The minimum for the Senate is nine. But the Constitution also set the precedent for relying upon disclosure rather than final prohibition. No person holding an office of profit or trust under the United States may accept any present, emolument, office, or title from any king, prince, or foreign state *without the consent of the Congress,* which, of course, ensures general knowledge of the fact.

The Federal Corrupt Practices Act and the Hatch Act prescribe outright exclusion from membership in the Senate or House in some cases. But the main reliance is upon giving full disclosure to campaign expenditures in the hope of warning the community of potential sources of bias or interest on the part of legislators.

The policy of enforced disclosure has often been made use of by the Congress. The postal registration law requires the disclosure of the identity of editors, managers, and owners of all publications using the mails under the second-class mailing privilege. The postal law also specifies that news and advertising must be separated and the latter plainly labeled. The Federal Communication Commission reports the ownership and control of radio stations and networks. The McCormack Act provided for the registration of foreign agents with the State Department where the list would be open to inspection. The Voorhis Act later required the registration of persons and organizations of certain types with the Department of Justice.

One decisive step toward bringing the legislative process into the full glare of publicity was the act requiring registration of lobbyists. However, the LaFollette-Monroney Act had a number of loopholes which further investigation and discussion may stop. What is the proper line to be drawn, for instance, between a lawyer engaged in legal business for a client, and lobbying? The Act also did not include government lobbyists. Obviously the activities of Defense, State, other departments and agencies are one of the important factors in security legislation. Is there an adequate record of the activities of the executive branch on the Hill? Is it possible to draw a useful distinction between the "lobbying" and "nonlobbying" activities of officials?

The Congress tries to protect itself from secret influences by laying down special requirements for those in contact with the two Houses in the course of duty. The press gallery is an accepted institution, and existing regulations are supposed to ensure that members of the gallery stick to their job of reporting. The current admission rules show what the Congress has learned to protect itself against:

Persons desiring admission . . . shall state in writing the names of all newspapers or publications or news associations by which they are employed, and what other occupation or employment they may have, if any; and they shall further declare that they are not engaged in the prosecution of claims pending before Congress or the departments, and will not become so engaged while allowed admission to the galleries; that they are not employed in any legislative or executive department of the Government, or by any foreign Government or representative thereof; and that they are not employed, directly or indirectly, by any stock exchange, board of trade, or other organization, or member thereof, or brokerage house, or broker, engaged in the buying and selling of any security or commodity or by any person or corporation having legislation before Congress, and will not become so engaged while retaining membership in the galleries. Holders of visitors' cards who may be allowed temporary admission to the galleries must conform to the restrictions of this rule.

Nothing in this proviso shall be taken to mean that admission shall be granted to any representatives of associations or publications for special economic, labor or business interests. And it shall be the duty of the standing committee, at their discretion, to report violation of the privileges of the galleries to the Speaker, or to the Senate Committee on Rules and Administration, and pending action thereon, the offending correspondent may be suspended. . . . Members of the families of the correspondents are not entitled to the privileges of the galleries.[13]

The policy of disclosure is a candid recognition that modern industrial society operates by persuasion that quickly turns into coercion if it is under cover. I have spoken of the "special elections" of everyday politics. Some events move so fast that representatives of the public interest mobilize too slowly. It has been suggested that Congress establish an Office of Public Counsel to make sure that special interest pressures are met in fair competition by counterpressures.[14] A trigger mechanism of this kind is able to spring latent motivations into immediate action.

### CHECKING UP ON RESULTS

Disclosure is a necessary though scarcely a sufficient condition of effective action on the part of Congress. Competition is not enough. The competitive strength of wise policies must be increased. This is the positive side of the democratic principle which not only opposes coercion but favors encouraging the use of the best minds and characters in the competitive struggle to guide national policy.

If policies in any field are to be subject to rational evaluation, there must be a checkup on results. In recent years Congress has given increasing support to programs directed at foreign and domestic audiences to be carried out by executive departments and agencies. The growing acknowledgment that "propaganda is here to stay" is removing some hypocrisies from public life. In the past, subterfuges of all sorts have been put up with in connection with information and propaganda. The wisdom and expediency of such programs were privately admitted, though publicly disavowed.

Although Congress is fully aware and positively concerned in our information-propaganda programs, neither the Senate nor the House has provided a suitable mechanism for checking on results. So far as the executive branch is concerned, the National Security Council can, if it will, coordinate information, propaganda, and security. The Budget Bureau looks into administrative operations in the light of fiscal needs and possibilities. The Congress has no independent audit of performance.

Some steps have already been taken toward evolving checkup mechanisms. An advisory board to the Assistant Secretary of State for Public Affairs and the Congress has been provided for by statute. The board is to report on the Voice of America. If the board were provided with funds for staff, a procedure could be set up for discovering the picture of America now prevailing in foreign countries and for estimating the influence of the Voice on this picture.

Individual members of Congress have made use of modern methods to keep in touch with constituents. The reasons for this were stated on the floor in these words by one Representative:

. . . obviously many of the pictures of public opinion on given issues which I had believed to be true were found to be very false.

I had been judging opinion on the basis of unsolicited letters and telephone calls from constituents. Like many others I tended to believe on a majority of questions that those who wrote, wired, or telephoned reflected typical opinion. They simply did not do so in most cases. Rather, they generally represented vocal minorities. Organized pressure groups and individuals have long since learned all the tricks of how to give members of Congress a false picture of public sentiment. There is one easy corrective—solicit opinion on a scale large enough to eliminate the possibility of error.[15]

The Congress has at its command a service agency through which inquiries of all kinds can be conducted. The Library of Congress is limited only by funds and not by know-how in these matters.

### CONGRESS CAN USE CIVILIAN PANELS

From time to time Congress has made use of the knowledge and public spirit of private citizens in connection with questions in need of special study. The Hoover Commission which advised on the reorganization of the executive branch is the most recent example. The ramifications of security policy are so wide that parts of the problems growing out of the continuing crisis can be assigned for advisory help to part-time civilian panels.

The advisory board set up in connection with the Voice of America is a mechanism which may be copied with advantage for other operations. The board is composed of private persons selected for independence of judgment and knowledge of the processes of communication in modern society. The board is a "task force" whose scope is clearly defined.

### CONGRESS CAN INFORM THE PUBLIC MORE FULLY

Individual Senators and Representatives have experimented extensively with means of providing their constituents with a well-rounded view of public issues. The Senate and the House have their own radio recording studios which are used to make reports by "cutting platters" for local stations. Printed reports are mailed to home audiences, especially to civic organizations which conduct forums on public issues.

Several possibilites exist which have not been fully utilized by the Congress as a whole. These relate to the handling of hearings and debates. In the interest of a comprehensive review of security needs, a full-dress debate on national security ought to become a fixture at certain regular times of year. If the President makes an annual report on security and freedom, transmission of the report can provide the proper occasion. Rather than stage a floor debate, more useful results may be obtained if the proposed national security committees arrange for hearings and discussion. "Security and Freedom Report Days" can do something to give the local leader of opinion and the private citizen a well-rounded view of the aims, present state, and future alternatives of national security policy.[16] Report days on security and freedom would be important enough to provide material for public-service programs by the radio stations of the country.

Perhaps the greatest opportunity for national service open to the members of the House or the Senate is that of clarifying the goals and alternatives open to the nation in the realm of security policy. The issues are not, as yet, fully understood in the constituencies. But it is already possible to show that the main problem confronting the American people as a result of the continuing crisis of national defense is not *whether* to have an American garrison but how much to include within it and how to organize it. The question of how much to take into the American garrison can be answered by deciding where Soviet aggression will be resisted by war, if necessary. A continuing source of insecurity in the postwar world has been uncertainty about the intentions and capabilities of the U.S.A. when the U.S.S.R. made an aggressive move. Will the U.S.A. permit further Soviet aggression? Until

1947 and 1948 the question could be raised for most of southeastern Europe—Czechoslovakia, Hungary, Poland, and Romania, for instance. By 1948 these nations were added to the Soviet zone by the "scissors," by the fifth column within and assistance from without. Until 1949 the question could be raised for China. Then most of China was added to the Soviet bloc. In 1950 the question can still be raised for southern Asia and the Near East, and Western Europe. Three obvious alternatives confront the American nation so far as the extent of the American garrison is concerned: first, include only the continental United States and immediate possessions, Canada, and South America (past the "hump" of Brazil); second, take in all the free and non-Soviet states of the globe; third, settle upon some intermediate zone. To create a garrison does not mean that the United States becomes the imperial center of a new empire but that the United States provides military, economic, diplomatic, and informational assistance in preparing to resist, and in resisting, aggression. The signing and the immediate implementation of the Atlantic Pact suggests that American policy and opinion are hardening in favor of a more comprehensive American garrison than the "little garrison" outlined as the first alternative. It is the opportunity and responsibility of the members of the Congress to aid the American people in deciding how far the security of the country requires that our garrison extend.

Upon the alertness, competence, and conscience of the members of the House and the Senate we must depend for what may prove to be the decisive acts essential to keeping an effective democratic process alive. Senators and Representatives are able to examine, both in open and closed hearings, members of the executive branch of the government and private individuals. On some occasions the legislators will in good conscience make facts available to the general public which in the judgment of the executive branch ought not to be disclosed. For such acts there are no rules of guidance beyond admonitions to reflect rather than to act on impulse.

### FAIR PLAY AT COMMITTEE HEARINGS

The concern of the Congress for individual freedoms can be expressed in providing a model of consideration for fair play in the hearings conducted by the several committees of the Senate and House. The criticisms of the methods employed by the House Committee on Un-American Activities has brought this question into the foreground.

It is tempting to propose that the Senate and the House adopt formal methods of disciplining members who fly in the face of public morals by smearing official and unofficial persons, violating both the rules of fair play and the imperative interest of the nation in unity. But the effective remedies under these conditions are not formal. Unless the consciences of fellow Senators and Representatives, and of leading constituents, are sufficiently outraged to put an effective moral and political stigma upon such conduct, the attempt to enforce formal discipline against elected representatives is likely to reward dishonorable men with the appearance of honorable martyrdom.

### NEW AGENCIES OF CONGRESSIONAL-EXECUTIVE ACTION

It may be possible to cope with the problems of security and freedom now before the country by tuning up the existing machinery at the Congressional and executive level. With small modifications of existing practice, a comprehensive view of security policy can be obtained by the Senate and the House, paralleling similar opportunities on the part of the Chief Executive. The public can benefit from the changes within each branch of the government, and especially from the cooperative timing of their activities.[17]

However, it may be advisable to go further if the modifications here proposed do not yield the desired results. In matters of high policy all sorts of party, factional, and personal factors can stand in the path of the adjustments essential to success. An unfortunate combination of circumstances might result in intensifying rather than alleviating tension between the executive and Congress.

We have learned in this country to use special devices to bring about harmonious action on some national and community issues. One device is the nonpartisan commission of citizens of acknowledged integrity, judgment, and competence. Such a commission is appropriate when the purpose is community-wide, depending upon a consensus in which it is believed party, pressure, and local considerations will play a minor role. All the informal (and some of the formal) mechanisms of accountability are available to register the success or failure of consensus. It is a sign of failure if the current stream of judgment begins to crystallize along the conventional lines of party, for example. When this happens, the commission or the agency or the individual has lost the capacity to fulfill the contemplated function.

There are many examples of devices depending upon consensus, covering a wide range of situations. Often we turn to an arbitrator or an umpire to lead parties to a controversy out of their dispute. We sometimes set up special commissions of inquiry, as after Pearl Harbor, to find what went on and what should be thought and done about it. An ex-president can be called upon to comb over the organization of the executive branch of the government as a whole, and propose what changes seem indicated.

We have many words to express the function served by these arrangements. It is possible to speak of a truly "integrated" solution. The idea of "trusteeship" is useful. The trustee is one who is expected to play a role that may diverge from his other private interests and preferences. He is supposed to have qualities of mind and character enabling him to rise above his ordinary preoccupations. Trustees are named for many collective purposes, ranging from the custody and administration of bequests to the championing of public viewpoints on boards of trustees.[18]

In the interest of salutary adjustments between Congress and the executive, new devices of rather inclusive scope have been established, including the Federal Reserve Board, the Federal Communications Commission, and the Federal Trade Commission. Such commissions, which are much more than advisory bodies, operate in the zone between the legislature and the executive. It would be false to imagine that they fit neatly into the textbook categories for describing the scope of authority and control.

It has been suggested that a special device is needed to assist the existing organs of government with the problems growing out of defense expenditure in peacetime.* The recommendation is that

a civilian commission should be established to be charged with the responsibility of scrutinizing and commenting upon general matters of defense policy and upon the efficiency of the conduct of the program.

Such a civilian commission should be in continuous session. The personnel should be highly competent and informed on all phases of defense strategy and tactics; it should be non-partisan and it should be non-representative; it should consist of patriotic citizens who would be willing to drop their ordinary activities and sacrifice their private interests to perform this new and vital public service.

It should be expected that such a commission and such a task would challenge the ablest men in the nation. These men should possess integrity, rare experience and qualities of judgment, and should further possess a sense of trusteeship with respect to their representation of a civilian point of view. Such men would com-

---

* A proposal advanced by a study group composed of Hiland G. Batcheller, Herbert Emmerich, William Tudor Gardiner, Beardsley Ruml, and Harry Scherman. Joseph E. McLean was secretary (1948).

mand the confidence of the President, Congress, the military, and the public generally.

In technical circles, ideas of this kind arouse some resistance for fear clear lines of responsibility will be blurred, and especially that tendencies toward party responsibility will be interfered with. These apprehensions place an exaggerated amount of confidence in party accountability as a means of combining integration with freedom. Modern politics calls for a varied set of instruments in the enforcement of accountability. Eternal vigilance is still the price of defending liberty and consent against tyranny and acquiescence.

# VI. WHAT THE COURTS CAN DO

To what extent can we rely upon the courts to protect our freedom and limit tendencies toward a garrison-police state? Of all the institutions of American government none has attracted so much world attention as the judiciary in our Federal system. The Supreme Court, the capstone of the pyramid of justice in this country, can put its own construction upon the Constitution, unbound by interpretations made by the Congress or the President. To the layman this means that "the courts can declare laws unconstitutional." The court is the final hurdle in the process of legislation. The House may say yes; the Senate may say yes; the President may say yes; but the courts may say no. This power of veto allows the court to perform the function which in some other systems of popular government is played by the upper chamber of a legislature, which acts as a revising body for the statutes passed by the lower house.

There are many factors which help explain "why the apparently helpless court succeeds." The veto power is a serious matter which the court came to exercise only with the gradual and growing support of the American people. The court has a special band of interpreters, public and private, the members of the legal profession. The profession has played such a prominent part in the life of the country that it is more than a witticism to say that ours is a government of "lawyers, not of men." In any case, not of laymen. In Parrington's phrase, we are a "lexocracy."

The sensitiveness of courts to public sentiment, and especially the difficulty of gauging public feeling other than that which is most vocal, and which may be closest to hysteria, is a factor limiting their effectiveness in protecting individual liberties in times of crisis. This can be concealed by using the opportunities for delay provided by legal procedure and technicality. Some of the most important decisions connected with the Civil War and the world wars were taken some time after the crisis atmosphere had abated. Hence, though the court is a bulwark of liberty, it cannot always be reached in a storm.*

Since the issue of the garrison-police state will largely be fought out in crises short of war, the courts can enter the arena with less fear of becoming targets of hysterical attack than in such an ultimate crisis as war. If courts act promptly when issues involving civil supremacy and civil liberty arise, the nation will have the best chance to combine security with freedom.

The Supreme Court is so prominent in the eyes of the public that we sometimes forget the more modest yet significant role of lower Federal courts and state judiciaries. Direct access to the Supreme Court is comparatively rare. Most matters come before it on appeal. The work of the lower courts in a crisis period promptly sets the tone of law enforcement. Inferior tribunals may be overruled on appeal, but timidity in defending the civil power and the liberty of the individual may contribute to an atmosphere of repression in which freedom is curtailed.

We often overlook the elementary fact that attorneys are officers of the court. The first responsibility of counsel for the prosecution or the defense is to the law of the land. The officer of the court who caters to popular passion or administrative pressure can do as much damage to national security and freedom as a paid agent of a foreign power. Of special importance for the law in action is the caliber of our prosecuting attorneys. These officials have

---

* It is somewhat exaggerated to say that "The nine Justices on the Supreme Court can only lock the door after the Liberty Bell is stolen" (Zechariah Chafee, Jr., *Free Speech in the United States,* Harvard University Press, Cambridge, 1941, p. 80).

a wide range of discretion in deciding whom to prosecute and particularly whom to harry with police measures short of prosecution. Such police measures can readily degenerate into instruments of persecution.

It takes courage to defend unpopular causes, and the history of the American bar is full of inspiring examples of attorneys who have braved the immediate disapproval of the community for the sake of evenhanded justice in litigation. When men of stature are willing to act on behalf of the calm consideration of passion-laden issues, the stability of our institutions is safeguarded if not ensured.

In this chapter attention is given for the most part to the relationship of judicial doctrines and procedures to the control of executive authority, civil or military, in defense crises. Relatively exempt from chronic consciousness of war, the American public has had very little experience in drawing the line between permissible and impermissible acts by the military. Our best informed opinion leaders are often uninstructed on these vital matters. What the courts of the nation are likely to do in the future can to some extent be forecast and understood by examining the precedents and principles which will be urged upon the judges by opposing attorneys. The outcome will depend upon all the factors that mold judicial decisions. Among these factors, precedent and principle obviously play a part.

Perhaps the outstanding achievement of our judiciary during the past twenty years—an achievement dramatized by the decisions of the Supreme Court—has been the revitalization of the due process clause in the Constitution that applies to state action: the due process clause of the Fourteenth Amendment. Not long ago the due process clause was chiefly invoked as a defense by interests claiming complete exemption from supervision by state governments. Today the clause in the Fourteenth Amendment has become a guarantee of Federal protection of the essential rights of the citizen from state interference.[1] As interpreted in a series of precedent-making decisions, it bars the overhasty legislature of a state from curtailing the rights of free expression and assembly guarded by the First Amendment; [2] it holds back the overzealous local official; [3] it requires the elements of a fair trial in state and local courts,[4] which would otherwise lie outside the scope of Federal justice. The Supreme Court has, by example and precept, created a climate of judicial opinion distinctly unfavorable to the abuse of individual civil liberties by agencies of government on any level.

The resistance which will be offered by the new freedom achieved under the due process clause to the stress of a continuing national emergency has yet to be tested. But we can determine something of its staying power by examining its history, and the history of other protective devices, under the pressure of previous emergencies, perhaps of greater intensity though of shorter duration. Of most importance is the behavior of the courts under actual stress of crisis rather than their resiliency in snapping back to "normal" after the crisis is over. The warping effect of crisis must not be underestimated.

When governmental action in crisis is subject to judicial examination, four issues may be distinguished: the affirmative power of the legislative or executive arm to meet the situation; the braking effect of due process restrictions; the scope of judicial authority to intervene; and the independence or timidity of the courts in fact.

### THE WAR POWER

Once war has been declared, the issue of affirmative power is no longer available to the judiciary in challenging the acts of the legislature and the executive. "The war power," according to the late Chief Justice Hughes, ". . . is the power to wage war successfully." [5] It is vested in the Federal government not merely by constitutional grant, but "as [a] necessary concomitant of sovereignty." [6] It has grown to include the most drastic economic controls—rationing, price-fixing, and the allocation of scarce materials by government order. It embraces the most stringent limitations on personal liberty—the draft acts, restrictions on the use of the mails, the internment of enemy aliens, and even, in World War II, of American citizens not charged with any offense.[7] Further, our experience in the period before Pearl Harbor demonstrated that even in advance of a declaration of war there was a sufficient arsenal of powers in the Constitution to make the transition to actual hostilities scarcely perceptible on the home front. The Congress was able to invoke its specific constitutional authority to lay and collect taxes for the common defense and the general welfare, to borrow money, to raise and support armies and to provide a navy, to regulate and call forth the militia, and, not least, to make all laws "which shall be necessary and proper" to carry out the specific grants of power. These provisions must be taken together with the executive authority of the President, as Commander in Chief, which itself has been broadly construed to permit carrying out the most generally expressed commands of the Congress, or even to allow acts in anticipation of those commands when the occasion requires.[8] Nor has the objection been urged with any success that the national government has invaded the area of local regulation in the name of national emergency.[9] In short, the judiciary has recognized the power of its two coordinate branches, acting in mutual concord, to occupy the entire field of governmental action to "provide for the common defense."

## DUE PROCESS RESTRICTIONS

From time to time throughout our history, however, the exercise of war or defense powers has been called into question by those who found their civil or economic claims limited thereby.

The courts have been fairly consistent in accepting that challenge, at least to the point of examining the facts and doctrines of the situation to determine whether the requirements of due process have been met. It can be concluded that governmental authority will not fail in crisis for want of specific constitutional authorization, but may be modified by specific constitutional limitations. It is possible to be a little more definite about the nature of the limitations invoked by the courts. Judicial criticism seems to run more strongly against acts which invade the more precise guarantees of the first ten amendments than against those which offend only the general prohibitions of the due process clause itself. This means that invasions of personal rather than property rights, and particularly those personal rights which protect a person accused of crime, will be most zealously resisted. Limitations on peacetime privileges are more likely to be countenanced if they have been authorized by legislative action, after due deliberation, than if they are imposed by executive fiat, either civil or military.

Let us consider some of the situations in which due process is likely to be invoked in connection with the administration of programs of national defense. Only in particular contexts can operative significance be given to an imperative as broad in its phrasing and as inclusive in its application as that no person shall "be deprived of life, liberty, or property" without "due process of law."

We can be fairly definite about the disposition of the courts when the due process argument is used to attack measures of economic control, administered with civil sanctions, which represent the considered judgment of Congress on military necessity. Conceding that all measures necessary to assure the triumph of our arms are within the authority of Congress to enact, the courts have found sufficient guarantee for the necessity of the measure in the deliberative processes of our representative national assembly. The appeal to due process has been conspicuously unsuccessful in blocking price and rent control, and against priorities and allocations legislation.[10] So long as the legislative act does not contemplate procedures specifically banned by the first ten amendments, and hence prejudged to be unnecessary in any crisis, the procedure chosen by the Congress will be deemed an appropriate and a due process in necessarily depriving individuals of some of their property rights.[11]

It is quite otherwise, however, when property is appropriated by executive order, unsupported by a general legislative command. This is not to say that the courts will frown on delegation of authority by Congress, even on an extensive scale, since they recognize the necessity for such delegation, with appropriate standards for guidance.[12] But the military commander or the civil executive who acts without Congressional authorization does so at his peril. This principle was established as early as the Mexican War, when a certain Lieutenant Colonel Doniphan, in command of an expeditionary force moving toward Chihuahua, required a trader who had joined the party to remain with the army column rather than to withdraw his wagons. Doniphan said that the trader was planning to do business with the enemy. As a consequence of his order, the trader lost all his property in the course of the expedition and sued Doniphan for its value. A jury brought in a verdict for the trader. The judgment was eventually affirmed by the United States Supreme Court on the grounds that only "immediate and impending" danger, not "remote or contingent" danger, would justify the seizure, and that "our duty is to determine under what circumstances private property may be taken from the owner by a military officer in a time of war." [13]

Defense preparations necessarily involve restrictions on human rights as well as on property rights. The most familiar example of such limitations is the peacetime Selective Service Acts immediately preceding and following World War II. Their constitutionality has not been seriously questioned,[14] although they affect the lives of those chosen for service as drastically as any other defense legislation yet enacted, except possibly that dealing with enemy aliens (and citizens regarded as of "enemy" origin or descent), discussed below. Military conscription has been sufficiently familiar, at least since the Civil War,[15] that its appearance in a national emergency seems to be taken for granted. The fact that it is employed in a period when the United States is engaged only in a cold war is not felt to raise new legal problems.

It was suggested, however, even toward the end of World War II, that more far-reaching invasions of human rights might be essential to national security. Legislation freezing defense workers in their jobs—the much-debated "labor draft"—was recommended but never adopted.[16] In a continuing emergency it may be proposed again and applied, if not wholesale, to workers in vital plants, such as those specialized to atomic energy. Legislation of this kind would clearly limit, and even obliterate, basic freedoms: the freedom to choose one's occupation,[17] the freedom to move from one part of the United States to another,[18] the freedom to bargain, individually or collectively, for the fruits of one's labor,[19] and perhaps even the freedom of assembly,[20] in that "frozen" workers would not be free to depart from their jobs and proceed, say, to Washington to present their grievances. Doubtless the last freedom is more useful to the judiciary as a peg on which to hang other rights [21] than it is to the employee himself. But the others are part of the everyday operation of a free society.

It is thinkable that the intensification of security precautions throughout the nation, and particularly in key defense areas, might produce a demand, justified or not, for the fingerprinting of every adult citizen, or perhaps even for a national system of passports and identity cards for travel within the continental limits of the United States. It may be urged upon Congress that guards be put at strategic points to check the papers of everyone who passes, and to subject vehicles to inspection without search warrant or probable cause to suspect the presence of contraband in any particular instance. The possibility, already mentioned in the press, that atomic weapons sufficient to destroy a city could be introduced by a *saboteur* carrying a salesman's sample case [22] is enough to indicate the frame of mind conducive to such measures. At present, statutes of this kind would appear to run counter to the prohibition in the Fourth Amendment against unreasonable searches and seizures.[23] But what seems unreasonable in reasonable times may look reasonable in unreasonable times.[24]

This much can be said about the prevailing disposition of the courts: A legislative declaration of the necessity for a restrictive measure is scrutinized with the greatest strictness when it is understood to deal with specifically protected rights. The special tenderness for those rights has been expressed in a much-quoted judicial footnote of the late Justice Stone, to the effect that "there may be narrower scope for operation of the presumption of constitutionality when legislation appears on its face to be within a specific prohibition of the Constitution, such as those of the first ten amendments, which are deemed equally specific when held to be embraced within the Fourteenth [*i.e.,* when applied to the several states]." [25] The Justice said that such legislation may restrict "those political processes which can ordinarily be expected to bring about repeal of undesirable legislation." [26] To the extent that these considerations continue to weigh with the courts, legislative judgment may be reexamined when it is felt that the restrictions imposed upon individual rights are more the outcome of popular hysteria than of deliberation. This reexamination is most likely in the case of local ordinances and state statutes arising from local or regional tensions that do not become a hysteria inundating the nation as a whole.[27]

Of all the rights protected by the first ten amendments, the one perhaps most essential to the political process is the right to free-

dom of expression. The courts have been proportionately solicitous of it. The familiar judicial formula for testing legislation
limiting freedom of expression is that there must be a "clear and
present danger" of serious harm to the body politic arising from
the expressions sought to be prohibited.[28] The formula entails an
independent estimate of the necessities of the situation, and imposes a rigorous standard of proof on the proponents of limitation.
In the case of security regulations, for instance, the judgment
whether given classes of information would be useful to actual
or potential enemies may be left to periodic review by an independent civilian administrative agency, such as the National
Security Council, rather than regarded as an issue for judicial
determination. But whatever limits or prohibits expressions of
opinion—on the ground that national security is endangered—
comes directly within the purview of the courts.[29] There they
act "not by authority of our competence but by force of our
commissions" [30] to apply the clear and present danger formula.

True, the application of this test after World War I cannot be
said to have exercised a positive check on postwar hysteria.[31] But
during the past generation the formula has been forcefully applied
in several lines of cases, one involving labor disputes [32] and another the activities of a particularly persistent and vociferous religious sect known as Jehovah's Witnesses.[33] In its most recent and
probably most extreme application, the Supreme Court has
thrown out the conviction by a lower court of a notorious
Coughlinite, an unfrocked priest, on a disorderly conduct charge
for delivering an inflammatory speech. The local ordinance had
been construed by the trial court to cover speech that merely
"stirs the public to anger, invites dispute, brings about a condition of unrest, or creates a disturbance." Said the Supreme Court:
". . . a function of free speech under our system of government
is to invite dispute." [34]

In the light of these recent and explicit statements, it is not unlikely that future legislation designed to curb expressions of opinion which are asserted to endanger national security will be subject to much closer judicial scrutiny than such measures have received in the past. It is not essential for the court to make a direct declaration of unconstitutionality.[35] By construing a statute in accordance with the presumption that the legislators would not have intended an unconstitutional interpretation, the courts can preserve their power of review in particular cases.[36] The Smith Act, which makes advocacy of overthrowing the government by force illegal, may be sustained as to constitutionality. However, a conviction based on the act would undoubtedly fail if it were based on the principle of guilt merely by association.[37] Propaganda aimed directly at discouraging enlistments or subverting members of the armed forces might be outlawed by statute and the prohibition sustained by the courts. But the same statute would not be recognized as supporting an indictment for urging repeal of selective service laws or a reduction of appropriations for the fighting services.

After all, in construing statutes as applied to particular cases, the courts are performing the judicial function in its most conservative traditional sense. In the exercise of this function the courts are most jealous of their peacetime prerogatives, and may be expected to be most effective, with certain exceptions, in limiting tendencies toward the garrison state. So long as the courts continue to function in civil and criminal matters, the standards and traditions of Anglo-Saxon jurisprudence will continue to soften the blows on our peacetime way of life of continued preparations for national defense.

### THE JUDICIAL FUNCTION OF THE EXECUTIVE: MILITARY LAW

Under what circumstances may the judicial function be assumed by the executive, whether military or civilian? Three forms are easily recognizable: military law, military government, and martial law.[38]

The rules of military law are laid down by Congress under its constitutional authority to "make rules for the government and regulation of the land and naval forces." They are executed by the Commander in Chief, through the appropriate branches of the National Defense Establishment. The members of the land and naval forces, and civilians who accompany them in the field, are subject to military law in war and in peace.[39] The decisions of military law tribunals, known as courts-martial, are not subject to appellate review by the courts, since they are not regarded as judicial acts. In fact there is no appeal other than the automatic review by higher echelons of the armed forces.[40] Military law is specifically exempted in its operation from the provisions of the Fifth Amendment, requiring trial by jury. It was thus recognized by the Founding Fathers as a separate and independent system for the administration of justice. It is possible to stretch the limits of its jurisdiction either by making soldiers of civilians, having them perform civilian tasks under military jurisdiction, or by extending the definition of "accompanying the armed forces in the field" to include civilian employees other than those who accompany troops or vessels on maneuvers or beyond the Interior Zone in wartime.[41] If these fairly obvious distortions are avoided, military law does not conflict in its normal operations with the continued functioning of civilian courts. It applies to a limited and easily distinguishable category of individuals, and only to that category.[42]

## MILITARY GOVERNMENT

Military government, by contrast, is defined not in terms of the people it covers but of the territory where it is in effect. When enemy territory is administered by an American occupation government, either civil or military, the judicial authority is known as military government. The doctrine is that the United States Constitution and the laws enacted under it do not apply on foreign soil except as they govern the actions of U.S. officials. However, military government tribunals make the law of the territory, under instructions from the military governor and his staff.[43] Again, the decisions of the executive tribunals are not subject to appellate review by United States courts. It is possible, by means of the extraordinary writ of *habeas corpus,*[44] to institute a judicial inquiry to determine the authority on which a prisoner is being held. Indeed the writ is available as well to prisoners held under military law. But once it is established that the tribunal holding the prisoner, whether for trial or under sentence, has proper jurisdiction, derived from the authorities on the occupied territory, the investigation is at an end.[45] The Supreme Court has recently gone further and held, though in a sharply divided decision, that an American official—in the case, General MacArthur— acting for an international tribunal may not be challenged by *habeas corpus* and need not answer to the writ in a United States court.[46] Another limitation is embodied in the very recent decision in *Johnson v. Eisentrager,* holding that our courts have no jurisdiction even to entertain petitions for *habeas corpus* by nonresident enemy aliens, despite the cessation of hostilities.

It has also been held, in the case of the eight Nazi saboteurs who landed on our coasts from a submarine, that they were triable by a military commission under the laws of war, although one of the saboteurs was, or at least had been, an American citizen.[47] The case provides no convincing precedent for executive action toward suspected spies and saboteurs apprehended in the United States. The fact that the saboteurs made what was in effect a small-scale surreptitious invasion in wartime likened their situation to that of the spy caught crossing no man's land into our lines.

The prerogatives of the civil judiciary are further protected by the constitutional provision that "no person shall be convicted of treason unless on the testimony of two witnesses to the same overt act, or on confession in open court." The clause indicates that a full judicial proceeding is contemplated and required, and recent decisions have strengthened it.[48]

Certain other precedents appear to contain more danger to the operation of the judicial system. After the termination of hostilities the Supreme Court denied a writ of *habeas corpus* to General Tomoyuki Yamashita.[49] The general had been sentenced for violation of the laws of war in that he failed to exercise his authority as commander to prevent his troops from carrying out many and brutal atrocities in the Philippines campaign. The trial had been conducted in American territory after the termination of hostilities by a military commission appointed by the commanding general in the area, acting under a general presidential directive. The proceedings of the commission were, to say the least, scarcely in accord with the standards of common-law justice as to reliability of evidence, specification of charges, and opportunity to prepare a full defense. The Supreme Court refused to intervene, affirming that it found sufficient authority in the constitutional provision that Congress may "define and punish . . . offences against the Law of Nations." The Court said that this included the international common law of war, against which Yamashita was alleged to have offended. Military commissions to try such offenses were recognized by Congress in the Articles of War, although the commissions are not subject to the standards of evidence and of procedure imposed under the articles.

The Court was careful to point out that it was dealing with an enemy combatant. But in failing to affirm any precise judicial standards for the trial of such a defendant, it left open certain questions which may rise to plague us in the future. It is not clear whether American citizens in occupied territory, not subject to the Articles of War, have any right to procedural due process from whatever courts are set up by American authorities even after the termination of hostilities. Since the status of occupied territory is said to be a political question with which our courts will not interfere,[50] the area beyond the reach of the Constitution may have a relatively permanent existence, sapping the strength of constitutional protections in other areas by example. It is, I think, clear that if we permit a garrison state to exist under our authority abroad, long after the ending of hostilities, we increase the likelihood of it at home.

## MARTIAL LAW

Martial law, which is the third form of assumption of judicial authority by the executive, is the least formalized of the three. A formal declaration of a state of martial law is superfluous when civil or military authority anywhere in U.S. territory takes over the dispensation of punishments for such offenses as it may specify (and perhaps also the adjudication of civil controversies).[51] Martial law is normally accompanied by suspension of the privilege of the writ of *habeas corpus.* According to the Constitution, the privilege of the writ may be suspended only when "in cases of rebellion or invasion the public safety may require it." Since the reference to suspension is found in the article prescribing the authority of Congress, it has been held that only Congress can provide for suspension.[52] Nevertheless, suspension of the privilege has been effected in fact by presidential proclamation, as at the beginning of the Civil War.[53]

The situation, however, does not rest here. The Supreme Court has said that suspension of the privilege of the writ does not suspend its operation. Even when it cannot be used to compel the "production of the body" in court, the courts can still inquire into the authority for detention and, if not satisfied, order release.[54] Nor does a proclamation suspending the privilege or declaring martial law provide any justification for invading private rights.[55] The courts abstain from interfering with the declaration itself [56] or with the calling up of the militia.[57] Such questions are described as political matters outside the scope of judicial review. Our judges hesitate to intervene in the arrest or temporary detention of any individual under a proclamation in the interest of maintaining public order.[58] The vital point, however, is that so long as the courts are open, they reserve to themselves the administration of justice and the holding to account of any authority that in their judgment trespasses on private rights in the name of a self-proclaimed emergency. Thus they held Colonel Doniphan to account a century ago.

The fundamental principle involved was expressed in the famous Civil War case of *Ex Parte Milligan*.[59] The salient facts can be briefly summarized. Lambdin P. Milligan, an Indiana Copperhead whose Southern sympathies had led him to plot rebellion against the Union, was seized by the military authorities in Indiana, tried before a military commission, and sentenced to death. At the time, the civil courts were open in Indiana and there was no actual or immediate danger of invasion. Milligan petitioned for *habeas corpus*, and the Supreme Court ordered his release. The Court might have rested its decision on the provision of the statute suspending the privilege of the writ, which required that political prisoners not indicted by a grand jury be set down behind the rebel lines. But a majority of the Court seized the occasion to hold that Congress not only had not but *could* not have provided for trial by military commission. Mr. Justice Davis, writing for the Court, declared that there can be no substitute for civil authority except "where the courts are actually closed, and it is impossible to administer criminal justice according to law." "Martial law," he observed, "cannot arise from a threatened invasion. The necessity must be actual and present; the invasion real, such as effectually closes the courts and deposes the civil administration." [60]

For many decades after the Civil War *Ex Parte Milligan* was invoked to protect rights jeopardized by unwarranted actions by state officers under color of martial law. The great test came on the heels of Pearl Harbor.[61] Immediately after that disastrous event, the civil governor of the Territory of Hawaii handed over his authority to the military, and martial law was proclaimed in the Islands. By order of the commanding general, all civil courts were closed on December the eighth. The military set up a system of provost courts, at first with exclusive jurisdiction, and later sharing certain functions with the civil courts, which were reopened on a limited basis.

The problems arising in this situation did not receive clarification by the Supreme Court until 1946. In August, 1942, a civilian stockbroker named White was convicted of embezzlement in a provost court and given a five-year sentence. In February, 1944, a civilian employee in the Honolulu Navy Yard (Duncan) was sentenced by a provost court to six months at hard labor for allegedly engaging in a drunken brawl with two armed sentries. White and Duncan both petitioned for *habeas corpus,* but their cases did not reach the Supreme Court until 1945, and the Court delayed handing down a decision for more than a year.[62]

When the decision was finally announced, the two men were released on the ground that the governor had lacked statutory authority to close the courts. This depended upon the interpretation given to a section of the Hawaiian Organic Act, which authorizes the proclamation of martial law in emergencies. Hence the majority did not seize the occasion to deal squarely with the constitutional issue, although Mr. Justice Murphy, in concurrence, relied on the *Milligan* case. It is not unfair to say that the tenor of the majority opinion was such that the two dissenting justices were perhaps justified in asking whether the decision would have been the same if it had been handed down in 1942 or 1944 rather than in 1946. So far as that goes, the *Milligan* decision came well after the surrender at Appomattox. The

*Duncan* and *White* cases are disquieting testimony to the difficulty of applying the open court principle under modern crisis conditions. There is no sure immunity from surprise attacks or from the necessity of advance preparation, especially at strategically vital spots.

What of the problem of preserving the judicial function for the judiciary in the face of *threatened* crisis? The Japanese Exclusion cases raised this issue; it cannot be said that it was squarely met.[63] American citizens of Japanese origin living in the so-called West Coast Defense Area were first required to submit to a curfew, then to register with the authorities, and finally to submit to removal en masse—100,000 of them—from the Pacific Coast region, where most Japanese-Americans lived, to camps in the Great American Desert. In the camps an attempt was made to separate the loyal from the disloyal and to allow those of demonstrated loyalty to go home. The screening process worked very slowly, however, and in at least one instance required judicial stimulus to bring about the release of an internee already cleared. Authority for the curfew and exclusion orders was provided in a general statute which authorized military commanders to apply restrictions on entering, leaving, remaining in, or committing specified acts in a military zone or area (*i.e.*, in any part of the United States so designated), and enforceable in the civil courts. The detention program, however, lacked statutory authority and rested upon an executive order. No effort was made to deal with these citizens on an individual basis, which is particularly striking since all internments or exclusions of Japanese elsewhere, including Hawaii, were individually ordered. Individual orders were also used for the internment of enemy aliens.

The response of the Supreme Court to the issues raised leaves much to be desired. Three aspects of the program—curfew, exclusion, and detention *after* loyalty clearance—were dealt with in three cases.[64] The overwhelmingly important issue of detention

was avoided in the two cases where it was raised.[65]  Without the
element of detention, which the Court refrained from reviewing,
the military cannot be said to have taken over a judicial function.[66]

Has the Court retreated from the strong position of *Ex Parte
Milligan?* The courts are not truly open to citizens who can be
deprived of their liberty and sent to a concentration camp by an
executive judgment that their presence in an area, as a group,
is dangerous to national security. They are even less available
if they refuse to consider the central issue raised by the plight
of the citizens. It has been suggested that the tone of the opinions
rendered in the American-Japanese cases is more disturbing than
the immediate outcome. When a member of the Court suggests,
even in dissent, that civil courts should not dirty their hands either
by enforcing or upsetting military orders, the complete abrogation
of the open court doctrine is in effect being advocated.[67]  The
suggestion has, at least up to now, been rejected, as the Hawaiian
martial-law cases subsequently showed. But the attitude is full
of danger.

On the whole, we can conclude that the courts of this country
have a body of ancient principles and recent precedents that can
be used to keep at a minimum unnecessary encroachments upon
private rights by the executive, civil or military. The vigor and
sensitiveness with which the due process clause has been affirmed
in the last two decades is, in particular, an important development.

Too much, of course, cannot be expected from judges in defending the judicial function from encroachment by those who
are overzealous and overfearful for national security. Courts
await the approach of litigants. They do not initiate proceedings
themselves. Likewise, they rely for the most part on enforcement
machinery outside the judicial system. The early attempts of

lower Federal courts to nullify martial law in Hawaii were largely ineffectual for that reason. But the doctrinal tools are available to judges with the courage to employ them, and examples of that courage are not lacking, from Chief Justice Taney, alone on circuit in Philadelphia in 1861, demanding the surrender of his prisoner in the face of an army,[68] to the Hawaiian judiciary after Pearl Harbor. Taney's demand was in vain, so far as the immediate situation was concerned, but it has been remembered, and it points a double moral: We cannot rely upon the judiciary standing alone to rebuild our liberties; but if we act to preserve them wherever they are threatened, the judges will not be the last to help us.[69]

While it is true that the existing body of doctrine and the present structure and operating methods of the courts can act as checks upon precipitate losses of freedom during crisis periods, the effectiveness of the courts can in all likelihood be improved by introducing some of the innovations which have been under test or discussion in recent years. Sentiment has been crystallizing in favor of a more comprehensive system of public defenders who will take their place opposite the prosecuting attorneys as agents of the court. It will be essential to equip them with investigating talent equal to that of the prosecutors. In general, the experiments with the public defender system have been restricted to providing assistance to the indigent. However, the stake of the community is so great in matters touching national security and individual freedom that public defenders should be assigned to aid the defense when security and freedom are involved.[70] Under present conditions every incentive is on the side of the prosecuting agencies to "make a record" by obtaining convictions, and there is no equal concentration of public interest on the other side. In the same way, the investigating agencies of the government tend to justify their appropriations on the ground that they contribute essential information to the successful prosecution of offenders.

The aim of the public defender and the investigating agencies assigned to the defense is to provide a counterweight in the government which makes sure that the stake of the community in a just outcome is supported by an organized concentration of appropriate skills and incentives.

# VII. WHAT THE PUBLIC CAN DO

WE COME FINALLY to the public, where under our form of government the ultimate responsibility lies for the review of security measures. No thoughtful person doubts that in popular government an informed public is essential to sound policy. But to be enlightened is no simple matter. A comprehensive view is more than passive exposure to a torrent of disjointed items even though the individual items are true. It is "no longer enough to report *the fact* truthfully. It is now necessary to report *the truth about the fact*."[1] We recognize that the President needs the benefit of staff counsel in evaluating security policies and that the Congress requires a comprehensive frame of reference. It is evident that the court system cannot operate without elaborate facilities and procedures for gathering, sifting, and interpreting evidence. The same is true of the individual citizen, however distinguished or obscure. The sovereign citizen needs help equivalent to the President's staff and to the proposed Senate and House committees on national security.

Although access to a stream of current intelligence is vital to proper action by the public, more is involved. It is essential to achieve and to sustain an active concern for the goal values of a free society. The consensus on goals must also be supplemented by a wide basis of agreement upon the specific institutions which embody these aims. (Among the specific institutions one of the most important is the method of amending the existing arrangements.)

Government is a two-way process in which officials and the rest of the community are interacting upon one another. The equilibrium which is essential to freedom can be upset under various circumstances in the direction of anarchy or despotism. During

a continuing crisis of defense the menace to freedom by a garrison-police state is far greater than the threat of anarchy. The
factors that tip the scales in favor of government in general during
such a crisis, and that also favor the centralization of government,
have already been noted. The executive branch is strengthened,
and power within the executive concentrates in the hands of the
armed services and the political police.

In considering what the public can do, the objective should be
the mobilization of every element that makes for the proper balance of national security and individual freedom. The conditions
that favor the abdication of freedom beyond essential limits must
be counterbalanced. Since these limits cannot be unequivocally
described in words, the heart of the matter is to see that individuals
who give full weight to freedom are charged with interpreting
the words.

Recognizing that the fate of the commonwealth is settled day
by day in the referendum of official-private relations, the purpose
here is to emphasize both the seriousness of the issues involved
and some feasible ways of coping with the crisis. It is no small
matter when the opinion leaders of the American people at every
level of government are alive to great issues. They can arouse
ever-widening circles of citizens to more active and effective participation. When the largest number are on notice, the likelihood
is that there will be more immediate awareness of, and resistance
to, the encroachments that mark the early stages of a potential
police state.

The suggestions given here are a fraction of what needs to be
done. Exhaustiveness is not essential, however, since we can rely
upon the initiative of the American people to invent and apply
more ways of meeting critical situations than can be conveniently
gathered between the covers of any book. This can be expected
from the political traditions and national character of Americans.
This volume is itself an example of private initiative, not only on

the part of the author, but of a private association whose leaders are willing to face the urgent issues of the time. In a deep sense, the response to be made by the American people in resisting unnecessary intrusions upon individual freedom have already been determined. Our predispositions of mind and character have been molded by the ceaseless interplay of everyday life during childhood, youth, and early adulthood.

Much can be done, however, in the current situation to encourage freedom-loving conduct and to deter dangerous activities. In an earlier chapter the "mechanics" of government were considered and the conditions were indicated under which an office becomes an "established practice." Once established in practice, the office provides an environment in which some intentions are strengthened while others are weakened. The same point applies to established practices which, though unofficial, shape politically significant conduct. In some degree, practices are open to change, whether by suppression or extension. The following are examples of the kinds of action now available to the American public for affecting official action relating to national security and individual freedom:

1. The public can provide an approving environment for the members of the press who live up to the best traditions of the free press during the continuing crisis. One means to this end is the establishment of a private commission to report upon the performance of the press. (In this context the term "press" covers all the mass media of communication, such as newspapers, magazines, radio, and film.)

2. To stimulate continuing attention and thought, the thousands of policy associations now existing at every level of national life can set up special committees on National Security and Individual Freedom. The policy associations include the political parties, pressure groups, and civic organizations at local, state, regional, and national levels.

3. Communities can strengthen and extend the recent movement toward creating councils on human rights which inquire into the level of local achievement and encourage corrective action. It is assumed that the committees make a conscientious search for revealing information.

4. As a means of emphasizing the importance of the issues involved, provision can be made to observe National Security and Individual Freedom Days at the time the President issues his report to the Congress on the State of the Union.

5. As a means of reducing the anxieties and suspicions that disturb the unity of the nation, a vigorous and continuing campaign utilizing the new instruments of mass communication for genuinely educational purposes can be carried out, preferably under private auspices. An example of this type of activity is the work that has been carried on by the Advertising Council, Inc., during the past five years.

6. As a check on official sources, and as a supplement to the daily and weekly press, unofficial sources of information and interpretation can be fostered throughout the nation.

## 1. THE RESPONSIBILITY OF THE FREE PRESS

The correspondents of the press associations and the principal newspapers and magazines are the front-line listening posts of the American people. On matters requiring quick action, the mind of the public will continue to be made up primarily on the basis of the news and comment in the columns of newspapers, the broadcasts of commentators, and the interpretative writing in the "news magazines" (which are often disguised magazines of opinion). The dependence of the ordinary citizen upon an "opinion leader" in his immediate circle does not abrogate the influence of the press, since the opinion leader obtains most of his current impressions from the stream of intelligence flowing through the mass media.

If the approval given to the members of the press who live up to the highest standards of American journalism is to be founded on a factual and balanced viewpoint, new institutions are needed to serve the seeing, reading, and listening public. The initiative has already been taken in many local communities for "listening councils" to evaluate the caliber of service performed by the radio stations. But a more comprehensive private agency is needed. The Commission on Freedom of the Press recommended the establishment of a new and independent agency designed to appraise and report upon the performance of the press. The commission suggested that such a body be independent of government and of the press, that it be founded by gifts, and that it be given a ten-year trial run.

An agency to report upon the performance level of the free press is more urgent now than when the commission made the original recommendation in 1947. Such an agency could be a powerful ally of the public as a whole and of the press itself in preserving the greatest possible scope for the information flowing to the American people.

## 2. COMMITTEES ON NATIONAL SECURITY AND INDIVIDUAL FREEDOM

It is essential to supply the press with an active, not a passive, audience if the needs of the nation are to be served. Studies of the impact of modern instruments of communication show that the audience often pays so little attention to what is said or printed that there is practically no result. Partly as a protective measure against overstimulation, such audiences live in a diffuse world of background noise furnished by musicians and speakers. Instead of contributing to public enlightenment or to a sense of responsibility for taking a more active part in building a sounder community, mass media operating under such conditions are the "opiates of the masses."

## What the Public Can Do

Under certain conditions, however, the mass media packs a terrific punch. One important finding concerns the interplay between the small group and the mass media. Audience impact is heightened when the mass audience is made up of a great honeycomb of small groups eagerly stimulating one another to pay attention and to react. Hence a technique for enlarging the effective role of the press (including, of course, the radio and the film) is to sharpen the connection between the small group and the large medium.

One way to introduce an active rather than a passive attitude toward news and comment on public affairs is through the policy association. The American people are a justly celebrated nation of joiners.[2] Whether it is a question of political parties, pressure groups, or civic bodies, Americans are accustomed to initiate and to manage private organizations on a grand scale.

It is not necessary, nor is it expedient, to set up a new network of private associations to deal with the problems of national security and individual freedom. It is possible to improve the effectiveness of the existing structure by setting up commitees in each organization to take the lead in reviewing national policy in the security field.

Some private associations are specialized to aspects of the security problem and have made important contributions to public opinion. The Council on Foreign Relations (New York City) and the Foreign Policy Association (in several cities) are concerned with many of the issues arising in national defense. There is a tendency, however, to detach foreign policy from the context of American life as a whole, a tendency which the formation of special committees on National Security and Freedom would do something to overcome. Many civic organizations are not limited to one set of questions. "City clubs" may spend as much time on state, regional, or national affairs as upon local matters, and could appropriately set up committees on national security and freedom. The forum movement, so greatly stimulated by World War I, dotted the country with free platforms for the discussion of controversial policies. Some forums use committees to look into specific questions and make recommendations. A committee on national security policy would fit into the mold.

The League of Women Voters is an excellent example of an organization which at first glance appears to limit its scope, but which does not in fact confine itself to "women's interests." Problems of security have always attracted the attention of the League, and committees on national security and freedom would be well within precedent. Among the general women's organizations the tradition of civic responsibility is well established.

Anyone acquainted with America knows that the most influential forums are often provided by organizations of businessmen. Chambers of commerce are active in thousands of communities. Committees of the chamber do faithful work on issues of the day. The idea of providing for a regular review of security and freedom is entirely consistent with the policy of the chamber. The lead in many places on questions of public policy is taken by service clubs like Rotary, Kiwanis, or Lions. Well schooled in the consideration of public issues, committees on national security and freedom would simply extend and intensify present programs.

The principal forums in farm communities are frequently provided by the American Farm Bureau Federation, the Grange, or the Farmers Union. In many city neighborhoods and mining towns the CIO or the AFL furnish forums. In common with most American organizations, the unions have paid increasing attention in recent years to security matters. Committees on national security and freedom would further this trend.*

* A more extended discussion of the committee in policy associations is in Appendix B.

### 3. COMMUNITY COUNCILS ON HUMAN RIGHTS

Within the past few years a new civic movement has made a mark in many communities throughout the land. After the report of the President's Committee on Civil Rights, the citizens of Montclair, N.J., took the initiative in making an audit of the extent to which Montclair lived up to the standards laid down in the report. The audit was made by the citizens, with some technical advice and aid from professional social scientists. When the picture began to form, action programs suggested themselves to many minds. The consensus was strong enough to bring about a number of private, semipublic, and official changes.[3]

The idea of keeping track of performance is, of course, no novelty in the business or civic life of the country. Private insurance companies rate communities as good or bad fire risks. Official, civic, and private agencies are involved in rating health, traffic, education, and other local activities. Hence the use of an audit to appraise the state of freedom is a rational extension of a well-established American practice.

In many places the council which has been organized in relation to human rights may well merge or at least work with committees on national security and individual freedom. The close coupling of security considerations with private rights poses the policy problems of the country in the clearest light.

### 4. OBSERVE NATIONAL SECURITY AND FREEDOM DAYS

A definite rhythm can be introduced into the consideration of security questions if the President issues an annual report on national security and freedom, and the Congress provides for an immediate appraisal of the report and of the position of the country. Committees of citizens' organizations can time their activities in relation to the President and Congress, arranging meetings for the consideration of official statements. The committeees can mobilize the best available talent to assist in the review. Scattered everywhere throughout America are persons competent to supply experience or judgment. The impact of security on the free market, freedom of information, and civil liberties can be assessed by qualified economists, businessmen, lawyers, political scientists, and sociologists.

It will be important for committees on national security and freedom to draw upon experts in presentation as well as in subject matter. The materials presented to audiences in the typical forum or lecture hall are usually in antiquated style. In business and education, visual aids are commonplace. But they are far from commonplace in civic meetings. However, local initiative is often able to leap over obstacles of this kind. Art classes in the schools prepare needed material. Commercial artists donate skill and experience. Throughout the country community leaders are often strikingly successful in forming citizen teams of many talents.

## 5. THE FULL USE OF MODERN MEDIA

The prominence of existing media and the extent and intensity of effort by party, pressure, and civic associations tend to obscure one simple fact: A very large part of the American people are not actively concerned with national issues.

I suppose every thoughtful American is startled by the results of some studies which have been made of the state of public information on policies of importance for the security of the nation. After sixteen months of debate and public discussion, and one month before Congress authorized the Marshall Plan, sixteen out of every hundred American voters had never heard of it. Only fourteen out of a hundred could be called informed, in the sense that they could give a reasonably accurate statement of the Plan's purpose. Although aware of the existence of such a scheme, seventy in each hundred were uninformed.[4]

## What the Public Can Do

Nor are these findings exceptional when matters of foreign policy, so vital to our security, are at issue. Actually the unaware group on the Marshall Plan was half as large as usual on such issues. (The informed group, however, was only about half the usual size.)

How is this possible in a country having access to the greatest network of mass communication on the globe? Nine out of every ten homes in America have radio sets. Two-thirds of the public claim to listen regularly to newscasts. Four-fifths of the public claim to read a daily or a weekly newspaper regularly. And half read magazines. Our media of mass communication are staffed by experts on arousing public interest. What do these results tell us about their efficiency?

It must be conceded that the level of public concern for national security and individual freedom depends upon many more factors in American life than the daily or weekly impact of the press. Why not, for instance, hold the schools responsible? If the schools did a proper job of preparing the audience for the mass media, would not the demand of the public automatically raise the competitive strength of the most enlightened and vigorous champions of the goal values of America?

The teachers have a partial answer to this, and to some extent a legitimate one, when they underline the neglect of schooling in America. It cannot be denied that from one point of view America is an unschooled nation. The census of 1940 (the last one available) showed that most of the population had gone little beyond the eighth grade. Only one person in seven who was twenty-five years of age or over had finished high school. And one in seventy had graduated from college. And there is evidence that informed interest in public affairs beyond the locality is positively related to the length of exposure to educational institutions. It was typical to discover that while 29 per cent of the voters with a grammar school background or less had not heard of the Marshall Plan, only 3 per cent of the college-educated Americans had not heard of it. (Incidentally, who might this 3 per cent be?)

Even when we have opened our eyes to the low exposure to schools of the population as a whole, the low level of persisting concern for the larger environment casts doubt upon the performance of the school system. Teachers have access to the population for at least eight formative years. Why has teaching not been more successful in enlarging the scope of curiosity and knowledge so that incentives to pay attention to the larger environment outlast the classroom?

One possible answer is that the struggle for a livelihood is so severe that only the immediate environment has any meaning to the lower income American. Some confirmation of this view is forthcoming from figures about knowledge of the Marshall Plan. Eighty-two per cent of the voters with incomes above the average could describe the purpose of the Plan. Eighty-eight per cent of voters with less-than-average income were unable to do so.

However, there are several grounds for rejecting the view that political indifference is always and everywhere a matter of income. The history of public affairs provides us with too many examples of political movements which have continued for years and enjoyed the active support of low-income farmers, craftsmen, and industrial workers.

The essential point is some failure of motivation, which is not of necessity related to the level of income. Rather, failures can be traced to unhappy experience with comprehensive political interests. If the cultivation of a comprehensive interest improves the position of the individual, we expect his interest to continue. Suppose, for example, that the individual is born into a home where the conversation is full of talk about major political issues and personalities. Assume, further, that the opinions of the growing youngster are welcome, and that his position within the family circle is improved by any sign of precocity in political knowledge and insight. Suppose that the command of political information and modes of discussion are approved by teachers and fellow pupils. It is not to be wondered at that the individual develops an image of himself in which he expects to win respect, and other advantages, from keeping well read and quick-spoken on public issues.

If this hypothetical analysis is applied to a group, it is possible to specify some conditions under which an active and comprehensive concern for politics is to be expected. Assume that a group of workers is engaged in an industry which competes strongly with foreign plants. Suppose that wages and conditions of work are driven down, on the plea of foreign competition. Then imagine that labor organizers succeed in establishing strong labor unions in the competing plants with one aim, that of protecting standards. It is not surprising to find that the group has a sense of interdependence and solidarity across national lines.

Summing up, the essential point is that participation in politics, in common with every human response, is a matter of relative expectations.[5] When the individual expects to be better off by cultivating broad, rather than local, interests, he will cultivate broad interests. A predisposition toward playing an active role in public affairs depends upon past success, appraised in terms of whatever values are sought (respect, affection, wealth, or power, for instance).

The connection between low incomes and political apathy, where it occurs, can have several roots. It may mean that the poorer families in a given community conceive of themselves as affected only by events in the immediate and controllable vicinity, not in the vague, vast, and utterly uncontrollable "world outside." It may also mean that children are sent to poor schools in which the teachers are as limited as the parents.

However, the significance of the connection between disinterest in the larger world and low income may be more complex. Studies of American communities have done much to disclose the nature of the environment in which political interests are at a minimum. The salient points can be briefly put. The main source of civic ignorance is indifference. Indifference is chiefly a matter of the class position of the home into which the individual is born and in which he is reared. The schools are the greatest agency now operating to enlarge the scope of civic knowledge and concern, but the effectiveness of schools depends to a very considerable extent upon the encouragement which is given at home to class-room achievement. Social scientists report that these differences in the rewarding of schoolroom effort and success are closely connected with the class structure of the country.

Many Americans are shocked when America is described in class terms. They think of classes as castes, as impassable chasms, and they are acutely aware that the American conception of human dignity calls for social mobility according to personal merit. But class is not necessarily caste; if individuals born into a given social status can move out of it, there is mobility, which is impossible in a smoothly operating caste system.

If you listen to the way people talk about one another in a given community, it appears that families are classified according to the respect in which they are held. It is typical to find "old families" and some who live "on the other side of the tracks." All sorts of subclasses can be distinguished between the extremes. Social scientists have taken the trouble to interview everyone in selected communities to find how each person is classified. Thus the meaning of class structure for education has been worked out in detail. At the lower end of the social scale the characteristic attitude is skepticism about the possibility of rising in the world by means of the skills made available in schools. The result is indifference or hostility to school achievement. Such homes do not provide the child with opportunities which are equal to those of children born in homes which encourage school success as a means to success in life.[6]

These findings put a grave burden on the schools and the mass media of communication, since these are the channels most capable of providing some compensation in the lives of young people for the failures of home and neighborhood to reward civic-mindedness. The mass media, too, are among the channels most capable of evoking a new spurt of interest in national affairs on the part of older persons. Among the other channels are policy associations and community organizations, both of which have been lacking in full effectiveness in appealing to the lower status groups. Local community studies have repeatedly shown that foreign policy associations, in particular, have a narrow class basis, often being restricted to the upper and upper-middle end of the social scale. In many cities and towns even the industrial workers are left in a civic vacuum.

Committees on national security and freedom can be used to overcome the narrow appeal of policy associations concerned with foreign affairs. People are not apathetic about what they think affects them and what they can do something about. Since individual freedom and national security are inextricably tied up with one another, the continuing crisis of defense provides an occasion on which all levels of the community can achieve heightened civic awareness. Obviously the state of free enterprise and of civil liberty are involved. The issues include freedom to organize and to bargain collectively, freedom to strike, freedom to organize new parties, freedom from unwarranted intrusion upon privacy.

Groups that have long been neglected generate an attitude of anxiety and suspiciousness that is a potential threat to the unity and strength of the nation. For many years observers of modern industrial civilization in this country and abroad have been impressed by the degree to which millions of individuals feel alienated from the world in which they live. Lacking a comprehensive picture of the routines of modern life, they are the prey to vague anxiety and generalized suspicion. This is a psychological process that operates with the devastating and surprising impact of an army of termites, hollowing out the substance of loyalty and obedience and leaving only the shell. Our capacity as a nation to endure the crisis, and if necessary to resort to a winning war, depends upon keeping the entire population genuinely devoted to the welfare of the commonwealth.

As a means of protecting both national security and individual freedom, we need to make fuller use of the new instruments of communication. Among modern media the greatest potentialities appear to be offered by film and television. Although film is by now a well-established tool of classroom teaching, the tool is used on a wholly inadequate scale.

What is the true significance of film and television for public opinion? These new instruments make it possible for the first time in large-scale modern communities for everybody to be exposed to what is going on. In the small town or the primitive tribe it is possible for the child to have brought to his attention the social context in its entirety. The explosive expansion of modern industrialism has enmeshed everybody in a social process extending far beyond his primary range of experience.

At first there was little specialized knowledge of the new world of industry. Today knowledge among specialists is catching up with needs. But the fundamentals of this knowledge need to become part of the common stock of culture if modern man is to feel at home in the world of science and technology. The new instruments of communication are at hand to aid in performing this essential job. The new gadgets can open the windows of the locality upon the region, the nation, and the world as a whole. The eye of the camera and the ear of the recorder reproduce what cannot be seen and heard at first hand. They bring into immediate experience what can otherwise be grasped only by travel and study expeditions. And film confers new concreteness on history.

Above all, the new instruments of communication enable us to catch up on our words. Until the invention of film and television we have had no suitable means of making words concrete without at the same time producing an excessively parochial outlook. The meaning of words depends upon a frame of reference. When we had to depend upon spoken or printed words, supplemented by still pictures, we lacked instruments capable of supplying the context for the words needed to describe the contemporary social process.

It is now possible to introduce the vocabulary of economics, political science, sociology, and all other human sciences and disciplines in an unambiguous way. And it is possible to exhibit significant samples of what is meant anywhere on the globe or any time in history. If the word is "national income," we can trace in films the items which are included or excluded by the economist. If defense expenditures are alleged to reduce the standard of living, we can follow the process step by step. Where expert opinion is in conflict or in doubt, alternative conceptions can be described. When we speak of the "free market" or "market restriction," the situations referred to by these words can be made definite, clear, vivid, and as comprehensive as desired. Since most of the vocabulary used in designating the social process is also employed in expressing preferences and determinations in reference to policy, it is essential at an early date to cultivate skill in disentangling one mode of statement from the other. It is possible to clarify the descriptive meaning of terms in the mouth of a speaker: "democracy," "despotism," "freedom," and the like. We can also recognize when statements are being presented by a speaker chiefly for their emotive significance to his audience.

If, as we are now told by some specialists, our methods of language instruction are obsolete, and more adequate use of visual materials can speed up the process by three or four years, the skill level of the public can be raised much more rapidly than hitherto imagined possible.

### 6. FOSTERING UNOFFICIAL SOURCES OF INFORMATION AND INTERPRETATION

The reincorporation of everyone into the commonwealth is a persisting problem of modern society that the urgency of crisis may provide the incentives to resolve. Certainly the harmonizing of mass media and policy organizations is one of the steps leading in the right direction. The crisis also provides a new imperative for coping with another chronic problem of a society that aspires toward freedom. This is the providing of sources of information and interpretation lying outside the official channels of government and proceeding at a more deliberate pace than is possible for the daily or weekly press.

One supplement of the daily and periodical press is the book and the personal message of experienced correspondents. It may be necessary for the correspondent in Moscow or Berlin to "pull punches" during his years of service or lose his usefulness by being thrown out of the country. Punches may also be pulled to avoid giving offense to owners and editors. (Sometimes editors are less exacting than readers who are deeply shocked when cherished stereotypes are violated. Reader activity, for instance, has influenced the published reports of events abroad. Catholic readers have put pressure on the press in connection with Spain, for instance; and Jews have had plenty to say about reporting from the Near East. For years the readers of liberal magazines raised a storm when anything was published that seemed unfriendly to Russia, which they mistook for a citadel of freedom.)

Whether he pulled punches much or little, there comes a time when "now it can be told." The public is greatly indebted to the books and lectures of foreign correspondents. It is almost invidious to name individual journalists who have played an important role in enlightening America. However, when we think of the Soviet Union, the name of William H. Chamberlain at once suggests itself.[7] During the early years of the Russian Revolution our most imaginative and perceptive journalists were tolerant and hopeful of the regime in Moscow. Chamberlain was a turning point in the literature of revaluation. His work was a warning that progress toward freedom was in temporary, if not permanent, abeyance in the Soviet Union, and that liberal support of the current regime was a doubtful asset to security or freedom. So far as Germany is concerned, the passionate tract by Edgar Ansel Mowrer, *Germany Puts the Clock Back,* was a landmark in crystallizing this nation's estimate of the Nazis.

There were, of course, journalists who went out of their way in praise of foreign tyrannies. In the free forum of America all voices are equally entitled to be heard, not to be believed; and the news "gets around" that Smith writes to please a foreign political party (Communist, Nazi, Fascist) or to please an American editor out to smear the New Deal or to cater to a reactionary clique of church politicians.

The mass media are supplemented every day by other communications originating with Americans abroad. There are specialized observers connected with American banking and business corporations engaged in foreign trade and investment. Some correspondents are staff members or influential figures in the vast system of private associations connected with churches, fraternal orders, service clubs, trade associations, trade unions, or scientific and professional societies.

Persons living abroad for any reason may affect American opinion. No proper assessment has been made of the impact of returned missionaries upon America's conception of national destiny, or image of other countries. Missionaries have touched and retouched our stereotypes of Asia, Africa, and the islands of the sea. Thousands of Americans have been brought up in missionary homes. (Remember the influence of Pearl Buck on our notion of the Chinese. Remember the background in China of Henry Luce.)

Mention of "the expatriates" calls up the memory of a host of artists and writers who left their mark upon what the American public thinks of Europe. The "emigration" of talented young people to Paris during the twenties came to an end when remittances ended in the crash of the thirties. In a sense this was the final immersion of Americans in the mother matrix of European culture. Afterward came the deluge in Europe and the discovery of America by the artists.

When diplomats and other officials return to private life, they occasionally become enlighteners of the public. William E. Dodd struck a powerful blow at Hitler when, after returning from Berlin, his diary was published. To go back further, there was the remarkable picture of Russo-British rivalry for the control of Persia painted by Morgan Schuster after returning from his post as financial adviser to the Persian government (*The Strangling of Persia*).

By far the greatest impact by an officer on professional and lay thought about security was made by Admiral Mahan in his books on sea power. Up to the present we have had no Mahan of diplomacy, economics, or propaganda. For that matter, we have had no Mahan of the land or air, or—more urgent matter— no Mahan of joint and combined strategy.

Mention of Mahan carries us away from unofficial channels of reporting and rumination upon events and toward more systematic interpretations of experience. In the last generation the American public has become conscious of being served by a distinguished gallery of foreign correspondents. Less obvious is the contribution of a growing corps of scholars and scientists.

In the forefront are the standards maintained by Foreign

*Affairs* under the editorship of Hamilton Fish Armstrong. When we go beyond the names known to the general public, new currents of thought become increasingly apparent. Before World War II a new note was struck in the analysis of America's place in the world when geographical factors affecting power were systematically examined by Nicholas Spykman at the Yale Institute of International Studies. New ground was occupied when Edward Meade Earle and his associates at the Institute of Advanced Study at Princeton developed a systematic program for studying the theory and practice of strategy. Meanwhile the older fields of geography, history, international law, and economics continued to expand, turning out specialists who staff many public and private agencies.[8]

Far removed from conventional ideas about the knowledge "proper" for national security policy is anthropology.[9] Yet field work in the Pacific laid the groundwork for much that was to prove directly useful during the war and afterward. More important was the growth, in conjunction with psychiatry and psychology, of a new frame of reference for high policy. The "scientific" or "engineering" approach was introduced into areas where formerly it was undreamed of. Ancient stereotypes about "savages" full of "superstition" went by the board. The arrogance of ignorance is no longer the norm for men in the foreign service or in advanced university work. Only a few years ago it was good form for all sorts of nonsense to be repeated by distinguished historians, international lawyers, and statesmen. For instance, we were repeatedly told that the people of Asia were unable to operate modern machinery—like planes—because there was something odd about their nervous system. Now we know that the oddity was the training of the men who said these things.

We are in the midst of profound revolutions of thought which we owe not to the propaganda releases of government but to the cumulative impact of events as these events are interpreted by scholars, scientists, philosophers, and artists. The "machine tools" of thought forged by important thinkers have been copied and applied by ever-widening circles of spokesmen of and to the public. Great names can be mentioned in this connection, although this does a certain injustice to the thousands of silent workers who quarry data and begin the processing of results. The modern outlook owes a great deal to the conception of personality and culture expressed by Durkheim, Max Weber, Sigmund Freud, Ruth Benedict, Elton Mayo, and others. For the understanding of the evolution of modern economic institutions, we have Sombart and a host of scholars to thank. Works of erudition and imagination like those of Toynbee have added their perspectives to our view of the past and present. The fact that some of these names are not American is a reminder of the intimate communion in which we live with the cultural tradition of the West.[10]

The events of recent years have given a new sense of timing to specialists in many fields of human endeavor. Timing comes from crisis consciousness. The shadow of the third world war hangs like a cloud on the horizon. Is it possible to employ the resources of the mind to reduce the dire peril in which we live? Is it possible to develop a strategy in the choice of problems for inquiry that will bring knowledge into close contact with crucial decisions? The idea is not for scholars and scientists to leave the test tube for the soapbox, but rather that the scarce supply of high-grade intellectual resources shall be turned toward crucial rather than trivial issues. (If a label is desired for this new sense of timing, I suggest terming it the "policy sciences" approach.)

A tangible result of the sense of timing is the growth of area programs of teaching and investigation. The central idea is to enable those who specialize on any phase of India, for example, to obtain enough knowledge of Indian history and culture to understand where their particular specialty fits into, and interacts with, the whole context of which it is part. All available experts are drawn into the area program in the hope of providing a grand mosaic of Indian civilization.

Systematic study is much more important to the public now than it was before World War II. In important areas normal information channels of the mass media are cut off. The methods of prewar reporting cannot be used in the Soviet Union or in many of the countries under Russian control. But this does not mean that the only remaining sources of information are spies. An alternative is the careful examination of "open" sources by scholars qualified to interpret the ripples and eddies on the surface of newspapers, magazines, books, films, statutes, regulations, resolutions, reports. All life is interrelated in any society; interrelations can be discerned by the inquiring mind properly equipped with knowledge and method.

Some area programs apply to the Soviet zone, and all available methods are applied as an aid to understanding what goes on. (Two of the chief academic centers are at Columbia and Harvard universities.) We must rely upon centers of this kind to keep the public informed of what is going on behind "curtains" of all kinds. The dissemination of their findings remains the primary responsibility of the mass media.

The media should perform the same function for all major interpretations of the world situation. That the American public is more serious than ever before in finding a clue to the worldwide predicament in which we live can be demonstrated in many ways. Large audiences are available for serious books and lectures on the goals, principles, and trends of the nation and the world community. Above all, perhaps, the quest of integration is the clearest evidence.[11] In American education, for example, unified courses in social science, history, the humanities, biology, and the physical sciences are emerging everywhere. The movement substitutes a coherent curriculum for the elective system which was so effective at one time in dissolving the stranglehold of the classicists upon our colleges. "Great issues" courses are now attempting to give a comprehensive view of the problems of citizenship. Parallel tendencies are visible at the junior college, senior and junior high school levels. The same forces are active at the apex of the academic pyramid where research teams are cutting across the department lines in graduate schools. Among the professional schools, like law, there are shifts of the same kind in legal education and research.[12]

The mechanism of committees on national security and individual freedom can accelerate both the demand for a comprehensive view and for unofficial sources of knowledge. Committees on national security can take the initiative in using and encouraging new sources apart from official information and propaganda. Every reviewing committee will become better acquainted with "who's who" on every major topic connected with security and freedom. The national network of security committees is a system of retail outlets for the gatherers and processors of information. They have a stake in encouraging private competition to offset government monopoly. In this struggle they can enlist the consuming public.

A security and freedom committee can in many places become an important institution for bringing scholars and men of action together. For many years, the huge academic structure of the United States was cut off from regular association with policy makers in government, business, and other institutions of American life. No mechanism was provided for keeping intellectual contact between the colleges, graduate schools, and professional schools on the one hand and decision makers on the other. Academic institutions were adapted to turning out specialists, but there were no specialists on the timing of knowledge in relation to the needs of policy.

There is no mystery about what is essential if the gap is to be bridged. A mechanism is necessary which brings scholars and policy makers into direct association on problems whose importance is obvious to all. Competent staff work needs to be done in preparing an agenda, but the results of research and study need to be pointed toward recommendations about policy.[13]

I cite a few examples of the new and modified institutions which America is developing to bring scholars and decision makers into fruitful working relationship. The Committee for Economic Development is a case in point. The most distinctive feature of CED is not that a highly competent staff is hired and given academic freedom to complete research projects in fields agreed to by the businessmen on the board of trustees. Nor is it the presence of an advisory board of academic specialists who take part in the discussion of projects, results, and recommendations. These important features can all be found in other organizations. The unique feature is that the businessmen take final responsibility for preparing policy statements. They give their own time to reading, debating, and drafting. Final recommendations are not the work of a technical staff countersigned by businessmen. On the contrary, the final product is the outcome of a processs of study, reflection, and writing in which the businessmen are genuinely active, not passive, participants.

The National Bureau of Economic Research is less in point, although some of the mechanisms tested by the Bureau affected the structure of CED and other agencies. The National Bureau of Economic Research exists, not to make recommendations, but to conduct research on fundamental problems connected with economic life. Control is in the hands of a board chosen in order to represent special constituencies without interfering with scientific objectivity. Management, labor, universities, and professional associations are all involved. The publications of the bureau are read and criticized at formative stages, and dissents are printed in the final version. The "right of footnote" has become one of the human rights of free expression.

An unofficial capstone to the system of security and freedom committees would be a national committee set up with a diversified board of trustees and a competent staff.

This agency might be included within the frame of a more comprehensive institution designed to act as an unofficial Institute of National Policy. Such an agency should not follow in the footsteps of the existing degree-granting academic establishments. It ought to exist for research, discussion, and recommendation. The permanent staff should be small. Most of the work could be done by staff members working on short-term or part-time assignment. And for every project area, continuing committees (and teams) should be set up to make policy recommendations. Team members would reside for various periods at institute headquarters.

If an Institute of National Policy is not set up, then there is a place for a less comprehensive institution specialized to national security and freedom: a Commission on National Security and Individual Fredom. The financing should be by grants from private foundations or similar sources (with no strings attached).

### HOLDING PUBLIC OFFICIALS ACCOUNTABLE

Informing the public is not enough. The public must act. It must hold public officials accountable.

The basic principle of accountability is to reward friends and punish enemies. We have previously spoken of "special elections" held every day in which any citizen can "register" and "vote." The vote may be by petition, public comment, or some other impact (positive or negative) upon officials.

The number one instrument of accountability in America is the daily press. The main contribution of the press is in sounding the alert when there is even the faintest suspicion that something contrary to public policy is on foot. The elementary job of the press is to yell "fire" and to get the citizens out of bed or the kitchen or the shop to look at their government. For instance: Is censorship going too far? Are pressure groups operating in the dark and spreading corruption? Are the political police extending their blacklist beyond the rather small number of truly sensitive spots in government and society?

The tradition of press initiative is not dead. The American people owe an incalculable debt to the members of the press who live up to it. I attach to this chapter a rather recent example of a Washington correspondent in action (see Appendix A). It is not the most sensational case that could have been taken. Nor is it trivial. It is not necessary to assume that Nat Finney was one hundred per cent right on the merits of the dispute. The fact that the Executive withdrew under the light of public discussion raises a presumption that Finney was right. And he won the support of his colleagues. The entire incident is an excellent example of what Americans are talking about when they quote Jefferson on the reliance of a free people upon a free press.

If officials are to be held fully accountable, the press must be joined by other agencies. The purpose of the proposed committees on national security and freedom is to increase the effectiveness of the existing system of civic institutions in America.

It is a mistake to suppose that the press and the pressure groups are limited to negative means of acting upon public officials. Praise and encouragement are more characteristic of America than negative incentives. Our technique of operation in business is to "make it worth his while," and this positive approach is carried over into all life situations even where money is not involved. We "accentuate the positive."

However, civic organizations are frequently behind time in the methods they employ. Some of our worthiest groups typically appear in the role of complainer, prosecutor, objector. A good example is the remarkable organization which Roger Baldwin has guided through a lifetime, the American Civil Liberties Union. Limited always by scarcity of funds and man-hours of available energy, the ACLU has kept its activities closely confined to the courtroom. It has not distinguished itself for the accolades that it has bestowed upon police officials, judges, prosecutors, and others who do a good job. The union has been too busy snapping at the heels of iniquity to do much to "accentuate the positive." [14]

An approach that joins the positive and negative incentives is the civic audit already referred to. The audit makes it possible to look at the civic picture as a whole, to identify current trends, and to encourage the critical consideration of future lines of action.[15]

### PREVENTING HYSTERIA

The measures which have been recommended in this discussion offer the best available defense against such extremes of crisis reaction as hysteria or complacency. During times of continuing crisis an undercurrent of insecurity creates explosive situations in which panics, persecution manias, and other psychic seizures can disrupt the life of the nation. Some of the most valuable studies of human behavior have been made on the "crowd mind." [16] The crowds of the French Revolution were stock examples, but the witchcraft persecutions, the "deportations delirium" of the 1920's in the United States, and lynch mobs are examples of the same phenomena. There is no great mystery about the behavior of crowds, although much remains to be known about them in detail. When the crowd demands the sacrifice of a public scapegoat, or turns into a roaring lynch mob, we are dealing with no supermind but with a special sort of relationship among individuals. The essential fact about the behavior of the individual in a crowd is that he acts regressively. He stops taking responsibility for his thoughts and actions. He returns to the attitudes appropriate to an immature phase of development when he depended upon outside guidance and care. The functions of the critical, reflecting mind are in abeyance, as are the limitations imposed by conscience. Since the person has abdicated his normal judgment, guidance and valuations are slavishly accepted from outside. The exhilaration of belonging to a crowd comes from the thrill of being identified with a human aggregate enormously bigger and stronger than one's puny self. In this aggregate one is absolved from the stress and strain of reflection or of self-control. (When individuals fall into the crowd state, they are not always destructive. On the contrary, they may tremble in religious ecstasy. Or they may face certain death with serenity.)

Since appalling damage can be done to the texture of civilization before balancing factors are brought into play, destructive crowd states are full of danger to the unity and security of the nation. It is not necessary to assume that the crowd response is wholly the result of sinister propaganda. Deliberate manipulation may be less important than spontaneous rumor.

How is the integrity of this country to be guarded from the devastating impact of destructive crowds? Where instant communications are in existence, psychic epidemics can spread across the continent in the twinkling of an eye.

One way to guard against the terror-stricken, hate-filled destructive crowd is to keep the tension level down by a process of enlightenment in which future possibilities are discounted in advance. If the potentialities of the world situation are fully discussed, and the factors affecting security and freedom are widely understood, new crises will be taken in stride. Enough cool heads will be left to keep the processes of orderly life intact. Among the possibilities to be discussed in advance are the dangers of the witch-hunting mentality. The signs of hysteria can be talked about before they appear, and thousands of opinion leaders can be alerted to recognize the sparks and keep from fanning the conflagration. The committees on security and freedom can learn about the psychology of rumor and of crowds. The continual investigation of this topic is a prophylactic against epidemics of the mind.[17]

The committees can use civil defense exercises for the sake of preparing the public in advance against the disruptive effect of surprise attack and sabotage. Defense exercises can familiarize everyone with the problems involved in "alerts" of various degrees, and reduce the likelihood of hysteria.

### PREVENTING COMPLACENCY

Security and freedom are threatened in some circumstances, not by tensions which create hysteria, but by fantasies which induce complacency. It is difficult for the American public to become reconciled to the grim fact of perpetual crisis and possible war. As a result, gestures of peace and friendship on the part of a member of the Russian elite are overreacted to by a significant number of opinion leaders and their constituencies. It is not necessary to assume that war is "inevitable" to maintain an attitude of hopeful restraint in interpreting gestures of this sort. In the past, these gestures have too often proved to be political tactics designed to confuse and divide rather than preludes to effective new initiatives. Hence the rational attitude is to welcome gestures of peace and friendship without inflating their importance.

The tendency of Americans to be complacent about peace and friendship in world affairs is imbedded in national character.[18] These American stereotypes have been formed by generations of experience in a continent free of instant threat of war. Even in the days of blockhouses and constant readiness to fight the Indian, the colonists did not transform themselves into a string of garrison states in which a large fraction of the population specialized in the profession of arms and power was given top priority among social values. Fighting was, for the most part, a part-time activity of the population as a whole. But the occasion and purpose of the fighting was to protect crops and homes. It was obviously not an end in itself but a means to other values. The Civil War, devastating as it was, seemed to be a temporary storm and no permanent harbinger of armed peace. The Spanish-American War was brief and episodic. Even World War I seemed only an interruption.

There has been much violence in America. Think of the homicide rate, of the Hatfield-McCoy feuds, of sheepherders versus cattlemen, of the Colorado coal strike and other labor-management bloodshed, of lynch mobs, and of gang wars in the field of mercenary crime. But so far as world politics are concerned, the American people have felt comparatively exempt from the expectation of violence. In this remote and poorly understood field, Americans applied ideal standards. By a paradox which has often astonished observers, Americans seem to expect nations to abide by a more stringent moral code than private individuals.

The point of view of the Russian elite is radically incomprehensible to most of those brought up in the American tradition. That leaders of a modern state can think of the world wholly in terms of power, and conceive of international relations as a series of engagements in a world civil war, is hard to admit. One has only to read the memoirs of former Secretary of State Byrnes or of General Deane to see by what reluctant steps even experienced American officials and officers came to recognize the truth.[19]

As in dealing with hysteria, the essential prescription against complacency is *continuous* consideration of national security and freedom. Attitudes which are based on knowledge are more stable than attitudes based on ignorance, save where the attitudes based on ignorance are inculcated by early experience. Such early attitudes are blinders which handicap the individual in learning from later experience. Even when some new slants have been reluctantly accepted, they are gladly thrown aside at the first development that seems to corroborate the underlying bias.

The most hopeful means of dealing with attitudes imbedded in national character is by insight methods. The distinguishing mark of such methods is explicit reference to, and examination of, the bias and its determining causes in experience. The problem is to create awareness of bias, much as the old-fashioned evangelists produced conviction of sin. In psychological terms, the process can be described as dividing the conscience against itself by bringing about a realization that the standards which presumably justify the bias are in fact falsely applied, and lead to other, if not indeed opposite, inferences. In this sense, conscience fission is no less fundamental than atomic fission.

The committees on national security and freedom can learn how to deepen their own insights and that of their constituents as a means of protecting the nation against complacency.

## INDIVIDUAL RESPONSIBILITY

In bringing to a close this discussion of what the public can do, mention must be made, however casual, of a factor of all-pervading importance. There is no substitute for character and intelligence combined in the national interest. When we think of character in this connection, we have in mind the man who is willing to take personal risks to further the common good as he conceives it. He is the man who "sticks his neck out." He is the one who seizes opportunities to contribute to the formation of policies consistent with the goals of a free society. He may, for example, resign his private activities and serve the community directly in civic or governmental agencies, not for the sake of furthering his own wealth or power, but in the hope of contributing directly to a more decent world. The responsible man will risk his survival interests to further his principled interests. He "speaks out of turn" for what he believes to be sound.[20]

The good citizen of a free society will be fully aware of the importance of civic discipline, including obedience to the lawful decisions of the community. The perversion of a public trust for private advantage is unthinkable to him. If the good citizen has a modern education and is equipped with proper instruments for examining himself, he will possess means of discerning personal biases which are ordinarily unconscious, and which defeat good intentions unless expertly exposed to conscious judgment.

Ever since serious reflection began on the relation between the good citizen of a free *society* and the good citizen of a free *government,* the possibility of conflict has been admitted. Acting through the channel of government, the community may authorize measures which in the judgment of the citizen are wrong or mistaken. The executives and administrators charged with responsibility for putting legislation into effect may, in the judgment of the citizen, be equally immoral or mistaken. If the citizen of the society is at the same time an official of the government, what is he to do? Obviously, he will make use of authorized channels of protest. But these may be very slow, or under the control of immoral and mistaken officials.

In our day the problem most frequently comes up in relation to official secrets. Typically, the most effective way to deal with mistaken or immoral colleagues and superiors is to "leak" to Congress or the press in violation of the law. No responsible citizen will resort to this practice lightly, despite the frequency of "government by leak." And like Socrates in ancient Athens, the truly good citizen will take the consequences of violating the lawful rule. If he continues to remain anonymous, as a self-appointed spy in the public interest, he will experience continuous conflict of mind which may eventually be resolved by submitting to legal process. In the United States it is likely that the fate of such a citizen will be milder than hemlock. The American common-wealth has pardoning and other technical means of dealing with men who violate the law in good faith for the intended benefit of all. It is, of course, essential to deal severely with the man who violates an official obligation for private gain.

There was a time in the history of this nation when it was not melodramatic to exclaim, "Give me liberty or give me death!" or to say that the tree of liberty must be watered by the blood of martyrs. In the developing crisis, the ultimate question for each of us may be: At what point do I risk death or want or humilia-tion on behalf of my conception of freedom? This question was not academic for the men and women of the resistance under the Nazis. It is not academic for millions now under the heel of Moscow. It is not wholly academic in America.

One of the tantalizing problems of history and political science is how to explain why the man who specializes in the control of coercion, especially in the management of weapons, is not always and everywhere the most important decision maker. A look into the past reveals the frequency with which the army did, in fact, usurp power. In modern times, however, we have seen some of the largest and strongest armies of history submit calmly to the control of party leaders, civilian executives and administrators. The late Professor Mosca came to the conclusion that the key factor in this has been the growing professionalization of the soldier.[21] The specialist on the tools of violence has come to think of himself as a technician who serves the state, and therefore obeys whoever speaks in the voice of the state. It is therefore argued that any attempt to interest the armed forces in political ideas, beyond stressing the vital importance of protecting public order, is dangerous to the principle and practice of civilian su-premacy.

In the developing world situation the distinction between mili-tary and civil spheres of action is breaking down. Under modern conditions of warfare everyone shares the risk, whether he wears a uniform or stays in the plant.[22] The dependence of warfare upon science and industry is also contributing to the breakdown of the functional distinction between those who specialize upon weapons and the rest of society. Furthermore, the increasing reliance of modern strategy upon the use of ideological weapons makes it unwise to rely upon a blind cult of "state loyalty" and "political neutrality." Under these changed circumstances the perpetuation of civilian supremacy would appear to depend not upon maintaining a specific set of governmental forms but upon ensuring the vitality of the value goals of the free society among all members of society, in or out of uniform.

The essential point was put in abiding form by President Woodrow Wilson in an address to the class of 1916 at the U.S. Military Academy:

> You are not militaristic because you are military. Militarism does not consist in the existence of an army, not even in the existence of a very great army. . . . The purpose of militarism is to use armies for aggression. The spirit of militarism is the opposite of the civilian spirit, the citizen spirit. In a country where militarism prevails the military man looks down upon the civilian, regards him as inferior, thinks of him as intended for his, the military man's, support and use; and just so long as America is America that spirit and point of view is impossible for us.[23]

Where there is sharing of risk and sharing of function, there must be sharing of purpose, if the purposes are to live. The security of the nation and the freedom of the individual depend upon the widest possible sharing of an enlightened sense of obligation to the goal values of the American commonwealth. This is "the civilian spirit, the citizen spirit." It is essential if in the continuing crisis of defense we are to achieve national security and individual freedom in a commonwealth garrison and to avoid serfdom in a garrison-police state.[24]

# APPENDIX A

THE FOLLOWING excerpts from the Minneapolis *Tribune* and
the *Star* show a press campaign that got results in blocking
certain kinds of regulations. It is a striking example of how an
alert Washington correspondent for a potent newspaper can get
results.* The campaign was reflected in the press all over the
country. The fact that the originating newspapers were Republican held back some Democratic papers in carrying the issue so
directly to the President. The title of the *Hearings* which were
launched as a consequence of the campaign: *Investigation of
Charges That Proposed Security Regulations under Executive
Order 9835 Will Limit Free Speech and a Free Press. Hearings
before a Subcommittee of the Committee on Expenditures in the
Executive Departments, House of Representatives, Eightieth Congress, First Session, November 14, 1947.*

Unless otherwise indicated the Minneapolis *Tribune* is the
paper from which the excerpt is taken. The lead sentences are
quoted. All are datelined Washington, D.C.

October 19, 1947. Exclusive by Nat Finney:

The Truman administration is about to put the ordinary affairs
of federal civilian agencies under a secret blanket modeled after wartime military security.

This was learned Saturday from Hamilton Robinson, chairman of
the Security Advisory Board of the State, War and Navy Depart-

* See the longer campaign by Bert Andrews of the *New York Herald
Tribune,* for which he won the Pulitzer Prize, devoted to the pressure put on
government employees by the loyalty investigations, called *Washington Witch
Hunt.*

ment coordinating committee, after a directive imposing secrecy upon the operations of the Veterans Administration "leaked."

October 20, 1947. Continued by Nat Finney; also by William H. Mylander:

State Department officials Monday attempted to minimize the significance of new government-wide secrecy regulations which would block the flow of information to the press and public.
"Nothing new about it."

October 22, 1947. Exclusive by Nat Finney:

Government information men, whose special job is to get out information about what federal departments are doing, said Tuesday that they could not function under the secrecy system now being proposed in Washington.

October 22, 1947. Exclusive by Nat Finney. (*Star*) :

No reporter would like to see a public official lose his job or go to jail for telling something he thinks the public ought to know.
Stripped down to its fundamentals that is what is involved in the new system of executive department secrecy the federal government is now considering.

October 23, 1947. Exclusive by Nat Finney:

The Minneapolis Tribune's Washington bureau Wednesday got a copy of the federal government's proposed secrecy rules for all executive departments and agencies.

October 23, 1947. Exclusive by Nat S. Finney (*Star*) :

Acting Secretary of State Robert Lovett today released a statement confirming the fact that a secrecy system for civilian agencies has been drafted and awaits White House approval.

October 24, 1947. By Nat Finney:

Acting Secretary of State Robert Lovett Thursday acknowledged government plans to put all executive departments under an army-navy style secrecy code.

# *Appendix A*

## October 25, 1947. By Nat Finney:

President Harry S. Truman's press secretary, Charles G. Ross, Friday said he would especially direct the President's attention to the plans of members of his administration to impose military secrecy procedures on civilian departments.

## October 28, 1947. By Staff Correspondent:

Rep. Kenneth B. Keating (R., N.Y.) said Monday he has written President Truman requesting an explanation of proposed government secrecy rules.

## October 29, 1947. By Nat Finney:

Strong criticism of the government plan to impose stringent secrecy upon information in civilian as well as military agencies brought its first results Tuesday.

A State Department announcement said that the original definitions of classified information drawn up at President Truman's request have been modified to remove some of the more objectionable phrases.

McDermott said . . . that they contained nothing new so far as the State Department is concerned, and that the amendments actually constituted a relaxation of State Department standards.

State Department reporters, however, expressed the belief that in the past, officials have had discretion to talk about information in restricted documents, while the new regulations would prevent that.

## October 31, 1947. By Nat Finney:

The Veterans' Administration Thursday was preparing to rescind the secrecy order that originally disclosed administration plans to impose military-type censorship on all civilian departments.

## November 5, 1947. By Nat Finney:

The Veterans' Administration Tuesday made a formal request to the Security Advisory Board of the State Department-War-Navy Coordinating Committee for an explicit statement of just what the federal government's secrecy rules now are.

## National Security and Individual Freedom

**November 6, 1947. By Washington Correspondent:**

The Veterans' Administration Wednesday rescinded regulations which set up a military-type classification system for censoring government information. These regulations have been in effect since July, and were first revealed by the Minneapolis Tribune October 19.

**November 7, 1947. By Staff Correspondent (*Star*) :**

President Truman, sharply criticizing the press for "setting up a straw man" Thursday indicated he would take no action at present on his subordinates' plan to impose censorship on all information from executive departments of the government.

**November 7, 1947. By Nat Finney (Copyright, 1947, Minneapolis Star and Tribune Co.) :**

[The following editorial interpretation of President Truman's action on censorship was written by N. F.]

President Harry S. Truman's irate refusal to call a halt to plans to impose censorship-at-the-source through all civilian departments of the executive branch can mean only one thing. He is determined to impose such censorship unless Congress stops him.

**November 7, 1947. By Staff Correspondent:**

President Harry S. Truman Thursday refused to take any action on his subordinates' plan to impose military-type censorship-at-the-source on civilian departments of the federal government.

**November 8, 1947. By Nat Finney:**

President Harry S. Truman disclosed Friday in a letter to Rep. Kenneth B. Keating (R., N.Y.) that he had not, on October 28, "ever heard of" plans to impose military type secrecy on civilian government departments.

Rep. Keating had sent the President clippings. . . .

**November 13, 1947. By Staff Correspondent:**

A Congressional investigation of the administration plan to impose war-style censorship regulations on government departments will

## Appendix A

begin Friday, under leadership of Rep. Clare Hoffman (R., Mich.), Chairman of the House Committee on Expenditures in the executive departments.

### November 15, 1947. By Jack Wilson:

A Congressional investigating committee Friday began questioning federal officials about a plan to censor information about government activities.

About all the committee got was the assurance of the officials that they didn't think the program would be so administered as to withhold information to which the papers were entitled. They admitted that it could be administered to do precisely that.

### November 19, 1947. By Nat S. Finney:

Administration plans for censorship of government information at the source were shelved Tuesday until Congress completes its probe of the whole proposal.

### January 15, 1948. By Nat Finney:

The department of National Defense has taken a further step toward re-establishment of voluntary censorship of information by calling to Washington a high official in the wartime censorship office, it was learned Wednesday.

He is Jack Lockhart.

Dr. Vannevar Bush, head of the research and development board, is quoted as saying that publication of the XSI supersonic plane data [by *Aviation Week*] gave vital information to Soviet Russia.

### January 16, 1948. By William H. Mylander:

[Second paragraph] He [the President] also declared that he doesn't see any necessity for revival of the wartime system of voluntary press censorship.

### January 23, 1948. By Nat Finney:

A group of about 20 top executives of the press, radio and motion picture industries will be taken behind the veil of American military secrecy so they can decide for themselves the importance of keeping an information lid on special military projects.

March 7, 1948:

The annual Raymond Clapper Memorial award for outstanding Washington reporting was presented Saturday night to Nat S. Finney, manager of the Washington bureau of the Minneapolis *Tribune.*

President Truman presented the $500 award at the 25th annual dinner of the White House Correspondents Association.

# APPENDIX B

I N CHAPTER VII it is recommended that all policy associations appoint committees on national security and individual freedom as a means of understanding and affecting public affairs. The following paragraphs expand the idea.

Churches lead in providing forums in many localities. The sponsor is often the Men's Brotherhood or a similar group. The gravity of the issues involved in national security and freedom policies cannot fail to interest churches irrespective of creed.

Often the initiative in providing a hall and a sponsor is in the hands of fraternal organizations. This is particularly true in residential areas occupied by immigrants who first relied upon benefit associations for personal security and social orientation.

Associations of veterans and reserve officers have a special claim to speak with authority and conviction on national security policies. It has been observed that associations of this kind often become self-absorbed. Hence local posts may make little effort to appraise the security problem as a whole. The appointment of a continuing committee of the sort here described would probably have an integrating effect.

Less prominent in the public eye than veterans or reserve officers are alumni of the foreign service, the State Department, and other civilian establishments with responsibilities in the foreign field. Thousands of Americans have had official experience abroad or in Washington which bears directly on national security problems. The idea of applying the reserve idea to the new specialists required for the conduct of foreign affairs under modern conditions is rather recent. (Information specialists and econo-

mists, for example, are relatively new.) The interest which the
alumni of these activities take in public policy should not be
underestimated. The publishers, editors, and correspondents who
were engaged in psychological warfare performed a great service
for the country in helping to save the Voice of America at a time
when Washington and the nation were not fully alive to the facts
of the postwar situation. Committees on national security and
freedom can be used to keep groups in existence who, from their
experience, have unusual contributions to make.

The usefulness of the committee mechanism is apparent when
we think of the network of professional associations which cobweb the nation. Bar associations are accustomed to speak up on
many controversial issues. A reviewing committee on security and
freedom provides a frame in which scattered initiatives can gain
coherence. Medical associations are less accustomed to touch on
a wide variety of public issues than the organized bar. Nevertheless, the threat and nature of modern war provides a new incentive
for physicians to keep in touch with national security problems and to give the community the benefit of considered judgment. This applies with particular force in the domain of civilian
defense.

Since atomic physicists have "known sin," public policy has
intruded into the laboratories. Scientific and engineering societies
exist in great profusion, and committees on national security and
freedom can keep professional opinion abreast of events.

The committee device has a special virtue for all who live
from government payrolls. There are many disadvantages which
stand in the way of complete outspokenness on public questions
by government employees. Nevertheless, the community needs the
judgment of such persons, since they are in many ways well qualified to speak. Organizations of public administrators (most of
them in the Public Administration Clearing House) can use committees to do jointly what individuals cannot wisely do alone.

## Appendix B

With so many Americans on government payrolls, a large fraction of the American public is disqualified from engaging fully
in the opinion-forming process. The active use of professional
associations enables us to strike a balance between the official
impartiality of the civil servant and the complete outspokenness
on controversial matters of the democratic citizen. We do not
need an enlarging class of second-class citizens.

Teachers of law, government, and the social sciences have not
yet established their identity in the minds of everyday Americans.
An "economist" is vaguely recognized, but who is a "political
scientist"? If the professional societies of social scientists appoint
committees on national security and freedom, conclusions may be
reached which the societies are willing to share with the public
at large. Over the years their appraisals may win the respect of
the community.

Americans act by committees in many places without being
aware of it. Newspapers and magazines hold editorial conferences
which sometimes come close to being committees of the whole for
the consideration of national policy. Since such committees are
under the pressures of the moment, comment is usually too hap-
hazard to constitute true review. The editorial process of many
publications would gain depth if committees were formally set
up to perform the reviewing function and report.

Some Americans come to be recognized leaders of opinion in
their own right rather than as spokesmen for specific interests.
Such men sit at the center of a cobweb of communication.
Lunches, dinners, committee meetings, telephone calls, memoranda—all are links in the endless chain of thought and talk about
policy. When one examines a specific cobweb, he discovers that a
few names often recur. They constitute the informal committee
that performs the staff advisory function. And the service is mutual. Opinion leaders may see the wisdom of adopting the committee idea more formally than hitherto in order to reach more

well-considered judgments than is possible under the daily pressure of business. In the modern world the individual Hercules is out of date. He needs help holding up the globe. He can use the committee mechanism to pass it around.

The committee procedure lends itself to the needs of universities, colleges, and other teaching institutions, where members of the community look in the hope of receiving helpful advice on public issues. The truth is that specialization has reached such a pitch in science and scholarship that many professors have quit talking to one another. They have lost the sense of participating in a joint enterprise. It is not simply that Smith knows about the atom and Jones knows about Chaucer. Or that Brown knows economics and White is a specialist in government. Economics is so refined that the mathematically trained theorist may have little in common with the economist who is arbitrating and studying labor-management controversies. Members of the same department or subdepartment may have no intellectual contact.

Universities and other intellectual establishments need a common frame of reference if the divisive tendencies of specialization are to be counteracted. The American university is no longer a universe, or even a pluriverse. It is a multiverse, with new activities popping off in all directions.

A common frame of reference can be found in relation to the goal values of a free society, and in the sense of timing introduced by continuing crisis. In the future, university presidents can go further than they have in the past in drawing upon the intellectual resources of their institutions to advise on national security and freedom. Formal or informal committees can be called into existence by faculties, departments, or interested individuals.

An audit of intellectual resources will frequently show that wide gaps exist. In most academic institutions, the whole field of military, naval, and air strategy is an unknown continent. Departments of political science, despite long concern with the "state," do not typically have seminars or courses on strategy, or on how the armed forces can be articulated with the needs of a free society. Departments of history do not typically have courses on military history. Departments of economics do not typically have courses on the problems of total or partial mobilization of an economy with minimum loss of freedom. Departments of philosophy do not typically have courses on the political and social ethics of coercion related to modern social situations.

In many institutions of learning, committees on national security and freedom can provide a nucleus around which activities of a unifying character can polarize. Intellectual tension between the whole and the parts can be kept creative by introducing a cross-disciplinary frame of reference. The policy committee can conduct conferences and seminars on the security position of the country and upon special questions that arise in auditing the situation. The committee can invite men of experience to participate for periods of varying length in programs of discussion and research. In this way a channel can be cut that associates men of affairs with specialists of a more academic sort. Students and faculty can benefit from the resulting struggle between the scholar to assimilate, and the man of affairs to make articulate, the fruits of experience.

# NOTES

## CHAPTER I

1. Harold D. Lasswell, "The Prospects of Cooperation in a Bipolar World," 15 *The University of Chicago Law Review* 877–901 (1948).
2. A concise review of French diplomacy in relation to the American Revolution is in Samuel Flagg Bemis, *A Diplomatic History of the United States*, 3d ed., Henry Holt and Company, Inc., New York, 1950, Chap. II. A more extended account is by Bemis, *The Diplomacy of the American Revolution*, Appleton-Century-Crofts, Inc., New York, 1935.
3. Tabulated in Bemis, *op. cit.*, p. 24.
4. On the Monroe Doctrine consult Arthur Preston Whitaker, *The United States and the Independence of Latin-America, 1800–1830*, Johns Hopkins University Press, Baltimore, 1941.
5. Concerning the Civil War period, refer to Dexter Perkins, *The Monroe Doctrine, 1826–1867*, Johns Hopkins University Press, Baltimore, 1933; especially pp. 318–548.
6. The changing structure of world politics is succinctly outlined in William T. R. Fox, *The Super Powers*, Harcourt, Brace and Company, Inc., New York, 1944; and Harold D. Lasswell, *World Politics Faces Economics*, McGraw-Hill Book Company, Inc., New York, 1945. For more detail: Max Beloff, *The Foreign Policy of Russia, 1929–1941*, Oxford University Press, New York, 1948–49 (2 vols.); Vera Micheles Dean, *The United States and Russia*, Harvard University Press, Cambridge, 1947.
7. *Summary Report (Pacific War)*, U.S. Strategic Bombing Survey, U.S. Government Printing Office, Washington, D.C., July, 1946.
8. A judicious appraisal of the weapons situation is in Hanson W. Baldwin, *The Price of Power*, Council on Foreign Relations, Harper & Brothers, New York, 1947.

9. Cited by Benjamin Jaffe, *Men of Science in America; The Role of Science in the Growth of Our Country,* Simon and Schuster, Inc., 1944, p. 49.

10. The standard summaries of the frequency of war are Quincy Wright, *A Study of War,* The University of Chicago Press, Chicago, 1942 (2 vols.); and Pitirim Sorokin, *Fluctuation of Social Relationships, War, and Revolution,* American Book Company, New York, 1937 (Vol. 3, of *Social and Cultural Dynamics*).

11. A convenient place to follow scientific opinion on atomic weapon capacities is the *Bulletin of the Atomic Scientists,* 1126 E. 59th Street, Chicago 37, and the *Scientific American.*

12. Samuel Eliot Morison, *The Rising Sun in the Pacific,* Little, Brown & Company, Boston, 1948. (Vol. III, Chap. V, *History of United States Naval Operations in World War II.*)

13. Milton Shulman, *Defeat in the West,* E. P. Dutton & Co., Inc., New York, 1948, Chap. X.

14. The most comprehensive attack on the President is by Charles A. Beard, *President Roosevelt and the Coming of the War,* Yale University Press, New Haven, 1941. Material on the other side can be found in Robert E. Sherwood, *Roosevelt and Hopkins; An Intimate History,* Harper & Brothers, New York, 1948, rev. 1950; and in the memoirs of Cordell Hull, and Henry L. Stimson (Stimson and McGeorge Bundy, *On Active Service in Peace and War,* Harper & Brothers, New York, 1948).

15. Franz Neumann's analysis of the dynamics of National Socialism in Germany is of more than passing worth (Behemoth, 2d ed., 1944). See also Robert M. MacIver, *The Web of Government,* The Macmillan Company, New York, 1947. Chap. IX, "The Ways of Dictatorship."

16. The methods of Soviet planning from the beginning are described by Alexander Baykov, *The Development of the Soviet Economic System,* The Macmillan Company, New York, 1947.

17. An accurate impression of the degree to which Soviet rulers rely upon the practice of keeping alive the fear of other countries can be obtained by reading the slogans issued annually by the Communist Party of the Soviet Union. See Sergius Yakobson and Harold D. Lasswell, "Trend: May Day Slogans in Soviet

# Notes

Russia, 1918–1943," Chap. 10 in Lasswell, Leites, and Associates, *Language of Politics; Studies in Quantitative Semantics,* George W. Stewart, Publishers, Inc., New York, 1949 (Library of Policy Sciences).

18. The platforms can be read directly in Kirk Porter, *National Party Platforms,* University of Chicago Press, Chicago, 1924.

19. Every standard economic history deals with the subject, of course. The standard synopsis is Willard Long Thorp, *Business Annals,* National Bureau of Economic Research, New York, 1926 (introductory chapter by Wesley C. Mitchell; foreword by Edwin F. Gay).

20. A standard survey is Lewis L. Lorwin, *Labor and Internationalism,* The Macmillan Company, New York, 1929.

21. The colorful account of Italian Fascism by the historian Gaetano Salvemini, *Under the Axe of Fascism,* has not been superseded (The Viking Press, Inc., New York, 1936). On modern dictatorships see Sigmund Neumann, *Permanent Revolution: the Total State in a World at War,* Harper & Brothers, New York, 1942.

22. Details are in William L. Langer, *The Diplomacy of Imperialism,* Alfred Knopf, Inc., New York, 1935 (2 vols.).

23. The tension between England and Germany can be followed down to the first war in Sidney B. Fay, *The Origins of the World War,* The Macmillan Company, New York, 1929 (2 vols.).

24. See the valuable survey prepared for the Committee on Foreign Affairs of the 80th Congress, 2d Session, entitled, "The Strategy and Tactics of World Communism," House Document No. 619. (A Report of Subcommittee No. 5. "National and International Movements" with Supplement I, "One Hundred Years of Communism, 1848–1948"; Supplement II, "Official Protests of the United States Government against Communist Policies or Actions, and Related Correspondence"; Supplement III, "The Coup d'etat in Prague"; Supplement IV, "Communism in the Near East," "Communism Machine"; Supplement V, "Five Hundred Leading Communists.") Government Printing Office, Washington, D.C., 1948. Consult also Arthur Rosenberg, *History of Bolshevism,* Oxford University Press, New York, 1934;

and F. Borkenau, *World Communism*, W. W. Norton & Company, New York, 1939.

25. On our intervention, read General William S. Graves, *America's Siberian Adventure*, Jonathan Cape, Ltd., London, 1931. We withdrew by April, 1920.

26. Despite all the talk about communism in the United States, there is no detailed history of the party which clearly shows the origin and turnover of members. Useful hints are found in some memoirs, notably Benjamin Gitlow, *I Confess; The Truth about American Communism*, E. P. Dutton & Co., New York, 1939. James Oneal and G. A. Werner, *American Communism*, E. P. Dutton & Co., New York, 1947, is almost barren of such information.

27. Outside the government, the National Bureau of Economic Research has made the greatest contributions to such investigations.

28. The significance of the surviving pattern of oriental despotism is being worked out by Karl August Wittfogel (forthcoming). On Soviet labor camps see David Y. Dallin and Boris I. Nicolaevsky, *Forced Labor in Soviet Russia*, Yale University Press, New Haven, 1947.

29. Arnold J. Toynbee, *A Study of History* (summary by D. C. Somervell), The Oxford University Press, New York, 1947; P. A. Sorokin, *The Crisis of Our Age*, E. P. Dutton & Co., New York, 1942. At the Hoover Institute and Library at Stanford University a research on "The World Revolution of Our Time" is under way, which is designed to evaluate various interpretations. (Directed by Harold Fisher, Easton Rothwell, and Daniel Lerner.)

CHAPTER II

1. Consult John R. Deane, *The Strange Alliance; The Story of Our Efforts at Wartime Co-operation with Russia,* The Viking Press, Inc., New York, 1947. General Deane was head of the Military Mission in Moscow. See also Chaps. XV and XVIII in Robert E. Sherwood, *Roosevelt and Hopkins, an Intimate History,* Harper & Brothers, New York, 1948.
2. John Lord O'Brian's important discussion is "Loyalty Tests and Guilt by Association," 61 *Harvard Law Review* 594 (1948).
3. A valuable case study of opinion formation is *The People's Choice; How the Voter Makes Up His Mind in a Presidential Campaign,* 2d ed., by Paul F. Lazarsfeld, Bernard Berelson, and Hazel Gaudet, Columbia University Press, New York, 1948.
4. See especially George E. G. Catlin, *A Study of the Principles of Politics,* Allen & Unwin, Ltd., London, 1930; Charles E. Merriam, *Systematic Politics,* University of Chicago Press, Chicago, 1945; R. M. MacIver, *The Web of Government,* The Macmillan Company, New York, 1947.
5. The present writer first dealt directly with the significance of the garrison state for modern politics in 1937, and again in 1941. The latter discussion is reprinted in Harold D. Lasswell, *The Analysis of Political Behaviour; An Empirical Approach,* Oxford University Press, New York, 1948. See also "The Interrelations of World Organization and Society," *Yale Law Journal* (Summer, 1946). A remarkable work of imagination is George Orwell, *Nineteen Eighty-Four,* Harcourt, Brace and Company, Inc., 1949.

CHAPTER III

1. Concerning goal values see Myres S. McDougal and Gertrude C. K. Leighton, "The Rights of Man in the World Community: Constitutional Illusions versus Rational Action," Symposium on International Human Rights, *Law and Contemporary Problems* (Summer, 1949). Reprinted *Yale Law Journal*, December, 1949.

2. General von Seeckt quoted in B. H. Liddell Hart, *The German Generals Talk*, William Morrow & Company, Inc., New York, 1948, p. 18.

3. Bernard Brodie discusses the principle of economy in "Strategy as a Science," *World Politics*, Vol. 1 (1949), pp. 467–488.

4. In 1795 Washington wrote to Major General Daniel Morgan: "Still it may be proper constantly and strongly to impress upon the Army that they are mere agents of Civil power: that out of Camp, they have no other authority, than other citizens [,] that offences against the laws are to be examined, not by a military officer, but by a Magistrate; that they are not exempt from arrests and indictments for violation of the law; that officers ought to be careful, not to give orders, which may lead the agents into infractions of the law; that no compulsion be used towards the inhabitants in the traffic, carried on between them and the army; that disputes be avoided, as much as possible, and be adjusted as quickly as may be, without urging them to an extreme: and that the whole country is not to be considered as within the limits of the camp." (March 27, 1795, *Writings*, XXXIV, 159–160.)

5. See Bruce Bliven's essay in Harold L. Ickes, editor, *Freedom of the Press Today*, Vanguard Press, New York, 1941.

6. See Raymond Clapper's essay in the volume just cited.

7. It is not implied that these principles are always lived up to in practice, as the discussion in Chapter VI will indicate.

8. Richard Centers, *The Psychology of Social Classes; A Study of Class Consciousness*, Princeton University Press, Princeton,

*Notes*

1949. A critical evaluation of current knowledge of class perspectives is "Public Opinion and Social Class," by Arthur Kornhauser in *The American Journal of Sociology,* Vol. LV (1950), pp. 333–345.

CHAPTER IV

1. See Chap. III of W. Ivor Jennings, *Cabinet Government*, Cambridge University Press, London, 1936.
2. The American Cabinet is considered in the standard books on the Presidency, such as E. Pendleton Herring, *Presidential Leadership*, Rinehart & Company, New York, 1940, and Harold J. Laski, *The American Presidency, an Interpretation*, Harper & Brothers, New York, 1940.
3. The details are given in studies of the Cabinet since 1890 by Richard Fisher to be published immediately by the Hoover Institute and Library as part of The Study of the World Revolution of Our Time, Stanford University, Calif.
4. For historical perspective an espionage and policy, see James Westfall Thompson and Saul K. Padover, *Secret Diplomacy; A Record of Espionage and Double-Dealing, 1500–1815*, Jarrolds Publishers, Ltd., London, 1937; and Richard W. Rowan, *The Story of Secret Service*, Doubleday & Company, Inc., New York, 1937.
5. The complex interaction between secrecy and security is indicated in James R. Newman and Byron S. Miller, *The Control of Atomic Energy*, McGraw-Hill Book Company, Inc., New York, 1947. See also the Symposium on "Atomic Energy for Lawyers," *The University of Chicago Law Review* (Summer, 1948), especially the articles by Byron S. Miller, Casper W. Ooms, and Herbert S. Marks; and Vannevar Bush, *Modern Arms and Free Men*, Simon and Schuster, Inc., New York, 1949.
6. Selectivity rather than blanket measures have served the security needs of countries that have gone through no less peril than our own. In Britain, for instance, the policy is to transfer an employee whose loyalty is in doubt to a position involving "nonsecret Government work."
7. See the discussion by Alfred Vagts, *A History of Militarism*, W. W. Norton & Company, New York, 1937, p. 371.

# Notes

8. Skilled selection of personnel is imperative for security and freedom. During World War II an epochal program was developed by Henry L. Murray and associates for the Office of Strategic Services. (See Assessment Staff, *The Assessment of Men*, 1948.) William J. Donovan, Wartime Director of OSS, and Mary Gardiner Jones have recommended that "the President might appoint a Commission to review the Loyalty Program and to examine into the feasibility of employing similar techniques in the screening of Government employees." "Program for a Democratic Counter Attack to Communist Penetration of Government Service," 58 *Yale Law Journal* 1239 (July, 1949). See also the proposal for a *National Personnel Assessment Board* in Harold D. Lasswell, *Power and Personality*, W. W. Norton & Company, New York, 1948, pp. 186–187.

9. The Federal Bureau of Investigation occupies a crucial though not a monopolistic position in the conduct of security investigations. The FBI states officially that it does no more than provide information upon which the appropriate agency is free to base its personnel choices. Unfortunately the material presented to the agency does not indicate the nature of the source relied upon for specific statements. It has often been suggested that all investigative agencies should adopt methods of reporting that provide a clue to the evidentiary worth of the sources used. For example: S1 could designate a trained agent of the FBI who has personally made the primary observation reported. S2 could refer to a similarly trained agent of another U.S. intelligence agency. S3 might refer to trained agents of foreign governments in whom the American agency has confidence. S4 can describe a private informant believed to be trustworthy who made the primary observation. S5 might designate a private informant believed to be trustworthy who transmits hearsay material in whose authenticity he believes. The rule could be adopted of adding the symbol "d" to the above categories when the person making the primary observation has some doubt about reliability. (Thus there may be doubt as to whether the person under surveillance met a foreign agent by accident or appointment.) The symbol "dd" can mean "very doubtful." SA can be assigned to anonymous informers—the lowest level

of credibility (such as the writers of unsigned denunciations). As matters stand at present, FBI and other intelligence reports are typically composed of undigested material ranging from declarations by trained agents who have made first-hand observations to malicious and unverified gossip.

Concerning the role of the FBI in the loyalty investigations see the article by Thomas I. Emerson and David M. Helfeld, "Loyalty among Government Employees," 58 *Yale Law Journal* 1 (December, 1948), and J. Edgar Hoover, "A Comment on the Article, 'Loyalty among Government Employees.'" 58 *Yale Law Journal* 401 (February, 1949).

After World War II several groups of veterans looked into the problem of "democratizing" the armed forces by providing a more satisfactory method of protecting the enlisted man, in particular, against arbitrary action by his superiors. This has led to the redrafting of regulations and to proposals for legislative action.

10. There is need of a procedure for dealing with Americans who were at one time members of a subversive organization but who have ceased to belong to, work with, or sympathize with such activities; and whose record is not known (or provable) by any police agency. In many cases the period of active association with the Communist Party, for example, was short and represented youthful enthusiasm, curiosity, or a brief period of personal despair. If investigation shows that since the severance the individual has, indeed, been a trustworthy citizen, the government should not be debarred from using his talents, and no word of the derogatory association should be circulated beyond the "confessional." Perhaps the "confessional" chamber for citizens should be under the auspices of the top review board for loyalty cases in the government (although several other agencies might be used). We are fully accustomed to applying the policy that lives ought not to be ruined by a load of errors from the past. Several devices have been used to enable individuals to begin anew. This is one purpose of bankruptcy acts and statutes of limitations. I remember the remark made by a very experienced, humane, though reputedly tough "red hater" in the Chicago Police Department that he was sometimes glad

that it was not always necessary to establish the identity of the young people who were brought in by the squad. He believed that the overwhelming number were involved as a result of private problems made acute by the Great Depression, and that it would be a handicap upon them in later years to be listed as communists, since nearly all of them would lose radical sympathies. The officer gave full cooperation in a research project which I was directing on the effectiveness of communist and other propaganda organizations in capitalizing for political purposes upon the Depression. [The results of the research, which was carried on under the auspices of the University of Chicago, were published in Lasswell and Blumenstock (Jones), *World Revolutionary Propaganda; A Chicago Study*, Alfred A. Knopf, Inc., New York, 1939.]

11. World War II produced an unprecedented burst of interest in the intelligence function from both secret and open sources. See particularly George S. Pettee, *The Future of American Secret Intelligence*, Infantry Journal, Washington, D.C., 1946; Sherman Kent, *Strategic Intelligence for American World Policy*, Princeton University Press, Princeton, N.J., 1949.

12. On the vital role of propaganda in modern world politics, see Lester Markel, editor, *Public Opinion and Foreign Policy*, Council on Foreign Relations, Harper & Brothers, New York, 1949; Charles A. H. Thomson, *The Overseas Information Service of the United States Government*, The Brookings Institution, Washington, D.C., 1948; Paul M. A. Linebarger, *Psychological Warfare*, Infantry Journal, Washington, D.C., 1948; Daniel Lerner, *Sykewar; Psychological Warfare against Germany, D-Day to VE-Day*, George W. Stewart, Publisher, Inc., New York, 1949.

13. The basic description of information and propaganda activity is still James L. McCamy, *Government Publicity; Its Practice in Federal Administration*, University of Chicago Press, Chicago, 1939. Leo C. Rosten analyzed the work of *The Washington Correspondents*, Harcourt, Brace & Company, Inc., New York, 1937. James E. Pollard has described the interrelations of *The Presidents and the Press* throughout American history, The Macmillan Company, New York, 1947.

14. The most famous statute is *38 U.S. Stat. 212* (October 22, 1913). Representative Frederick H. Gillette, Massachusetts Republican, brought the attention of the House to the announcement of an open competitive examination for a publicity expert in the Office of Public Roads, Department of Agriculture, whose duties would be to prepare news releases and get them in newspapers.

15. The Commission on Freedom of the Press recommended a more positive role for democratic government in these words: "Government may and should enter the field of press comment and news supply, not as displacing private enterprise, but as a supplementary source." *A Free and Responsible Press*, University of Chicago Press, Chicago, 1947, p. 128. See also Zechariah Chafee, Jr., *Government and Mass Communications*, University of Chicago Press, Chicago, 1947, Vol. 2. If the function of supplying information and propaganda is to be properly carried out, it must rest upon knowledge of the attitudes prevailing in the audience to be reached. Presidents usually read several newspapers to keep in touch with the popular mood. It has long been customary to have clippings from the national press available on request of the Chief Executive. At times systematic summaries and graphs have been prepared for the use of the White House and other executive agencies (by Emil Hurja in the thirties, for example). Detail about the intelligence operations of the Department of State are given by W. Phillips Davison in Lester Markel, editor, *Public Opinion and Foreign Policy*, Harper & Brothers, New York, 1949, Chap. 6. Rensis Likert, now of the University of Michigan, is one of the most effective social psychologists in introducing modern methods of attitude research into Washington practice. Many private and public agencies have been drawn upon, especially those developed by George Gallup, Elmo Roper, and Paul Lazarsfeld (Bureau of Applied Social Research). During the war some military policies were affected by the systematic polling of American soldiers. The results have been reassessed for scientific purposes by Samuel O. Stouffer and colleagues in the four-volume *Studies in Social Psychology in World War II*, Princeton University Press, Princeton, N.J., 1949–50. Extensive efforts

were also made by private and public agencies to analyze foreign broadcasts, newspapers, magazines, and other channels of communication for intelligence purposes. Consult Harwood L. Childs and John B. Whitton, editors, *Propaganda by Short Wave,* Princeton University Press, Princeton, N.J., 1942; Ernst Kris, Hans Speier and associates, *German Radio Propaganda; Report on Home Broadcasts during the War,* Oxford University Press, New York, 1944; H. D. Lasswell, Nathan Leites and associates, *Language of Politics; Studies in Quantitative Semantics,* George W. Stewart, Publisher, Inc., New York, 1949.

16. Under a civilian chairman the NSRB consists of the following secretaries: State, Treasury, Defense, Agriculture, Commerce, Interior, Labor. In 1950 all of the Board's authority was vested in the chairman, and a vice-chairman was provided for.

17. Few points have been more unanimously agreed to than the necessity of providing for a competent civilian staff to serve the Secretary of Defense. Otherwise there is no means by which the Secretary can obtain a comprehensive view of the needs of the armed forces as a whole, divorced from the conscious and unconscious biases of the separate interests involved. This is a crucial spot for civilian preview and review of decisions related to the armed forces. The changes initiated following the Hoover recommendations have been in this direction. See *Digest of Reports of the Commission on Organization of the Executive Branch of the Government,* prepared by the staff of the Committee on Expenditures of the Executive Departments, U.S. Senate, 81st Cong., 1st Sess. *U.S. Government Printing Office,* Washington, D.C., 1949. The organization of the Joint General Staff has an important bearing upon the effective application of the principle of civilian supremacy. It is argued that if the chief of the JGS is given much weight his influence as mouthpiece for the armed services would put entirely too much power in his hands in relation to the President as Commander in Chief. The President would be at a great disadvantage in obtaining a picture, through official channels, of the degree of unanimity and the range of alternatives considered in arriving at any given set of proposals. Hence "government by leak" and intrigue would be confirmed in our system, with the resulting

dangers of abuse. It is essential that some formal means be adopted which will enable the President to obtain a full and direct picture of the complex pattern of assumptions that go into the making of vital plans.

18. See John Perry Miller, *Pricing of Military Procurement,* Studies in National Policy, Yale University Press, New Haven, 1949.

19. On many of the issues touched upon here consult Jerome G. Kerwin, Editor, *Civil-Military Relationships in American Life,* University of Chicago Press, Chicago, 1948. The contributors include Waldemar Kaempffert, Dixon Wecter, Hanson W. Baldwin, Paul H. Appleby, T. V. Smith, Quincy Wright, Adlai Stevenson, Charles E. Merriam.

CHAPTER V

1. A review of the many proposals along this line is included in George B. Galloway, *Congress at the Crossroads,* The Thomas Y. Crowell Company, New York, 1946. See also Robert Heller, *Strengthening the Congress, A Progress Report,* National Planning Association, Washington, D.C., 1946. Majority and Minority Policy Committees are put in the "vital necessity" list.

2. For example: Woodrow Wilson, *Congressional Government,* Houghton Mifflin Company, Boston, 1885; Samuel W. McCall, *The Business of Congress,* Columbia University Press, New York, 1911; William Macdonald, *A New Constitution for a New America,* Huebsch, New York, 1921; William Y. Elliott, *The Need for Constitutional Reform,* McGraw-Hill Book Company, Inc., New York, 1935; Thomas K. Finletter, *Can Representative Government Do the Job?* Reynal & Hitchcock, Inc., New York, 1945.

3. Basic data on voting behavior are in Harold F. Gosnell, *Democracy the Threshold of Freedom,* The Ronald Press Company, New York, 1948; H. L. G. Tingsten, *Political Behaviour; Studies in Election Statistics,* P. S. King & Staples, Ltd., London, 1937.

4. The factors in decentralization are well brought out in E. E. Schattschneider, *Party Government,* Rinehart & Company, Inc., New York, 1942; and in other standard books on political parties by Charles E. Merriam, Harold F. Gosnell, Peter H. Odegard and E. A. Helms, V. O. Key, Jr., W. E. Binkley, and A. N. Holcombe.

5. Arthur N. Holcombe worked out this interpretation in detail in *The Middle Classes in American Politics,* Harvard University Press, Cambridge, 1940. See the factors weighed in C. E. Merriam and H. F. Gosnell, *American Party System* (4th ed.), The Macmillan Company, New York, 1949.

6. Two emphases, rather than contradictions, are involved: Emphasis A will be supported by those who use government with

alacrity for policies which they believe will directly improve the general standard of living. Emphasis B includes those who back such programs with misgivings on the ground that their long-range effectiveness for the purpose is doubtful. Adherents of B are embarrassed and handicapped by the applause of "reactionary" elements who are in fact against the objective of improving the standard of living of the whole people. Adherents of A are obviously on the side of immediate popularity. If democratic processes are kept alive, the only hope of those holding view B is in a gigantic job of public education which will enable the community as a whole to understand how and when living standards over the long run may be compromised by immediate improvements now.

In passing, we may note that the differences between persons, factions, and parties with emphasis A or B will be sloganized in many ways. Without identifying the object referred to in each case, we can at least foresee the following forensic pairs: socialism versus liberalism; welfare state versus freedom state; laboristic versus business state; communist versus fascist; statism versus individualism; neo-capitalism versus *laissez faire* capitalism; welfare state versus the exploitative state; benevolent state versus the umpire state; spending state versus the progressive state; regimentation versus enterprise. . . .

7. Harold J. Laski, *The American Democracy,* The Viking Press, Inc., New York, 1948, p. 88.

8. See "The Parliamentary and Presidential Systems" by Don K. Price in 3 *Public Administration Review* (Autumn, 1943), 317–334, and the rejoinder by Harold J. Laski (Autumn, 1944), 347–359. Also Charles E. Merriam, *Systematic Politics,* University of Chicago Press, Chicago, 1945, Chap. IV.

9. Psychology, psychiatry, and anthropology have brought about a renewal of interest in theories of national character. A succinct review and appraisal by Nathan Leites appears in the first issue of *World Politics* (October, 1948), "Psycho-Cultural Hypotheses about Political Acts." See Gabriel Almond, *The American People and Foreign Policy,* Harcourt, Brace & Company, Inc., New York, 1950.

10. An important attempt to appraise the impact of the Great De-

pression of the thirties on an American city in the Middle West was made by Robert S. Lynd and Helen Merrell Lynd, *Middletown in Transition; A Study in Cultural Conflicts,* Harcourt, Brace & Company, Inc., New York, 1937. The original survey of the city had been made in 1924–1925 and published as *Middletown; A Study in Contemporary American Culture,* Harcourt, Brace & Company, Inc., New York, 1929.

11. A guide to some modern conceptions of personality in politics is H. D. Lasswell, *Power and Personality,* W. W. Norton & Company, New York, 1948 (Salmon Memorial Lectures in Psychiatry, New York Academy of Medicine, 1947).

12. On disclosure measures see "Improving the Legislative Process: Federal Regulation of Lobbying," Comment, 56 *Yale Law Journal* 304–332 (January, 1947); Zechariah Chafee, Jr., *Government and Mass Communications,* University of Chicago Press, Chicago, 1947, 2 vols., Chap. 20; Bruce Lannes Smith, "Democratic Control of Propaganda through Registration and Disclosure," 6 *Public Opinion Quarterly* (1942), pp. 27–40.

13. Available in the current *Congressional Directory.* In 1929, E. Pendleton Herring, Jr., counted about 400 national pressure groups with headquarters in New York or Washington. (*Group Representation before Congress,* Brookings Institution, Washington, 1929, pp. 276–283.) Ten years later there were about the same number. (Temporary National Economic Committee, *Economic Power and Political Pressure,* Monograph No. 26, Washington, D.C., Supt. of Documents, 1941, pp. 197–201). In 1938 there were 1,505 national and regional and 6,000 state and local trade associations, which touched government at many points. (Temporary National Economic Committees, *Trade Association Survey,* Monograph No. 18, Washington, D.C., Supt. of Documents, 1941.)

14. By Walton H. Hamilton, *Hearings before the Joint Committee on the Organization of Congress,* pp. 715–716.

15. Representative Corbett of Pennsylvania, *Congressional Record,* March 15, 1946.

16. Giraud Chester analyzed the content of the Senate debate on the Selective Training and Service Bill of 1940, and emphasized the success of the discussion in disclosing the issues. ("Con-

temporary Senate Debate; A Case Study," 31 *Quarterly Journal of Speech,* December, 1945).

17. A device intended to bring about closer relations between Congress and the executive on security matters, and involving no formal change, has been recommended by Hansen W. Baldwin: "To insure that the citizen's point of view is represented in the National Security Council two key members of Congress, the Chairmen of the Senate Committee on Foreign Relations and the House Committee on Foreign Affairs for instance, might be invited to sit on special occasions as advisory members of the Security Council, at least on all discussions of public opinion." In Lester Markel, editor, *Public Opinion and Foreign Policy,* 1949, p. 118.

18. Beardsley Ruml, *Tomorrow's Business,* Rinehart & Company, Inc., New York, 1945, has suggestive things to say about trusteeship.

CHAPTER VI

1. See Hamilton and Braden, "The Special Competence of the Supreme Court," 50 *Yale Law Journal* 1319 (1941) for a classic treatment of this change in the climate of judicial opinion. The key cases are collected in Harris, "Due Process of Law," in "Symposium, Ten Years of the Supreme Court: 1937–1947," 42 *American Political Science Review* 32 (1948). The proposition that the specific provisions of the First Amendment were incorporated by reference into the Fourteenth Amendment, so as to make them applicable to the states, was accepted by the Supreme Court, at least by way of dictum, as early as 1925, in *Gitlow v. New York, 268 U.S. 652.* Whether all ten amendments in the Bill of Rights are incorporated is still being bitterly debated by the Court, with the negative of that proposition temporarily in the ascendancy, by a vote of 5 to 4, in *Adamson v. California, 332 U.S. 46 (1947).* See Comment, "The Adamson Case: A Study in Constitutional Technique," 58 *Yale Law Journal* 268 (1949).

2. See *e.g., DeJonge v. Oregon, 299 U.S. 353 (1937)* (criminal syndicalism statute).

3. See, *e.g., Saia v. New York, 334 U.S. 558 (1948)* (sound-truck ordinance subjecting use of trucks to uncontrolled discretion of local police chief).

4. See, *e.g., Ashcraft v. Tennessee, 322 U.S. 143 (1944).* (Coerced confession); but note the limitations on review of state court action, as contrasted with the more stringent attitude toward inequalities in the lower Federal courts, discussed in Comment, "The Adamson Case," *supra* note 1, at 279–286.

5. Chief Justice Hughes, in *Home Building & Loan Association v. Blaisdell, 290 U.S. 398, 426 (1934).*

6. Mr. Justice Sutherland, in *United States v. Curtiss-Wright Export Corp., 299 U.S. 304, 317 (1936).*

7. The best concise account of the impact of World War II on our existing constitutional system is contained in Corwin, *Total War*

*and the Constitution* (1947). Other references on specific parts of the war effort appear below.

8. See Corwin, *supra* note 7. See also the same author's *President's Control of Foreign Relations* (1917) for a discussion of the views of the Fathers.

9. For significant examples of cooperation, see Mermin, "Cooperative Federalism Again: State and Municipal Legislation Penalizing Violations of Existing and Future Federal Requirements," 57 *Yale Law Journal* 1, 201 (1947). See also Clark, *The Rise of a New Federalism* (1938), for World War I experience; reports of the various State Defense Councils established even before the declaration of war in World War II to collaborate with Federal authorities; *e.g., New York State War Emergency Act and Other Emergency Laws* (New York State War Council, 1945).

10. See, *e.g., O'Neal v. United States, 6 Cir., 140 F. 2d 908 (1944),* cert. denied, *322 U.S. 729* (priorities and allocations); *Yakus v. United States, 321 U.S. 414 (1944); Bowles v. Willingham, 321 U.S. 503 (1944)* (World War II price and rent control); *Woods v. Cloyd W. Miller Co., 333 U.S. 138 (1948)* (postwar rent control); and cf. *Block v. Hirsch, 256 U.S. 135 (1921)* (post-World War I rent control); *Hamilton v. Kentucky Distilleries Warehouse Co., 251 U.S. 146 (1919)* (World War I prohibition).

11. It should be noted that legislation such as the Emergency Price Control Act of 1942 contained provisions for eventual judicial review of specific orders issued by the Administrator, although the absence of provision for prior review before the orders became effective did not make the Act unconstitutional, *Bowles v. Willingham, 321 U.S. 503 (1944),* nor did the provision for review only by a specially constituted Emergency Court of Appeals, *Yakus v. United States, 321 U.S. 414 (1944).* The Court made it clear, in the *Willingham* opinion, that the standards by which individual orders would be judged did not require absolute equality of hardship, observing that "A member of the class which is regulated may suffer economic losses not shared by others. . . . But that has never been a barrier to the exercise of the police power." *Id.* at 518. And *cf. Ainsworth v. Barn*

# Notes

*Ballroom Co., Inc., 4 Cir., 157 F. 2d 97 (1946)* (military authorities are not responsible for consequential damages resulting from order placing dance hall off limits for military personnel).

12. *Bowles v. Willingham, supra* note 11, at 512; *Yakus v. United States, supra* note 11, at 423.
13. *Mitchell v. Harmony, 13 How. 115, 133–35 (U.S. 1851).*
14. This issue was settled in the Selective Draft Law cases, *245 U.S. 366 (1918)*. It did not reach the Supreme Court in World War II, but the constitutionality of the 1940 (prewar) and 1941 Acts was determined favorably in all of the five Federal judicial circuits where it reached the appellate level. It was not until after the termination of hostilities, however, that the Supreme Court worked out a satisfactory procedure for judicial review of selective service classification. *Estep v. United States, 327 U.S. 114 (1946)*. See Cornell, "Exemption from the Draft: A Study in Civil Liberties," 56 *Yale Law Journal* 258 (1947).
15. Compulsory service during the American Revolution was limited to a compulsion by local authorities to serve in the militia, which was then levied on by the Congress. A direct draft was debated during the War of 1812 and the Mexican War, but no action was taken. The first direct draft law, relying on the constitutional power "to raise and support armies" rather than, as previously, on the power "to provide for calling forth the militia," was enacted during the Civil War, and the first draft law involving foreign service came during World War I. See Selective Draft Law Cases, *supra* note 14, at 384–388.
16. See "Presidential Message on the State of the Union," January 11, 1944, *U.S. Code Cong. Service No. 1,* p. 3.3 (1944), and *H.R. 3944, 78th Cong. 2d Sess. (1944).*
17. *Yick Wo v. Hopkins, 118 U.S. 356 (1886).* But *cf. Kotch v. Board of River Port Pilot Commissioners, 330 U.S. 552 (1947),* noted in 56 *Yale Law Journal* 1276 (1947).
18. *Cf. Crandall v. Nevada, 6 Wall. 35 (U.S., 1868); Corfield v. Coryell, 6 Fed. Cas. No. 3,230 (C.C.E.D. Pa. 1823),* at p. 552; and concurring opinion of Mr. Justice Douglas in *Edwards v.*

*California, 314 U.S. 160, 177 (1941);* and *cf. Truax v. Raich, 239 U.S. 33, 39 (1915)* as to aliens.

19. That this freedom has been severely restricted by state and Federal legislation is, of course, evident, and indeed it is generally acknowledged that reconciliation of individual and collective bargaining requires restrictions on both. But peonage in any form, even when authorized by state statute for default on a contract for services to be rendered, is still held to contravene the Thirteenth Amendment. *Pollock v. Williams, 322 U.S. 4 (1944).*

20. Generally applied to local gatherings, as in *DeJonge v. Oregon, 299 U.S. 353 (1937).*

21. The legislation invalidated in the *Crandall* case, *supra* note 18, was a Nevada tax on all persons leaving the state by common carrier.

22. See Note 13, *supra.*

23. If information justifying a search or seizure is received by the officers concerned in sufficient time to obtain a warrant, a search or seizure without a warrant will be improper, *Trupiano v. United States, 334 U.S. 699 (1948).* But this decision has been significantly limited by the holding in *United States v. Rabinowitz, 339 U.S. 56,* that a search may be made without a warrant, as an incident to a lawful arrest, at least where it is not a "general" or "exploratory" search. And if the officer has no time to obtain a warrant, as in a search of an automobile on the highway, he must have "a belief, reasonably arising out of the circumstances known to the seizing officer, that [it] contains that which by law is subject to seizure or destruction." *Carrol v. United States, 267 U.S. 132, 149 (1925),* followed in *Brinegar v. United States, 338 U.S. 160 (1949).*

24. *Cf.* Mr. Justice Jackson, dissenting, in *Brinegar v. United States, supra* note 23, at 1823. "Undoubtedly the automobile presents peculiar problems for enforcement agencies, frequently a facility for the perpetration of crime and an aid in the escape of criminals. But if we are to make judicial exceptions to the Fourth Amendment for these reasons, it seems to me they should depend somewhat upon the gravity of the offense. If we assume, for example, that a child is kidnaped and the

# Notes

officers throw a roadblock about the neighborhood and search every outgoing car, it would be a drastic and undiscriminating use of the search. The officers might be unable to show probable cause for searching any particular car. However, I should candidly strive hard to sustain such an action, executed fairly and in good faith, because it might be reasonable to subject travelers to that indignity if it was the only way to save a threatened life and detect a vicious crime. . . ."

25. Chief Justice Stone in *United States v. Carolene Products Co., 304 U.S. 144, 152, note 4 (1938).*

26. *Ibid.* And see discussion of the footnote in Braden, "The Search for Objectivity in Constitutional Law," 57 *Yale Law Journal,* 571, 579 (1948).

27. In the past decade the Supreme Court has invalidated only two Federal statutes on the grounds that they violated constitutionally protected individual rights. *Tot v. United States, 319 U.S. 463 (1943); United States v. Lovett, 328 U.S. 303 (1946).*

28. The formula is the special contribution of Mr. Justice Holmes, who first enunciated it as dictum, speaking for the Court in *Schenck v. United States, 249 U.S. 47 (1919),* affirming Schenck's conviction. He employed it again, in dissent, in *Abrams v. United States, 250 U.S. 616, 624 (1919),* and likewise in *Gitlow v. New York, 268 U.S. 652, 672 (1925).* The ideas behind these, as behind so many other of his dissents, have since become accepted law.

29. "Those who begin coercive elimination of dissent soon find themselves exterminating dissenters. Compulsory unification of opinion achieves only the unanimity of the graveyard. . . . We set up government by consent of the governed, and the Bill of Rights denies those in power any legal opportunity to coerce that consent. Authority here is to be controlled by public opinion, not public opinion by authority." Mr. Justice Jackson, speaking for the Court in the second flag-salute case, *West Virginia State Board of Education v. Barnette, 319 U.S. 624, 641 (1943).*

30. *Id.* at 640.

31. The Supreme Court upheld all the appealed convictions under

the Espionage Act, refused to interfere with censorship by the Postmaster General, and upheld the constitutionality of state restrictions. See Fraenkel, "War, Civil Liberties and the Supreme Court," 55 *Yale Law Journal* 715, 717–718 (1946).

32. See Teller, "Picketing and Free Speech," 56 *Harvard Law Review* 180 (1942); Dodd, "Picketing and Free Speech—a Dissent," *Id.* at 513, and Reply by Teller, *Id.* at 532.

33. See Corwin, *The Constitution and What It Means Today* (8th ed., 1946) 189–191.

34. *Terminiello v. Chicago,* 337 U.S. 1, 4 (1949).

35. See note 27, *supra.*

36. *Cf.* modification of the provision in the Taft-Hartley Act, section 304, barring political expenditures by unions, in *United States v. Congress of Industrial Organizations, 335 U.S. 106 (1948); United Staes v. Painters' Local Union No. 481, 2 Cir., 172 F. 2d 854 (1949).*

37. The doctrine of guilt by association was expressly disavowed in *Schneiderman v. United States, 320 U.S. 118 (1943).*

38. The classic formulation of this tripartite distinction appears in the concurring opinion of Chief Justice Chase in *Ex Parte Milligan, 4 Wall. 2, 141–142 (U.S. 1866).* For general discussion, see Fairman, *The Law of Martial Rule* (2d ed., 1942); Fairman, "The Law of Martial Rule and The National Emergency," 55 *Harvard Law Review* 1253 (1942); Fairman, "The Supreme Court on Military Jurisdiction," 56 *Harvard Law Review* 833 (1946); Corwin, *supra* note 7, c. iii; Wiener, *A Practical Manual of Martial Law* (1940); Miller, "Relation of Military to Civil and Administrative Tribunals in Time of War," 7 *Ohio State Law Journal* 188, 400 (1941).

39. Articles of War, 10 U.S.C. c. 36 (1947); *Manual for Courts-Martial* (1943); Winthrop, *Military Law and Precedents* (2d ed. 1920); Tillotson, *Articles of War Annotated* (1942). The Second Article of War, 10 U.S.C. Par. 1473 (1947), deals with jurisdiction of courts-martial.

40. See Fairman, *supra,* note 38.

41. See Morgan, "Court-Martial Jurisdiction over Non-Military Persons under the Articles of War," 4 *Minnesota Law Review* 79 (1920); Shapiro, "Jurisdiction of Military Tribunals of the

## Notes

United States over Civilians," 12 *California Law Review* 75 (1924) ; and annotations to A.W. 2 in Tillotson, *supra* note 40.

42. For recent discussion of some of the problems arising within that special area, see *Report of War Department Advisory Committee on Military Justice,* December 1946; Wallstein, "Revision of the Army Court-Martial System," 48 *Columbia Law Review* 219 (1948).

43. *Fleming v. Page, 9 How. 602, 614 ff. (U.S. 1850).* For a recent and authoritative discussion of problems arising out of our first large-scale venture in military government, see Fairman, "Some New Problems of the Constitution Following the Flag," 1 *Stanford Law Review* 587 (1949).

44. See note, "The Freedom Writ—The Expanding Use of Federal Habeas Corpus," 61 *Harvard Law Review* 657 (1948).

45. *Ex Parte Vallandigham, 1 Wall, 253 (U.S. 1864).* There has been some extension, in practice, of judicial reexamination of court-martial judgments, by extending the concept of what is "jurisdiction." See Note, "Collateral Attack on Courts-Martial in the Federal Courts," 57 *Yale Law Journal* 483 (1948). But this development received a severe setback in *Humphrey v. Smith,* 336 U.S. 695 (1949), where the Court held that failure to conduct the pretrial investigation required by A.W. 70 did not deprive a court-martial of jurisdiction.

In seeking *habeas corpus* to examine into the judgments of a military government tribunal, petitioners encounter a further problem—the technical one of finding a court with original territorial jurisdiction to receive the petition. See *Ahrens v. Clark,* 334 U.S. 188 (1948), and the suggestion of Fairman, *supra* note 43, at 643, that the United States District Court for the District of Columbia is the proper court to entertain such petitions.

46. *Hirota v. MacArthur, 338 U.S. 197 (1948),* concurring opinion by Mr. Justice Douglas at 199. Mr. Justice Douglas argued that as an American official, the General must answer to the writ even when acting for the Allied Powers, but that the tribunal was properly constituted under the Congressional power "to define and punish offenses against the law of nations" and the executive power to conduct the foreign affairs of the United

States, and that its judgment was therefore not reviewable by the courts.

47. *Ex Parte Quirin, 317 U.S. 1 (1942)*. Fairman, *supra* note 43, at 604–605, argues that this case represents a fourth kind of military jurisdiction, "over persons accused of violations of the laws of war." See Note, "Federal Military Commissions," 56 *Harvard Law Review* 631 (1943). And see C⟶win, *supra* note 7, at 117–122, for a similar view.

48. In fact the evidentiary standards for conviction of treason were raised by the wartime decision in *Cramer v. United States, 325 U.S. 1 (1945)*. The fact that Quirin and his companions all entered the United States in enemy uniform in time of war serves to distinguish their case so that it does not undermine the presumably exclusive judicial jurisdiction over offenses amounting to treason.

49. *327 U.S. 1 (1946)*. Note Mr. Justice Rutledge's strong dissent at p. 41, taking the view that the protections of the Fifth Amendment are everywhere applicable.

50. *Neely v. Henkel, 180 U.S. 109 (1901)*.

51. See Fairman, Wiener, *op. cit. supra* note 38, both for elaboration and documentation of the doctrine, and for specific examples of its employment in war and in peace.

52. *Ex Parte Merryman, 17 Fed. Cas. 144, No. 9487 (D. Md. 1861)* per Taney, C. J.

53. *The War of the Rebellion: Official Records, Second Series,* H.R. Doc. No. 558 56th Cong., 2d Sess. 564 (1901).

54. *Ex Parte Milligan, 4 Wall. 2 126–7 (U.S. 1866)*.

55. *Sterling v. Constantin, 287 U.S. 378 (1932)*.

56. *Luther v. Borden, 7 How. 1 (U.S. 1849)*.

57. *Martin v. Mott, 12 Wheat. 19 (U.S. 1827)*.

58. *Moyer v. Peabody, 212 U.S. 78 (1909)*.

59. *4 Wall. 2 (U.S. 1866)*. See Klaus, *The Milligan Case* (1929); Fairman, *Mr. Justice Miller and the Supreme Court* (1939) c. 4.

60. *Id.* at 127.

61. See Fairman, "The Supreme Court on Military Jurisdiction: Martial Rule in Hawaii and the Yamashita Case," 56 *Harvard Law Review* 833, 834–866 (1946); Frank, "Ex Parte Milligan

v. The Five Companies: Martial Law in Hawaii," 44 *Columbia Law Review* 639 (1944); Anthony, "Martial Law in Hawaii," 30 *California Law Review* 371 (1942); "Martial Law, Military Government and the Writ of Habeas Corpus in Hawaii," 31 *California Law Review* 477 (1943); "Hawaiian Martial Law in the Supreme Court," 57 *Yale Law Journal* 1 (1947); Armstrong, "Martial Law in Hawaii," 29 *A.B.A.J.* 698 (1943); McColloch, "Now It Can Be Told: Judge Metzger and the Military," 35 *A.B.A.J.* 365 (1949); Radin, "Martial Law and the State of Siege," 30 *California Law Review* 634 (1942); Corwin, *op. cit. supra* note 7, at 100–105.

62. *Duncan v. Kahanamoku, 327 U.S. 304* (1946) (together with *White v. Steer*, combined opinion).

63. See Rostow, "The Japanese American Cases—A Disaster," 54 *Yale Law Journal* 489 (1945); Dembitz, "Racial Discrimination and the Military Judgment: The Supreme Court's Korematsu and Endo Decisions," 45 *Columbia Law Review* 175 (1945); Freeman, "Genesis, Exodus and Leviticus: Genealogy, Evacuation and the Law," 28 *Cornell Law Quarterly* 414 (1943); Wolfson, "Legal Doctrine, War Power and Japanese Evacuation," 32 *Kentucky Law Journal* 328 (1944); Comment, *Yale Law Journal* 1316 (1942); Corwin, *op. cit. supra* note 7, at 91–100.

64. *Hirabayashi v. United States, 320 U.S. 81* (1943); *Korematsu v. United States, 323 U.S. 214 (1944); Ex Parte Mitsuye Endo, 323 U.S. 283 (1944).*

65. The *Korematsu* and *Endo* cases, *supra*.

66. *Schueller v. Drum, D.C.E.D. Pa., 51 F. Supp. 383 (1943); Ebel v. Drum, D.C.D. Mass., 52 F. Supp. 189 (1943); Scherzberg v. Maderia, D.C.E.D. Pa., 57 F. Supp. 42 (1944).*

67. Mr. Justice Jackson, in *Korematsu v. United States, 323 U.S. 214, 247–248 (1944).*

68. *Ex Parte Merryman, 17 Fed. Cas. 144, No. 9487 (D. Md. 1861).* For a disapproving view see Fairman, "The Law of Martial Rule and the National Emergency," 55 *Harvard Law Review* 1253, 1278–81.

69. There are many obscure technical matters of grave significance

for security and freedom upon which the courts will or ought to have an opportunity to pass. Can the executive branch of the government endanger the rights of parties to a litigation by withholding documents on the plea of protecting national security? See the Note, 59 *Yale Law Journal* 993 (1949) on "Government Privilege against Disclosure of Official Documents." The scope of the activities permitted to the police remains a twilight zone into which the Supreme Court has been rapidly moving (as rehearsed above). But what, after all, is permissible in search and seizure? What of the violations of privacy inherent in wire tapping and related methods of surveillance? Are the methods of lie detection invasions of privacy that violate the rule against self-incrimination? What about "voluntary" submissions as part of a system of "administrative" tests to determine fitness for a job? (Are not the coercive implications such that the policy against self-incrimination is actually violated?) Do not the various "oath" requirements flagrantly conflict with the policies expressed in statutes of limitations? (If the person must disclose that he once belonged to a certain class of political organizations, under pain of prosecution for perjury, he may be making harmful disclosures about his early errors, as well as incriminating himself.)

70. On the public defender idea and a number of other recommendations see Judge Jerome Frank, *Courts on Trial; Myth and Reality in American Justice,* Princeton University Press, Princeton, 1949.

CHAPTER VII

1. The Commission on Freedom of the Press, *A Free and Responsible Press,* University of Chicago Press, Chicago, 1947, p. 22.
2. Current news almanacs report on the network of civic organizations in the U.S. The American Legion has almost 17,000 posts. The General Federation of Women's Clubs has over 14,000 affiliates. Altogether Lions, Rotary, and Kiwanis have more than 12,000 clubs. The Army Information Division has begun to organize army advisory committees in each army area made up of community leaders in every walk of life. The aim is to set up 600 committees with about 9,000 members. Eventually these will be correlated with the other branches of the armed forces.
3. A guide to "Community Self Surveys: An Approach to Social Change" is in the *Journal of Social Issues* (Spring, 1949).
4. See Martin Kriesberg, in Lester Markel, editor, *Public Opinion and Foreign Policy,* Harper & Brothers, New York, 1949, Chap. 2.
5. It should be noted in order to avoid misunderstanding that "expectations" may be conscious or unconscious, and that they interact with "demands" and "identifications."
6. The technique developed by Warner and his associates is outlined in W. Lloyd Warner, Marchia Meeker and Kenneth Eells, *Social Class in America; A Manual of Procedure for the Measurement of Social Status,* Science Research Associates, Chicago, 1949. See Allison Davis, "Socialization and Adolescent Personality," *Forty-third Yearbook of the National Society for the Study of Education* (Part 1); Allison Davis and Robert J. Havighurst, *Father of the Man,* Houghton Mifflin Company, Boston, 1947; Allison Davis and John Dollard, *Children of Bondage,* American Council on Education, Washington, D.C., 1940.
7. Among Chamberlain's books are *The Russian Revolution, 1917–1921,* The Macmillan Company, New York, 1935, 2 Vols.; *Soviet Russia,* Little Brown & Company, Boston, 1930.

8. See Nicholas J. Spykman, *America's Strategy in World Politics; The United States and the Balance of Power,* Harcourt, Brace & Company, Inc., New York, 1942; Edward Mead Earle, *Makers of Modern Strategy; Military Thought from Machiavelli to Hitler,* Princeton University Press, Princeton, N.J., 1943; Quincy Wright, *A Study of War,* University of Chicago, Chicago, 1942, 2 Vols.

9. Clyde Kluckhohn undertakes to explain the significance of anthropology to the layman in *Mirror for Man; The Relation of Anthropology to Modern Life,* McGraw-Hill Book Company, Inc., New York, 1949. He is Professor of Anthropology at Harvard University.

10. The tremendous expansion of modern social science has far outrun the popular interpreters of knowledge. Stuart Chase caught several aspects of the subject in *The Proper Study of Mankind—An Inquiry into the Science of Human Relations,* Harper & Brothers, New York, 1948. An "inside job" remains to be done.

11. An example is the Conference on Science, Philosophy and Religion, initiated by Louis Finkelstein, president of the Jewish Theological Seminary of America in 1939. The proceedings have usually been published through Harper & Brothers.

12. A sign of the times is the investigation by the professional philosophers of how they can be more effective. See *Philosophy in American Education,* by a Committee of the American Philosophical Association, Harper & Brothers, New York, 1945.

13. A great impetus to public thought and action in the field of Negro-white relations was provided by the publication of *An American Dilemma; The Negro Problem and Modern Democracy* by Gunnar Myrdal and associates, Harper & Brothers, New York, 1944, 2 Vols. See also *To Secure These Rights,* Report of the President's Committee on Civil Rights, Washington, 1947.

14. A compact review of the work of the American Civil Liberties Union, the National Association for the Advancement of Colored People, and the Commission on Law and Social Action of the American Jewish Congress in 58 *Yale Law Journal* 574–598 (March, 1949).

## Notes

15. Saul D. Alinsky, *Reveille for Radicals*, University of Chicago Press, Chicago, 1946, is a report on how a gang area can be changed by the proper use of social method.
16. The classical essay by Gustav Le Bon on "The Crowd" is superseded by the work of modern social psychologists. For example, Hadley Cantril, *The Psychology of Social Movements*, John Wiley & Sons, Inc., New York, 1941.
17. A case study of radio-induced panic by Hadley Cantril and associates is *The Invasion from Mars, A Study in the Psychology of Panic, with the Complete Script of the Famous Orson Welles Broadcast*, Princeton University Press, Princeton, N.J., 1940. See *The Psychology of Rumor*, by Gordon W. Allport and Leo Postman, Henry Holt & Company, Inc., New York, 1947. The term "rumor" is defined as "a specific (or topical) proposition for belief, passed along from person to person, usually by word of mouth, without secure standards of evidence being present."
18. See Gabriel Almond, *The American People and Foreign Policy*, Harcourt, Brace & Company, Inc., New York, 1950.
19. James F. Byrnes, *Speaking Frankly*, New York, 1947; John R. Deane, *Strange Alliance*, The Viking Press, Inc., New York, 1947.
20. A forthcoming study of David Riesman deals with the transition which he sees in our culture between the "inner directed" personality and the "other directed" type. "Speaking out of turn" is becoming less and less characteristic of modern man by reason of factors which Riesman's analysis does much to illuminate. Hence the problem of individual responsibility is more far-reaching than appears at first glance.
21. The details of the analysis are in Chapter IX of Gaetano Mosca, *The Ruling Class*, McGraw-Hill Book Company, Inc., New York, 1939.
22. The most important studies of the militarizing trends in modern times are by Hans Speier in *Social Research*, publication of the Graduate Faculty of the New School for Social Research, New York.
23. The context of the quotation is:
    "You know that the chief thing that is holding many people back from what is called preparedness is the fear of militarism.

You are not militarists because you are military. Militarism does not consist in the existence of an army, not even in the existence of a very great army. Militarism is a spirit. It is a point of view. It is a system. It is a purpose. The purpose of militarism is to use armies for aggression. The spirit of militarism is the opposite of the civilian spirit, the citizen spirit. In a country where militarism prevails the military man looks down upon the civilian, regards him as inferior, thinks of him as intended for his, the military man's, support and use; and just so long as America is America that spirit and point of view is impossible with us. There is as yet in this country, so far as I can discover, no taint of the spirit of militarism. You young gentlemen are not preferred in promotion because of the families you belong to. You are not drawn into the Academy because you belong to certain influential circles. You do not come here with a long tradition of military pride back of you.

"You are picked out from the citizens of the United States to be that part of the force of the United States which makes its policy safe against interference. You are the part of American citizens who say to those who would interfere, 'You must not' and 'You shall not.' But you are American citizens, and the idea I want to leave with you boys today is this: No matter what comes, always remember that first of all you are citizens of the United States before you are officers, and that you are officers because you represent in your particular profession what the citizenship of the United States stands for. There is no danger of militarism if you are genuine Americans, and I for one do not doubt that you are. When you begin to have the militaristic spirit—not the military spirit, that is all right—then begin to doubt whether you are Americans or not.

"You know that one thing in which our forefathers took pride was this, that the civil power is superior to the military power in the United States. Once and again the people of the United States have so admired some great military man as to make him President of the United States, when he became commander-in-chief of all the forces of the United States, but he was commander-in-chief because he was President, not because he had been trained to arms, and his authority was civil, not military."

· 232 ·

# Notes

A recent example of the confidence felt by the American people in the citizenship as well as the professional competence of its soldiers is the selection of General Eisenhower as president of Columbia University. Eisenhower referred to the point in his address at the installation ceremonies:

"If this were a land in which the military profession is a weapon of tyranny or aggression—its members an elite caste dedicated to its own perpetuation—a lifelong soldier could hardly assume my present post. But in our nation the army is the servant of the people, designed and trained exclusively to protect our way of life. Duty in its ranks is an exercise of citizenship. Hence, among us, the soldier who becomes an educator or the teacher who becomes a soldier enters into no foreign field but finds himself instead engaged in a new phase of his fundamental life purpose—the protection and perpetuation of basic human freedoms."

24. During the crisis the chief problem of civil defense is to recapture the alertness of an earlier day in the history of our country when risks were shared by every member of the frontier community. The traditional figure from the history of the colonies and from the westward moving frontier is the farmer with a gun in easy reach ready to move with his family if necessary to the blockhouse or the stockade. Under the technological conditions now prevailing, the frontier is determined by the airways that lead to the principal industrial centers. The interconnections between the armed forces and civilian society have been ably reviewed by General C. T. Lanham under the title "Our Armed Forces: Threat or Guarantee," in *Years of the Modern; An American Appraisal,* edited by John W. Chase (Longmans, Green & Co., New York, 1949). He quite properly emphasizes the mixture of ignorance, contempt, and apprehension that characterizes the approach of so many members of our society to the military problem in times of peace, and the dangers that are the result of such perspectives. The armed forces are thereby deprived of the personnel most predisposed by character and training to sustain democratic values and the principle of civilian supremacy.

# A NOTE ON THE COMMITTEE
# FOR ECONOMIC DEVELOPMENT
# AND ITS RESEARCH PROGRAM

THE COMMITTEE for Economic Development was organized in August, 1942, by a group of business leaders who were convinced that attainment and maintenance of high employment after the war could not and need not be left to chance. They foresaw an opportunity to achieve unprecedented peacetime prosperity if business were ready to swing rapidly to peacetime production at the war's end and the government were prepared with policies and measures that would assist the reconversion and contribute to subsequent high production.

Recognizing that this undertaking comprised two distinct though related sets of problems, the CED provided for two areas of action: (1) a Field Development Division to supply to businesses, large and small, in every part of the land, information and aid in planning for peacetime production and employment; (2) a Research Division to study the economic problems of the immediate postwar transition years as well as the basic long-range problems in maintaining high production and employment.

It was generally agreed in informed quarters that high-level employment at the close of the war would require civilian jobs for 7 to 10 million more workers than had been employed in 1940. This meant that business had to plan a postwar volume of business greater than any prior peacetime year—in fact, an over-all increase some 30 to 45 per cent above 1940.

Through the Field Development Division, nearly 3,000 county and community committees were established. More than 65,000 businessmen served as members of these committees, responsible for getting information concerning postwar markets and job requirements to the local manufacturer, merchant, and other businesses, and responsible, likewise, for prodding the individual businessman, hard driven though he was with war work, to lay plans for peacetime.

Tested procedures for making both production and employment plans were made available by the national CED office. Specialists in industrial management, in product design, in advertising and selling, and in training of sales personnel placed their skills at the service of all cooperating businessmen, without cost, through handbooks, films, training courses, business clinics, and forums for the local committees. An outstanding achievement of the Field Development Division was a postwar market analysis, carried out with the cooperation of leading industrial firms and trade associations, covering more than 500 finished-goods products. A greatly enlarged peacetime market was forecast by this survey; the report, *American Industry Looks Ahead,* was released to business and the public in August, 1945.

How thoroughly and carefully the local work was done was evident when, at V-J Day, the CED was the only major organization to state that, contrary to prevailing opinion, there would not be a job slump immediately following the war. Its reports from business throughout the country indicated preparedness to move rapidly into peacetime production. Its wartime "plan jobs" assignment concluded, the Field Development Division was discontinued early in 1946.

Plans for high-level production and employment will not flourish long unless national policies prevail that make such plans feasible. To define what these national policies of government, business, and labor should be to encourage high production and employment is the special task of the CED Research Division. This is the purpose of the research studies of which this volume is the sixteenth.

## The Committee for Economic Development

To the long-range economic questions involved in this undertaking were added the particular economic problems arising out of the war. Six studies dealing primarily with the economic problems of the transition from a war to a peace economy were completed during the war years. Of the studies concerned with the long-range fundamental problems involved in maintaining high productive employment, nine have been issued.

The present report on national security and individual freedom may seem to be a departure from research directed to economic problems. But the social conflict now dominant in the world is peculiarly entangled with two kinds of security—economic and national, neither of which can be wholly dissociated from the other. And both aspects of security are intimately related to freedom.

The authors of these research reports had already won distinction in their own fields. Perhaps more important is the fact that they had demonstrated not only the competence but also the vigor of thought which these complex problems demand. Knowing, however, that the problems that would be scrutinized—taxation, monetary policy, international trade, agriculture, and the like— are not separate ones, but are integrated and must be studied in relationship one to the other, the CED sought to make possible an exchange of information and views by the experts and, equally important, between the scholars and businessmen.

What may be a unique scheme of conferences was established, the objective being to blend the experience and judgment of the business world with the scholars' knowledge of the action of economic forces. A Research and Policy Committee consisting of knowledgeable, successful businessmen was set up; to this group was added a Research Advisory Board whose members are recognized as among our leading social scientists; and, finally, a small central research staff was appointed, in addition to the persons who would be responsible for the research reports.

The author of the report thus has the benefit of criticism and suggestion by many other competent minds. He is able to follow closely the development of the reports on other economic matters that affect his own study.

No effort is made to arrive at absolute agreement. There is no single answer to the problems that are being studied. What is gained is agreement as to the determinative factors in each problem, and the possible results to be achieved by differing methods of handling the problem. The author of the report has full responsibility and complete freedom for proposing whatever action or solution seems advisable to him. There is only one rule—the approach must be from the standpoint of the general welfare and not from that of any special economic or political group; the objective must be stable high production and employment in a democratic society.

The author is free to present his own conclusions and does not speak for the Research and Policy Committee or for the Research Advisory Board. In turn, the Research and Policy Committee usually prepares its own Statement on National Policy for the problems under study. This may endorse all of the recommendations arrived at in the research report, or it may disagree with some of them.[1] The statements are based on thorough study and discussion of relevant materials, including the reports. Their outstanding characteristic is that they offer informed, responsible thinking by the businessmen themselves. They are not a staff product countersigned by businessmen.

As the second half of the twentieth century opens, several facts are clearly evident affecting the American economy. First, there is the fact that the USA is a central force in the maintenance and development of the democratic free society. Second, we are necessarily a major source of aid in the recovery of the nations

[1] A listing of CED policy statements and copies thereof are available from CED headquarters.

still burdened by the social and economic dislocations of a destructive depression and the world's worst war. Third, the peoples in the underdeveloped areas of the world look to us for economic assistance and counsel in bettering their living conditions. Fourth, in the normal trading of the world, we now constitute the largest single factor.

The health of the American economy has extraordinary significance in these conditions. Can it continue its dynamic growth, improving living standards throughout our own nation, and contributing to their betterment elsewhere? Can extreme swings in the economy—the boom and bust—be eliminated?

The work of the past eight years has strengthened conviction within CED that these are attainable goals. Continued close study of the economy is vitally needed. It is no simple or static mechanism. Equally necessary is a greater dissemination of the knowledge gained. The American economy is not run by a few businessmen, government officials, farm and labor leaders. More knowledgeable action by many businessmen, labor leaders, farmers, and consumers is requisite to the goals. To both these purposes—more knowledge of our economy and more widespread use of the knowledge—CED continues to work.

The following is a description of the research studies published or under way, with the transition period studies shown first:

A. *The Transition from War to Peace:*

 1. *The Liquidation of War Production,* by A. D. H. Kaplan, The Brookings Institution. The problems involved in the cancellation of war contracts and the disposal of government-owned surplus supplies, plants, and capital equipment are analyzed quantitatively as well as qualitatively. How much war plant did the government finance, and what part of it could be put into civilian production? What criteria should prevail in selecting the producers to

be released first from war manufactures as the war production program is curtailed? How and when should surplus goods be sold? Rapid resumption of peacetime production, with conditions favorable to high levels of employment, is the gauge by which the recommendations are measured.

2. *Demobilization of Wartime Economic Controls,* by John Maurice Clark, Professor of Economics, Columbia University. When and how should the wartime controls be removed? The interdependency of the wartime controls of production, man power, prices, wages, rationing, credit policies, and others is made clear. How relaxation of each control may affect the peacetime economy—in terms of demand and supply, and therefore in terms of jobs and production levels—is weighed. The conditions that can be expected to prevail at different stages of the transition from a wartime to a peacetime economy are outlined, with emphasis on the variables with which we must be prepared to deal. Professor Clark does not overlook the significance of attitudes and objectives.

3. *Providing for Unemployed Workers in the Transition,* by Richard A. Lester, Chairman, Department of Economics and Social Institutions, Princeton University. An estimate of the size and the duration of transition unemployment. The efficacy of public works employment, relief employment, the adequacy of unemployment compensation, wartime savings, dismissal pay, and the like are appraised. A program is developed to provide for the maintenance of workers who may be out of jobs in the transition from war to peace.

4. *Financing Business during the Transition,* by Charles C. Abbott, Professor of Business Economics, Harvard University. The sources upon which business has relied for its

capital are examined, along with the current financial condition of large and small corporations. These two are balanced against the likely needs of financing by industry for reconversion and expansion in the transition years following the war.

5. *Jobs and Markets,* by Melvin G. de Chazeau, Albert G. Hart, Gardiner C. Means, Howard B. Myers, Herbert Stein, and Theodore O. Yntema. The problem of controlling aggregate demand in the several transition years during which the nation will endeavor to move from the high plateau of wartime production and employment to a similarly high level of peacetime productivity. The deflationary elements as well as the prevailing dangerous inflationary forces are examined. A program of fiscal, monetary, and price control policies is presented to speed civilian production and to counter inflation and depression in the return to free markets.

B. *The Long-term Fundamental Problems:*

1. *Production, Jobs and Taxes,* by Harold M. Groves, Professor of Economics, University of Wisconsin (published). A study of the federal tax structure as it affects the creation of jobs. A second volume, *Postwar Taxation and Economic Progress* (published), concludes Professor Groves' analysis of the relationship of taxation to economic development, and presents an approach to taxation that would make for constructive tax policy. The second report inquires into the problems of state and local, as well as federal, taxation.

2. *Agriculture in an Unstable Economy,* by Theodore W. Schultz, Professor of Economics, The University of Chicago (published). An investigation going to the roots of the "farm problem." The significance of ex-

cess labor resources on farms, the failure of price mechanisms to induce shifts of resources out of agriculture, the differences between the farm and industrial sectors in responding to reduced demand. The importance to farmers of continued prosperity in business. A solution to the farm problem without resort to price floors or restrictions on output.

3. *International Trade and Domestic Employment,* by Calvin B. Hoover, Chairman, Department of Economics, Duke University (published). An examination of the kind of foreign trade policies and mechanisms we can adopt that will increase our gains from international trade and also contribute to world peace. A statement of the requirements in terms of the economies of other countries as well as our own.

4. *Controlling World Trade—Cartels and Commodity Agreements,* by Edward S. Mason, Dean, Graduate School of Public Administration, Harvard University (published). The conditions that brought forth cartels and intergovernmental commodity agreements and the way in which both types of international business organization operate are presented as background to a searching appraisal of their role in the political-economic machinery of future world trade. American attitudes as well as American objectives in foreign trade are reviewed.

5. *Small Business: Its Place and Problems,* by A. D. H. Kaplan, The Brookings Institution (published). An inquiry into the part that small business plays in a free enterprise economy and as a facet of democracy. With these as basic points of reference, the position of small business in the economy today is compared with its past. An evaluation is made of social and economic factors affecting the entry of small businesses, their chances for survival and

growth. What small businessmen need to do for themselves and what the community should do for small business is examined in detail.

6. *Monetary and Credit Policies,* by E. A. Goldenweiser, Institute for Advanced Study, Princeton, N. J. An initial volume, *Monetary Management* (published), appraises the powers of and the demands on a central banking authority in the current situation, and under conditions which may be anticipated in the next several years. A full study by Dr. Goldenweiser, now in preparation, will examine the position of money in an advanced industrialized economy. It will enquire into credit and debt policies as related to booms and busts. Is it possible to keep money movements from reinforcing and exaggerating an upward or a downward swing in the economy? Can the money supply and credit policy be used effectively to counter the ups and downs? What is the significance for monetary policy of the large public debt?

7. *National Security and Individual Freedom,* by Harold D. Lasswell, Professor of Law, Yale University (the present volume). This study examines the significance for the fundamental values of a democracy of the conflict, now dominant in the world, between statism and democracy. Specifically, it looks at the continuing crisis of defense as it may affect these four principles of a free society: civilian supremacy, freedom of information, civil liberties, a free economy.

The need formally and continuously to appraise security measures for their toll of freedom arises not only from the fact that freedom is at the heart of our society, but also that individual freedom and a free economy are integral to our economic strength and thus to our national security. The author proposes methods whereby the government and the people would obtain a better over-all grasp of the security program and its relationship to individual freedom. How such an understanding would contribute to unity within our nation, and help to reduce costly wastes, is discussed. The lack of machinery for such a review and reporting to the people reflects the fact that the USA has by choice and by the benefit of distance been able in the past to put its mind to peaceful pursuits, and not to war or defense.

8. *Fiscal Policy,* by Herbert Stein, CED Research Staff. An analysis of the relationship of federal taxation and expenditures to the maintenance of stable employment and high productivity. Particular attention will be given the impact of budgetary policy since the federal budget is likely for some years to represent a far greater percentage of the nation's income than ever before in peacetime.

9. *Analysis of Fiscal-Monetary Policy between World War I and World War II,* by Bertrand Fox, Professor of Business Administration, Harvard University. An examination of fiscal-monetary policies in the inter-war years, and what we can learn from experience with them.

10. *Production versus Inflation,* by John Maurice Clark, Professor of Economics, Columbia University. Under what conditions does an increase in demand lead to an expansion of production; under what conditions does it lead to an inflation of prices? What needs to be done so that demand results in increased production and not increased prices alone? Two other CED studies—on price-wage relations and on labor-management relations—are, in part, addressed to this same problem.

11. *Labor-Management Relations,* by Douglass V. Brown, Professor of Industrial Management, and Charles A.

Myers, Professor of Industrial Relations, Massachusetts
Institute of Technology. An examination of the growth
and character of the business structure along with the
growth and character of unions and the labor movement.
What objectives have business and unions in common, and
what objectives conflict? What is the bearing of each of
these on: the maintenance of high employment; uninter-
rupted supply, as a factor of major importance to the
public at large; costs and prices? This study is related also
to the CED study of price-wage relations and the study
of production versus inflation.

12. *Price-Wage Relations,* by Edward S. Mason, Dean, Graduate School of Public Administration, Harvard University.

13. *What Can Individual Business Contribute to Stable
High Production and High Employment?* by Melvin de
Chazeau, Professor of Business Economics and Policy,
Cornell University.

14. *Business Inventories and Their Effect on Business Movements,* by Ragnar Nurkse, Professor of Economics, Graduate Faculty of Political Science, Columbia University.

15. *What Can State and Local Governments Do to Contribute
to Business Stability?* by Clarence Heer, Professor of Economics, University of North Carolina.

16. *Facilitating the Flow of Savings into Private Investment,*
by Homer Jones, Research Staff, Federal Reserve System.

17. *Stabilizing the Construction Industry,* by Miles L. Colean,
Consulting Economist, and Robinson Newcomb, Con-
struction Economist, Staff of the Council of Economic
Advisers.

18. *Money Flows and Cash Balances,* by Morris Copeland,
Professor of Economics, Cornell University. This study

was initiated at the instance of the CED under the auspices of the National Bureau of Economic Research and has been taken over and continued by the Federal Reserve Board. The first report in this project—*A New Federal Financial Statement*—was issued by the NBER in December, 1947.

19. *Controls vs. Prices in the Allocation of Resources,* by Arthur Smithies, Professor of Economics, Harvard University. In carrying a large armaments production program in peacetime, what conditions may arise affecting prices and the availability of materials for defense uses, as against civilian uses? What criteria should determine the choice between direct controls of particular commodities or reliance on price to increase output or limit demand. How do these choices relate to inflationary conditions? The unsettled state of world affairs and the possibility that we may have a long period with heavy defense spending make this enquiry necessary.

C. *Supplementary Papers:*

1. *World Politics Faces Economics,* by Harold D. Lasswell, Professor of Law, Yale University (published). A discussion of the interrelationship of economic and political factors shaping the world political structure, with particular reference to the relations of the United States and Russia.

2. *The Economics of a Free Society,* by William Benton, Chairman of the Board, Encyclopaedia Britannica, Inc. (Published in October, 1944, issue of *Fortune* Magazine.)

3. *Personnel Problems of the Postwar Transition Period,* by Charles A. Myers, Professor of Industrial Relations, Massachusetts Institute of Technology (published). An exam-

ination of the problems that would confront employers in connection with the rehiring of servicemen and war workers, and issues arising in the shift of the work force from wartime to peacetime production.

4. *Distribution of Income,* by William Vickrey, Associate Professor of Economics, Columbia University.

# EXCERPTS FROM BY-LAWS OF THE COMMITTEE FOR ECONOMIC DEVELOPMENT CONCERNING THE RESEARCH PROGRAM

*Article 5. Research and Policy Committee*

It shall be the responsibility of the Research and Policy Committee to initiate studies into the principles of business policy and of public policy which will foster the full contribution by industry and commerce to the attainment and maintenance of high and secure standards of living for people in all walks of life through maximum employment and high productivity in the domestic economy. All research is to be thoroughly objective in character and the approach in each instance is to be from the standpoint of the general welfare and not from that of any special political or economic group.

*Research Reports*

The determination of whether or not a research report shall be published shall rest solely with the Research Director and with the Research Advisory Board. . . . The Research Director shall, after consulting with the Chairman of the Research Advisory Board, appoint a Reading Committee of three members of the Research Advisory Board. Thereupon, as a special assignment, each member of the Reading Committee shall read the manuscript and fifteen days after its assignment to him shall signify his approval or disapproval for publication. If two out of the three Reading Committee members signify their approval, the manuscript shall be published at the expense of the Corporation. If two out of the three disapprove, the manuscript shall not be published at the expense of the Corporation. . . . Upon approval for publication a copy of the manuscript shall be sent to each member of the Research Advisory Board. Fifteen days shall then be allowed to the members of the Research Advisory Board and the Research Director to submit signed memoranda of comment, reservation or dissent. Should a member of the Research Advisory Board or the Research Director so request, his memorandum, which must be signed, shall be published with the manuscript. . . . In the event a research report it not approved for publication as above provided, the individual or group making the research shall neverthless have the right to publish the manuscript.

*Supplementary Papers*

There shall be an Editorial Board for Supplementary Papers to consist of the Research Director, two members of the Research and Policy Committee and two members of the Research Advisory Board. The members from the Research and Policy Committee and the members from the Research Advisory Board shall be appointed by the respective Chairman of these bodies. The Research Director shall be the chairman of the Editorial Board and shall act as Editor of the Supplementary Papers.

The Research Director may recommend to the Editorial Board for publication as a Supplementary Paper any manuscript (other than a research report) . . . which in his opinion should be made publicly available because it constitutes an important contribution to the understanding of a problem on which research has been initiated by the Research and Policy Committee. On specific authorization by the Research and Policy Committee, he may also have prepared and recommend for publication as a Supplementary Paper a manuscript on any subject outside the scope of the formally initiated research program. . . . If a majority of the members of the Editorial Board vote for publica-

· 249 ·

tion, the manuscript shall be published as one of a series of Supplementary Papers, separate and distinct from the Research Reports. . . . Upon approval for publication . . . fifteen days shall be allowed to the members of the Research Advisory Board and the Research Director to submit signed memoranda of comment, reservation or dissent. Should a member of the Research Advisory Board or the Research Director so request, his memorandum, which must be signed, shall be published with the Supplementary Paper. . . .

Publication does not necessarily constitute endorsement . . . by the Committee for Economic Development, the Board of Trustees, the Research and Policy Committee, the Research Advisory Board, the research staff, or any member of any board or committee, or any officer, of the Committee for Economic Development.

# RESEARCH AND POLICY COMMITTEE

· 251 ·

# National Security and Individual Freedom

· 253 ·

# INDEX

## A

Adams, John, 59
Agriculture, Department of, 95–96
Airplanes, 6–7
Alien and Sedition Acts (1798), 46
American Civil Liberties Union, 180
Anthropology, 173–174
Armaments, 25–28
Army in government, 59–61
Atomic bomb, 6–8, 25–26
Atomic Energy Commission, 30, 65, 78, 92, 94
Attorneys, 134–135
Audio-visual education, 168–169

## B

Baldwin, Roger, 180
Bill of Rights, 45, 64–68, 137–138, 141–142
Bipartisan policy, 37–38, 108–109
Books as information sources, 170–174
Britain, government, 109–110, 113–115
Brookhaven Interuniversity Laboratory, 29
Buck, Pearl, 172
Business in police state, 47–48
Byrnes, James F., 183

## C

Cabinet, 84–86
Cabinet system of government, 105, 109, 113–115

Capitalism, Marxist theories, 12–13
Censorship in defense, 89
Centers, Richard, 72
Centralization of government, 29–30
Chafee, Zechariah, Jr., 134
Chamberlain, William H., 171
Chambers of Commerce, 160
Citizen, responsibility of, 184–187
Civic organizations, 156, 159–161, 167
Civil liberties, 57, 65–68, 180
Civil War, American, 5, 148
Civilian authority, in Defense Department, 98–100, 213–214
  in National Security Council, 80, 84, 87, 89, 91–93
Civilian executives, 41–45
Civilian panels in Congress, 126, 131
Civilian supremacy, 57–63, 97
Clapper, Raymond, 65
Class consciousness, 72, 166–167
Cominform, 17
Commission on Freedom of the Press, 158, 212
Committee for Economic Development (CED), 97–98, 177, 235–239
  by-laws of, 248–250
  Field Development Division, 235–236
  Research Advisory Board, 237, 253
  Research and Policy Committee, 237, 251–252

# Index

Committee for Economic Development, Research and Policy Committee, research studies published by, 239–247

Committees, of citizens, 156–162, 167, 176, 195–199

Congressional, 105–107, 115

Communication, media of, 156–158, 162–170, 175

Communism, 11–20, 31–32

Communist Party, in Russia, 14–17, 21–22

in the United States, 18, 210–211

Complacency, prevention of, 182–184

Congress, civilian panels in, 126, 131

committees, 105–107, 115

public influence on, 115–121

responsibility of, 38–41, 103–105, 126–132

war authority, 136–137, 139

Conscription, 139–140

Constitution of the United States, 59–60, 64, 68–69, 133, 135, 137 (*See also* Bill of Rights)

Correspondents, newspaper, 170–171

Council of Economic Advisers, 28, 79, 83

Council on Foreign Relations, 159

Councils on human rights, 157, 161

Counterespionage, 88

Courts, responsibility of, 45–46, 133–136, 141–143

war authority, 136–143 (*See also* Supreme Court)

Crowd, behavior of, 180–182

## D

Davis, David, 148

Deane, John R., 183

Declaration of Independence, 58

Defense, Department of, 78–80, 93, 98–100, 213–214

Defense, national, 2–7, 52–53

expenditures for, 26–28

government control in, 27–30

and individual freedom, 23–24

secrecy in, 30–33

Despotism, 9–11, 20–22

Dodd, William E., 172

Doniphan, Alexander W., 139, 148

Due process clause, 135–143

## E

Earle, Edward Meade, 173

Education, 163–164, 166–167, 175–176, 198–199

Eisenhower, Dwight D., 233

Espionage, 88, 145

*Ex parte Milligan*, 148–149, 151

Executive branch, 41–45, 81–82

judicial function of, 143–151

Expression, freedom of, 141–143

## F

Federal Bureau of Investigation, 44, 209–210

*Federalist, The,* 54, 60, 69

Films, 156, 168–169

Finney, Nat, 179, 189–194

*Foreign Affairs,* 172–173

Foreign policy, 3–7, 52–55

Foreign Policy Association, 159

Forums, 160, 195

Fourteenth Amendment, 135–136, 141

Franklin, Benjamin, 7–8

Free economy, 57, 68–74, 96–98

Freedom Day, 127, 157, 161–162

## G

Garrison-police state, 21–22, 47–49

# Index

Germany in World War II, 9, 24–25

Government, centralization of, 29–30

and free economy, 70–74, 96–98

Government control in defense, 27–30

Government departments and security, 41–45

Government employees, loyalty of, 32, 43–45, 209–211

## H

*Habeas corpus,* writ of, 145–149

Hamilton, Alexander, 54, 60, 63

Hawaii, martial law in, 149, 151–152

Hearings, Congressional, 104, 127, 129

Hitler, Adolf, 9

Hoover Commission, 63, 81–83

Human rights, councils on, 157, 161

Hydrogen bomb, 7–8, 26

Hysteria, prevention of, 180–182

## I

Indifference, 162–169

Individual responsibility, 184–187

Industry, government control of, 27–30

Information, Congress responsible for, 104, 121–126

freedom of, 57, 63–65

and propaganda, 93–96

and security, 30–36, 91–92

sources of, 157, 162–178, 195–196

Institute of National Policy, proposed, 178

## J

Jackson, Andrew, 61

Japanese in the United States, 150–151

Jefferson, Thomas, 63–64

Joint committees in Congress, 107

Journalists, 170–171

Judicial function of executive, 143–151

Judiciary (*see* Courts)

## L

Labor and communism, 18, 31, 45

League of Women Voters, 160

Library of Congress, Legislative Reference Service, 103–104, 126

Lobbying, 103–104, 121–124

Loyalty, of government employees, 32, 209–211

investigations of, 43–45, 90, 209–211

Luce, Henry, 172

## M

Madison, James, 23, 63, 69–70

Magazines, 156–158, 163, 170

Mahan, Alfred T., 172

Marshall Plan, public opinion of, 162–164

Martial law, 147–151

Marxism, 12–13, 19–21

Military and civilian authority, 41–43, 58–63

Military government, 144–147

Military law, 143–144

Milligan, Lambdin P., 148–149, 151

Missionaries, 171–172

Mobilization, emergency, 140

Monopolies, regulation of, 70, 72

Monroe Doctrine, 5

Morris, Gouverneur, 60

Mosca, Gaetano, 186

Moving pictures, 156, 168–169

Mowrer, Edgar Ansel, 171

# Index

## N

National Bureau of Economic Research, 177–178
National Science Foundation, 29
National Security Act, 79
National security committees in Congress, 104, 106–107, 127
National Security Council, 42, 79–80, 82–84, 87, 89–93, 96, 98–101, 108, 125, 142
National Security Day, 127, 157, 161–162
National security policy, 50–52, 57
National Security Resources Board, 28, 79–80, 83, 96–98
National War College, 101
Newspapers, 156–158, 163, 189–194

## P

Police, political, 41, 43–45, 80, 87–90
Police state, 20–22, 47–49
Policy associations, 156, 159, 167, 195–199
Political parties, 36–38, 108–113
Polls, public opinion, 120
President, and Congress, 108–111, 114
responsibility of, 76–84, 90–102
war authority, 137
Press, freedom of, 64–65, 94, 156–158, 189–194, 212–213
and government, 120, 123–124
responsibility of, 178–179, 189–194
and security, 33–36
Pressure groups, 120, 126, 179
Price control, 74, 98
Princeton, Institute for Advanced Study, 173
Private enterprise, 68–74

Propaganda, communist, 11–20, 31–32
Congressional inquiries, 103–104, 121–125
and information, 93–96
Public officials, accountability of, 178–180
Public opinion, influences on, 34–36
and information, 162–170
Public responsibility, 154–157

## R

Radar, 10, 26
Radio, 127, 156–158, 163
Revolution, American, 4
Roosevelt, Franklin Delano, 9, 110
Russia, armaments, 25–26
foreign policy, 3, 127–128
industrialization, 11
police state, 20–22
propaganda, 11–20
in World War II, 9–10, 24–25

## S

Schools, 163–164, 166–167
Schuster, Morgan, 172
Scientists, 172–174
Secrecy, in defense, 30–33, 89–92
and despotism, 9–10
Security, and foreign policy, 52–55
and freedom, 23–24
regulation of information, 30–33
Security committees in Congress, 104, 106–107, 127
Security policy, 50–52, 57
Selective Service Acts, 139–140
Smith Act, 143
Smyth Report, 92
Social security, 112
Speech, freedom of, 142

# Index

Spykman, Nicholas, 173
State, Department of, 78, 93, 96
Stone, Harlan F., 141
Supreme Court, 133–136, 139, 142, 145–151

## T

Taney, Roger B., 152
Taxation, 97
Television, 168–169
Third International, 14–15
Tito, Marshal, 21
Trade unions, communism in, 31, 45
Two-party system, 108–113

## U

United Nations, 2
United States, foreign policy, 3–7, 52–55, 127–128
  security policy, 50–52, 57
  in World War II, 9–10, 24–25

## V

Vice-President, 84, 86–87
Virginia Declaration of Rights, 58
Visual education, 168–169
Voice of America, 95, 125, 126, 196

## W

Washington, George, 58–59, 61
Weapon parity, 25–26
Wilson, Woodrow, 120, 187, 231–232
World politics, 3–6
World War I, 6
World War II, 6, 9–10, 24–25, 139–140

## Y

Yale Institute of International Studies, 173
Yamashita, Tomoyuki, 146
Yugoslavia, 21